Oregon Trail

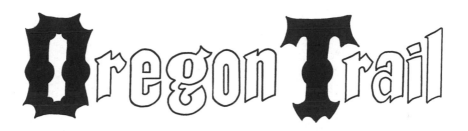

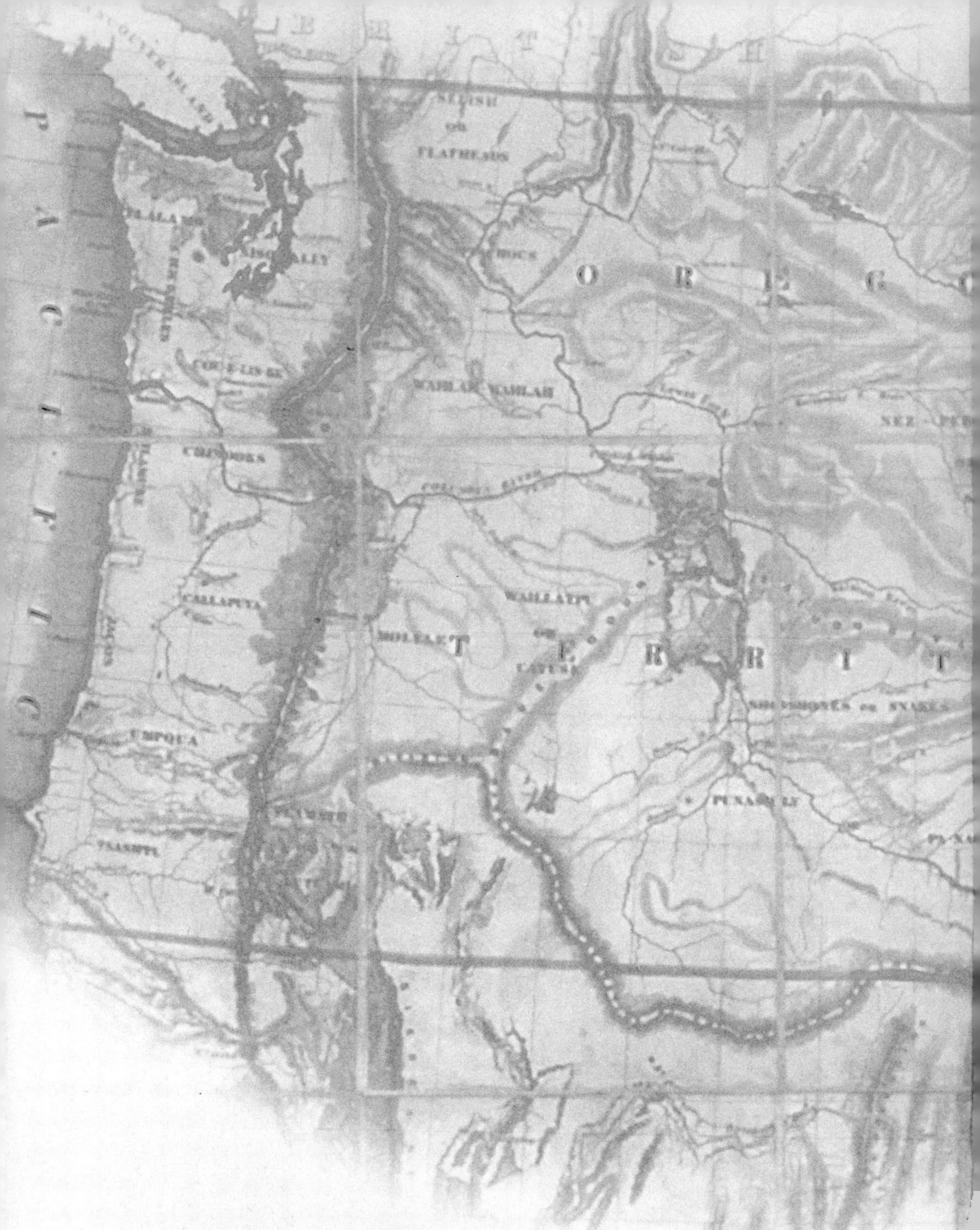
SELISH
OR
FLATHEADS
WAHLAH WAHLAH
CHINOOKS
CALLAPUYA
UMPQUA
WAILLATPU
OR
CAYUSE
SHOSHONES or SNAKES

Oregon Trail

The Road to Destiny

Frank Young & David Lasky

SASQUATCH BOOKS
SEATTLE

Printed in the United States of America
Published by Sasquatch Books
Distributed by PGW/Perseus
17 16 15 14 13 12 11 9 8 7 6 5 4 3 2 1

Cover illustration: David Lasky
Cover design: Rosebud Eustace and Sarah Plein
Interior design and illustrations: David Lasky

Library of Congress Cataloging-in-Publication Data is available.

ISBN-13: 978-1-57061-649-5
ISBN-10: 1-57061-649-3

Sasquatch Books
119 South Main Street, Suite 400
Seattle, WA 98104
(206) 467-4300
www.sasquatchbooks.com
custserv@sasquatchbooks.com

SUSTAINABLE FORESTRY INITIATIVE
Label applies to the text stock
Certified Fiber Sourcing
www.sfiprogram.org

Dedication

Frank Young wishes to thank:
James Gill, Heidi Hollister, David Lasky, Bob Mecoy, Michael Komlos, Michael McCarty, Lois Regen, Don Roff, Autumn Taylor-Roff, Paul Tumey, Rosa, and Naraya (RIP). Special thanks to David A. Young, whose kindness and patience helped this book happen.

David Lasky wishes to thank:
Leeann, Mom, Dad, and Jason. Frank Young and Bob Mecoy. The Benincasa family. Kate Lebo. Helen Parson, Steve Leiber, and other friends who cheered me on as I drew this book. Special thanks to Sean Robinson for his assistance in inking some of the scenery!

The Oregon Trail Journey of the Weston Family, 1848

PACIFIC OCEAN
Oregon City
Salem
CASCADE MTS.
COLUMBIA RIVER
BLUE MTS.
SNAKE RIVER
Fort Hall
Soda Springs
ROAD TO CALIFORNIA
SOUTH PASS
Devil's Gate
Independence Rock
Fort Laramie
Scotts Bluff
Chimney Rock
Courthouse Rock
Pawnee Territory
PLATTE RIVER
Independence
St. Louis

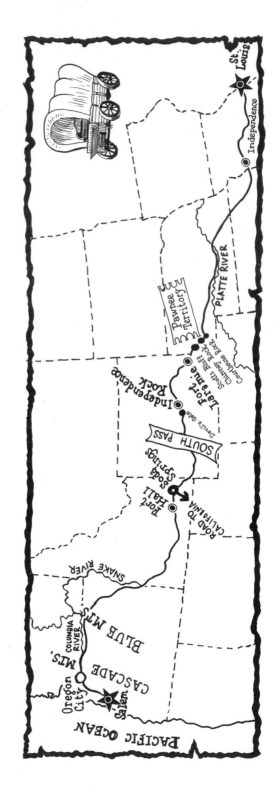

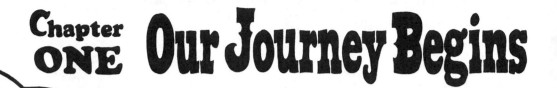

Chapter ONE Our Journey Begins

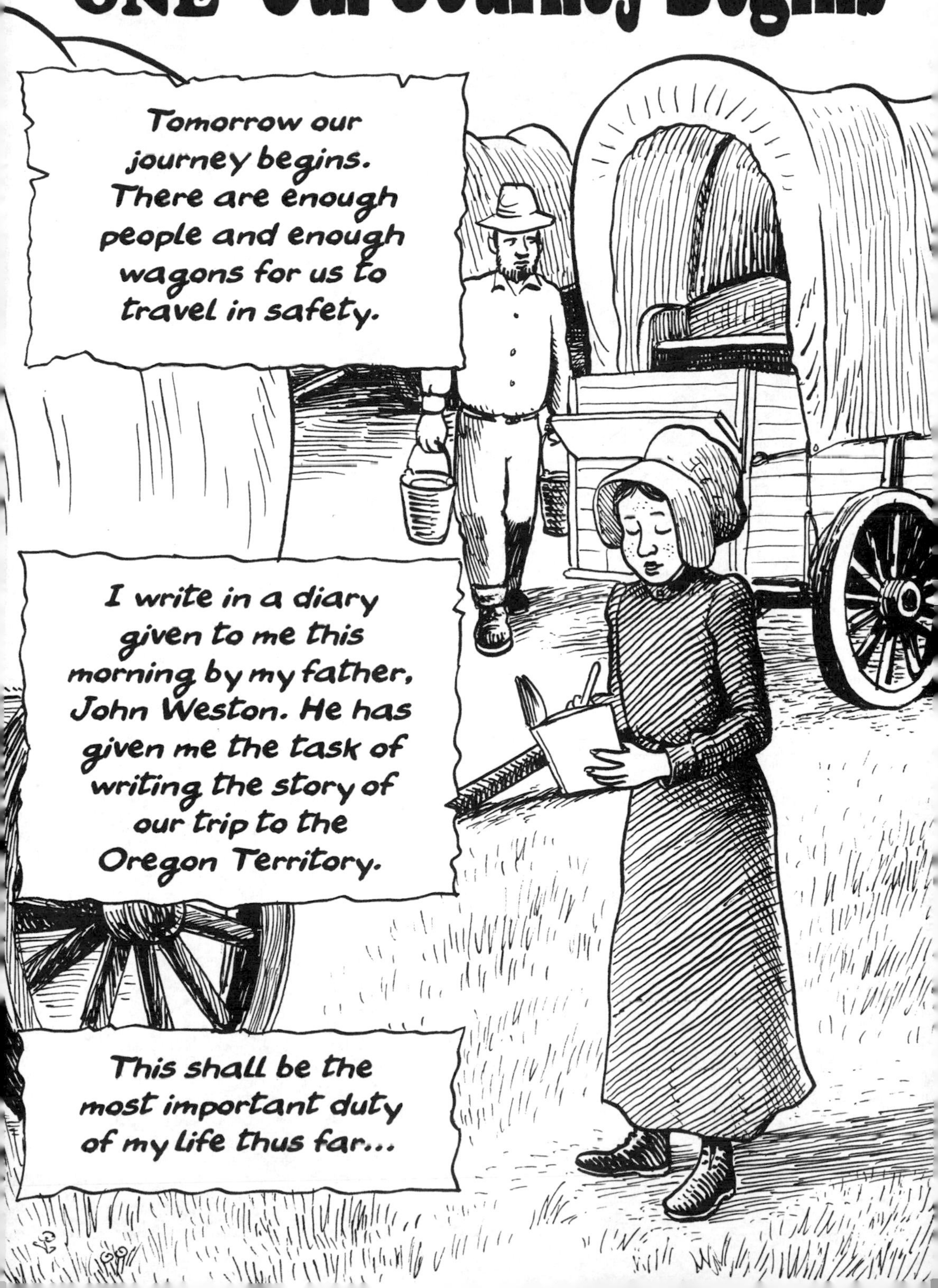
Tomorrow our journey begins. There are enough people and enough wagons for us to travel in safety.
I write in a diary given to me this morning by my father, John Weston. He has given me the task of writing the story of our trip to the Oregon Territory.
This shall be the most important duty of my life thus far...

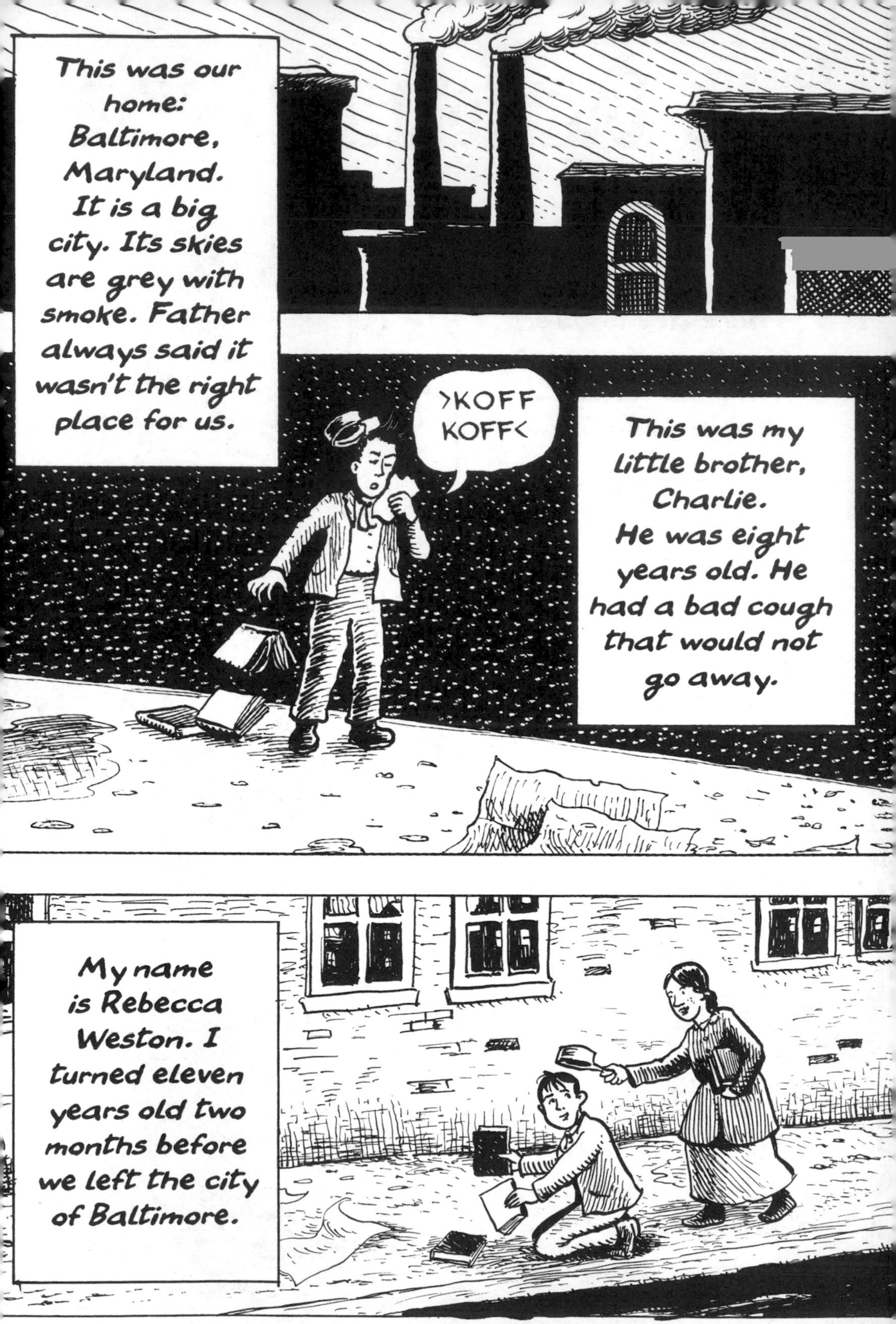
This was our home: Baltimore, Maryland. It is a big city. Its skies are grey with smoke. Father always said it wasn't the right place for us.
>KOFF KOFF<
This was my little brother, Charlie. He was eight years old. He had a bad cough that would not go away.
My name is Rebecca Weston. I turned eleven years old two months before we left the city of Baltimore.

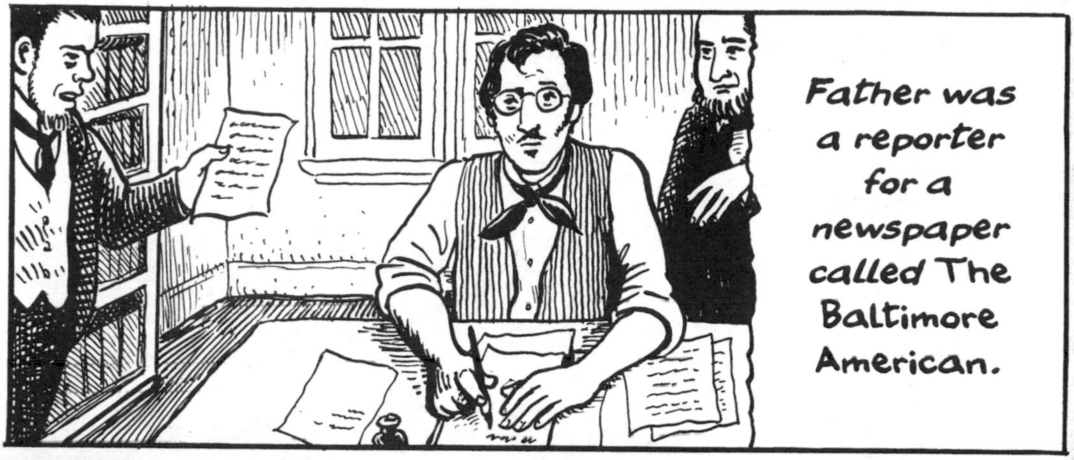
Father was a reporter for a newspaper called The Baltimore American.

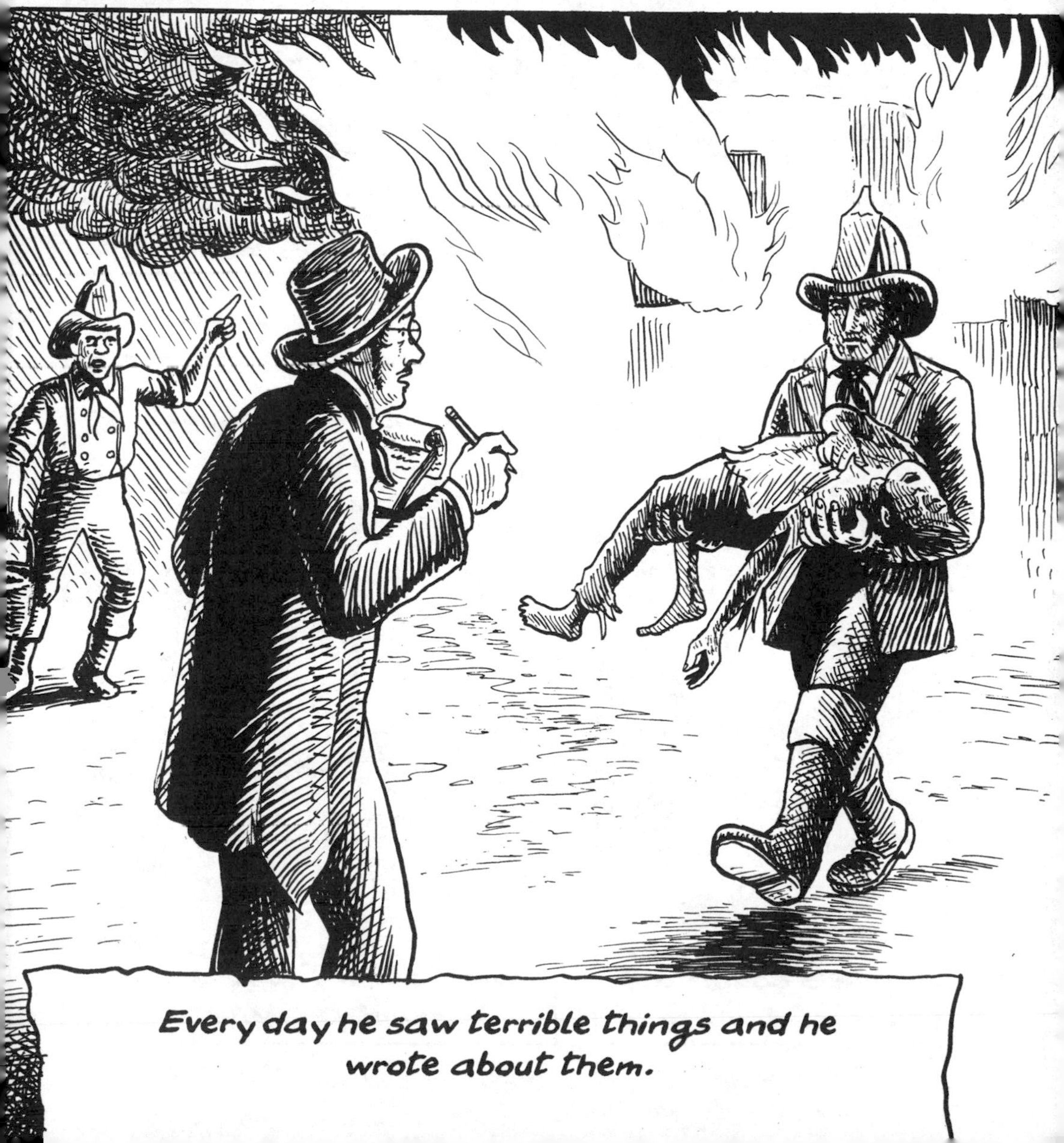
Every day he saw terrible things and he wrote about them.

Father was not happy with this life. He wanted something better for all of us.

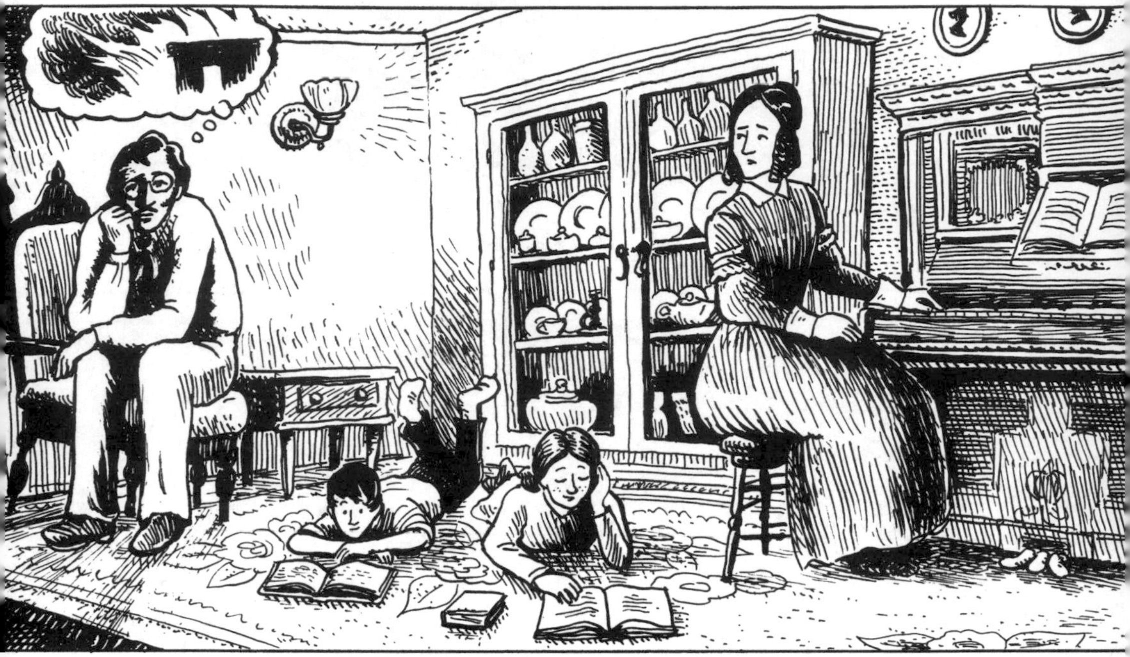

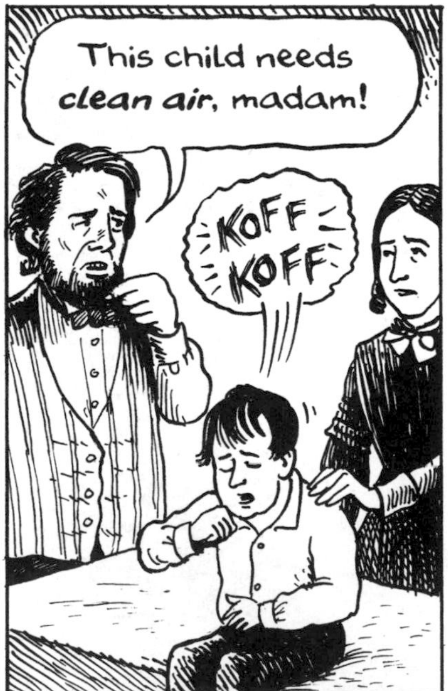
This child needs clean air, madam!
KOFF KOFF

Charlie's cough got worse and worse...

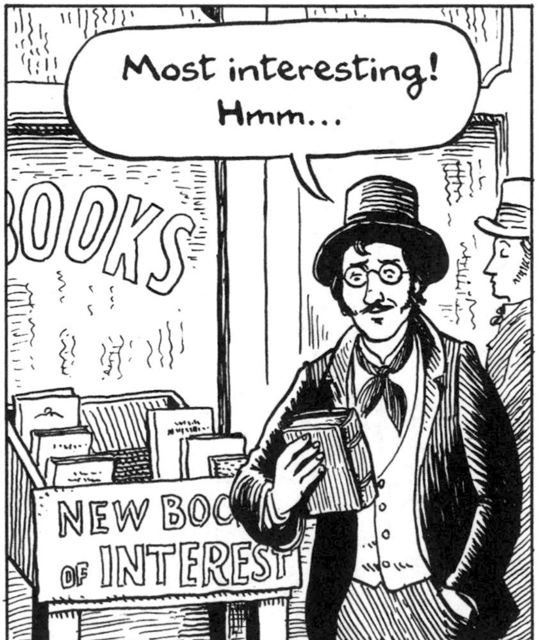
Most interesting! Hmm...
OOKS
NEW BOO
OF INTEREST

and Father found a book about the West.

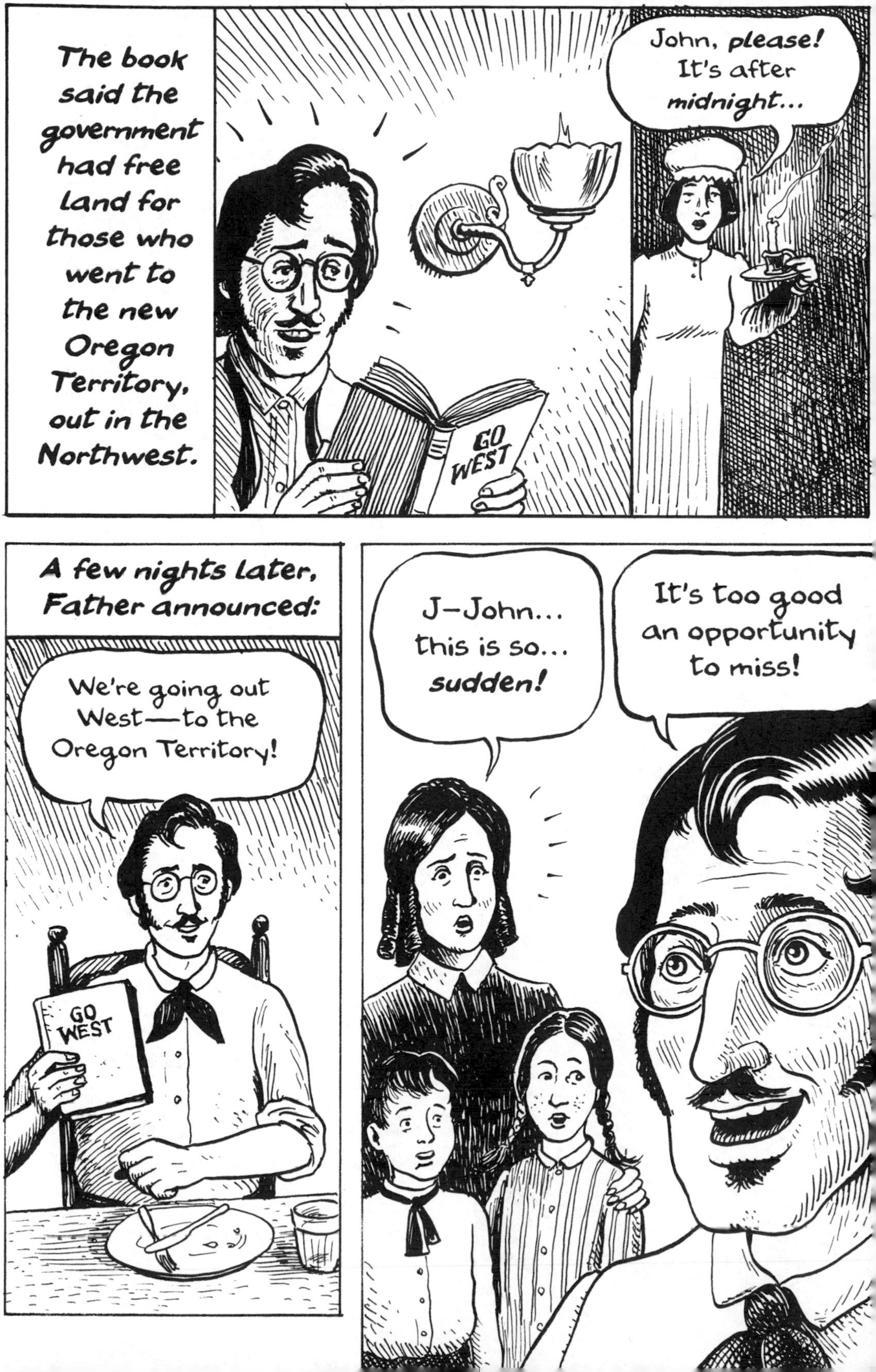
The book said the government had free land for those who went to the new Oregon Territory, out in the Northwest.
GO WEST
John, please! It's after midnight...
A few nights later, Father announced:
We're going out West—to the Oregon Territory!
GO WEST
J-John... this is so... sudden!
It's too good an opportunity to miss!

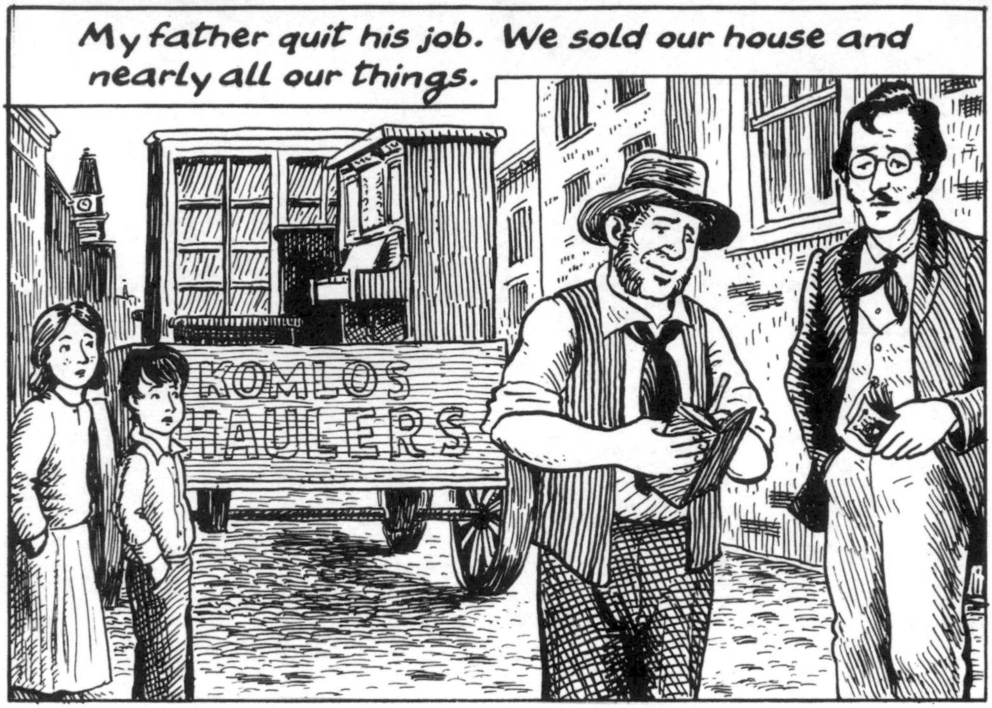
My father quit his job. We sold our house and nearly all our things.
KOMLOS HAULERS

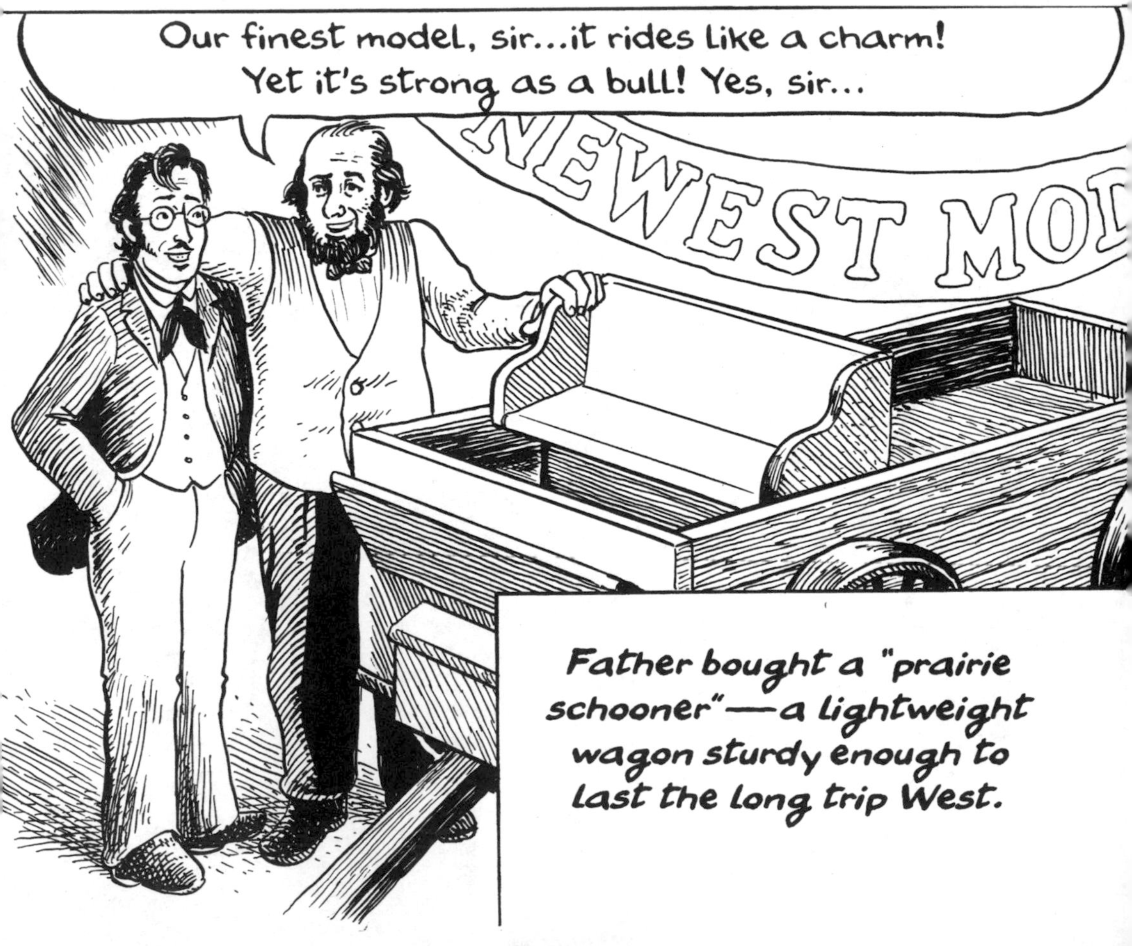
Our finest model, sir...it rides like a charm! Yet it's strong as a bull! Yes, sir...
NEWEST MOD
Father bought a "prairie schooner"—a lightweight wagon sturdy enough to last the long trip West.

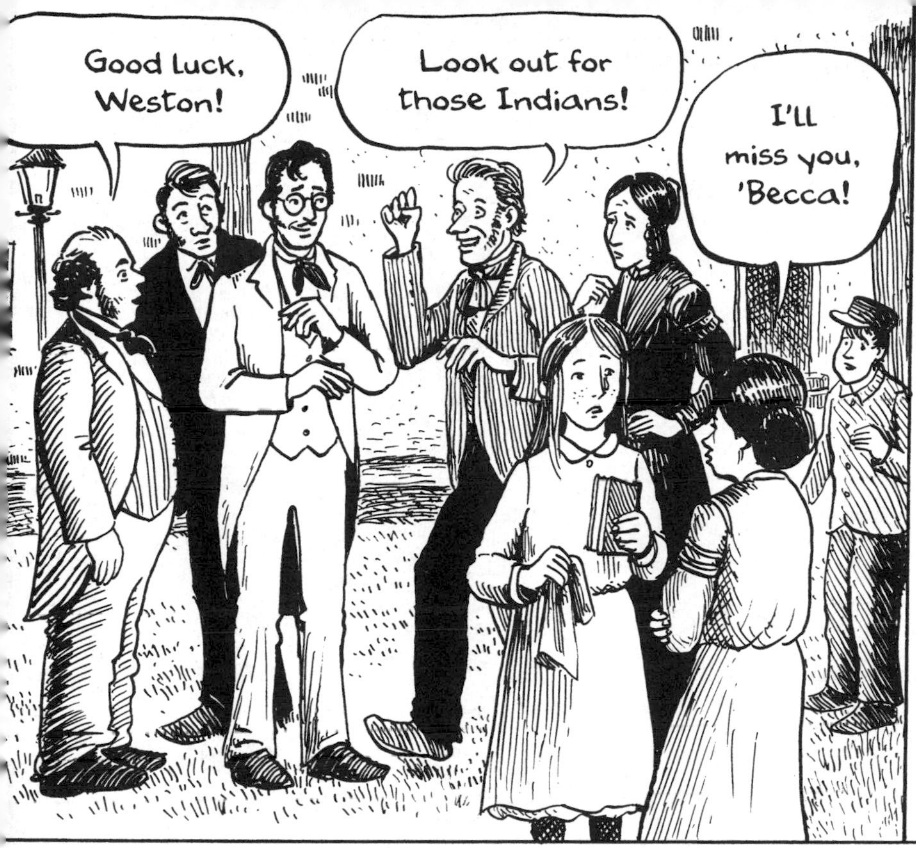
Good luck, Weston!
Look out for those Indians!
I'll miss you, 'Becca!

We said farewell to friends and family in Baltimore.

It was a sad day.

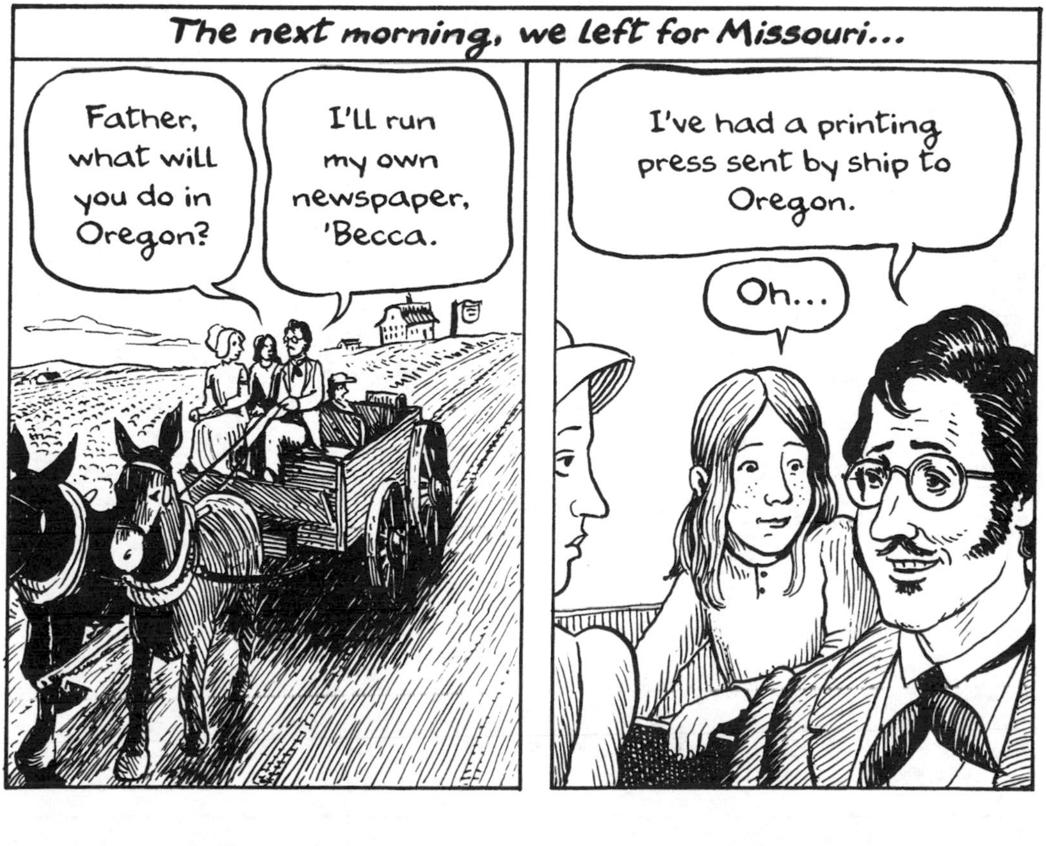
The next morning, we left for Missouri...
Father, what will you do in Oregon?
I'll run my own newspaper, 'Becca.
I've had a printing press sent by ship to Oregon.
Oh...

Forty–five days later, we arrived in Missouri...

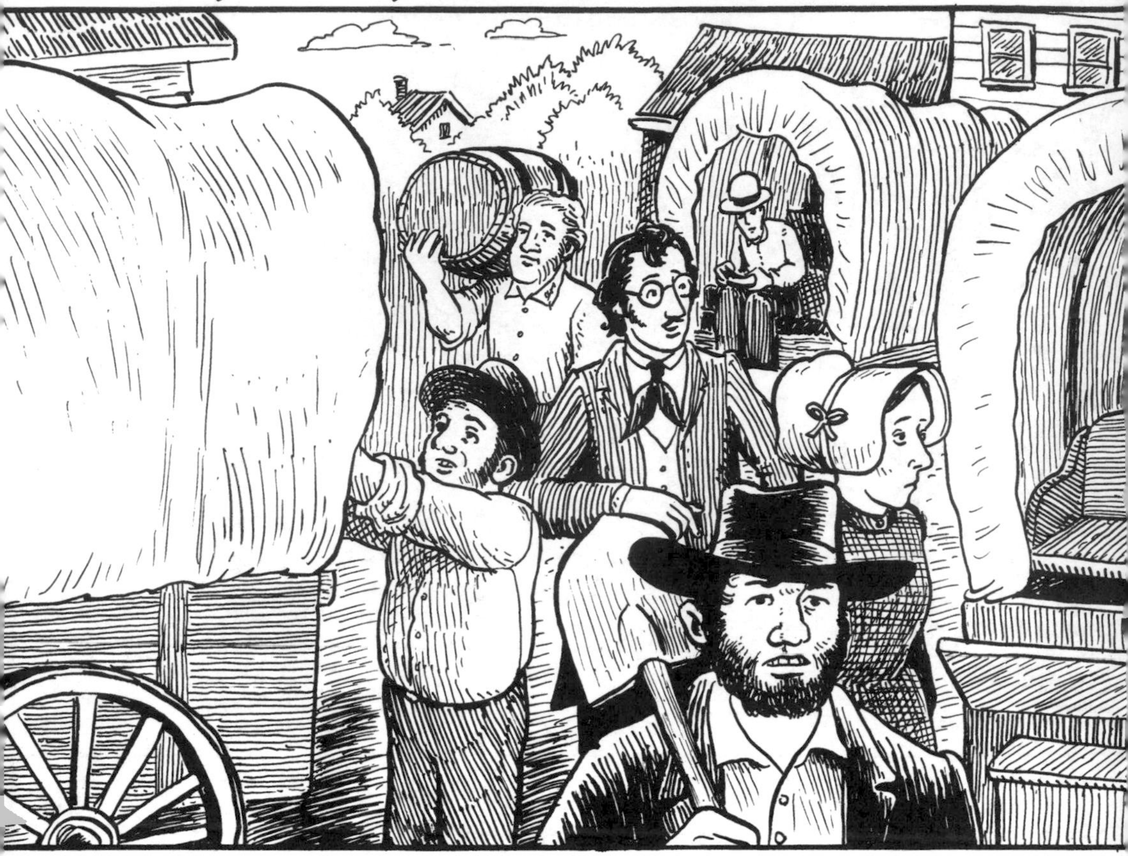

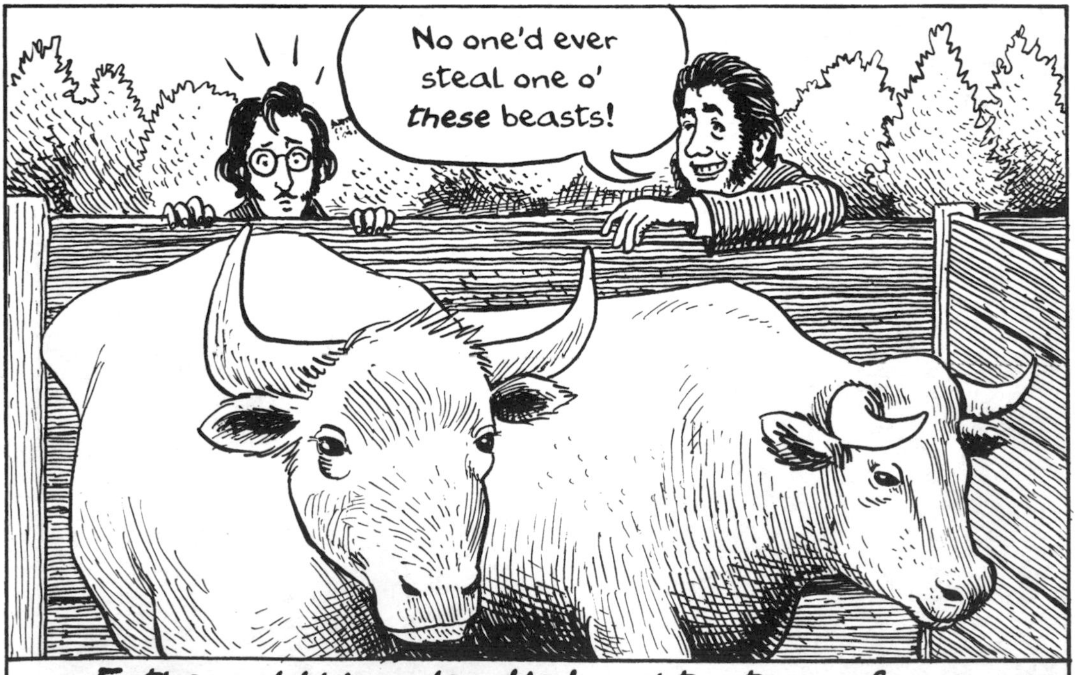
No one'd ever steal one o' *these* beasts!

Father sold his mules. He bought a team of oxen.

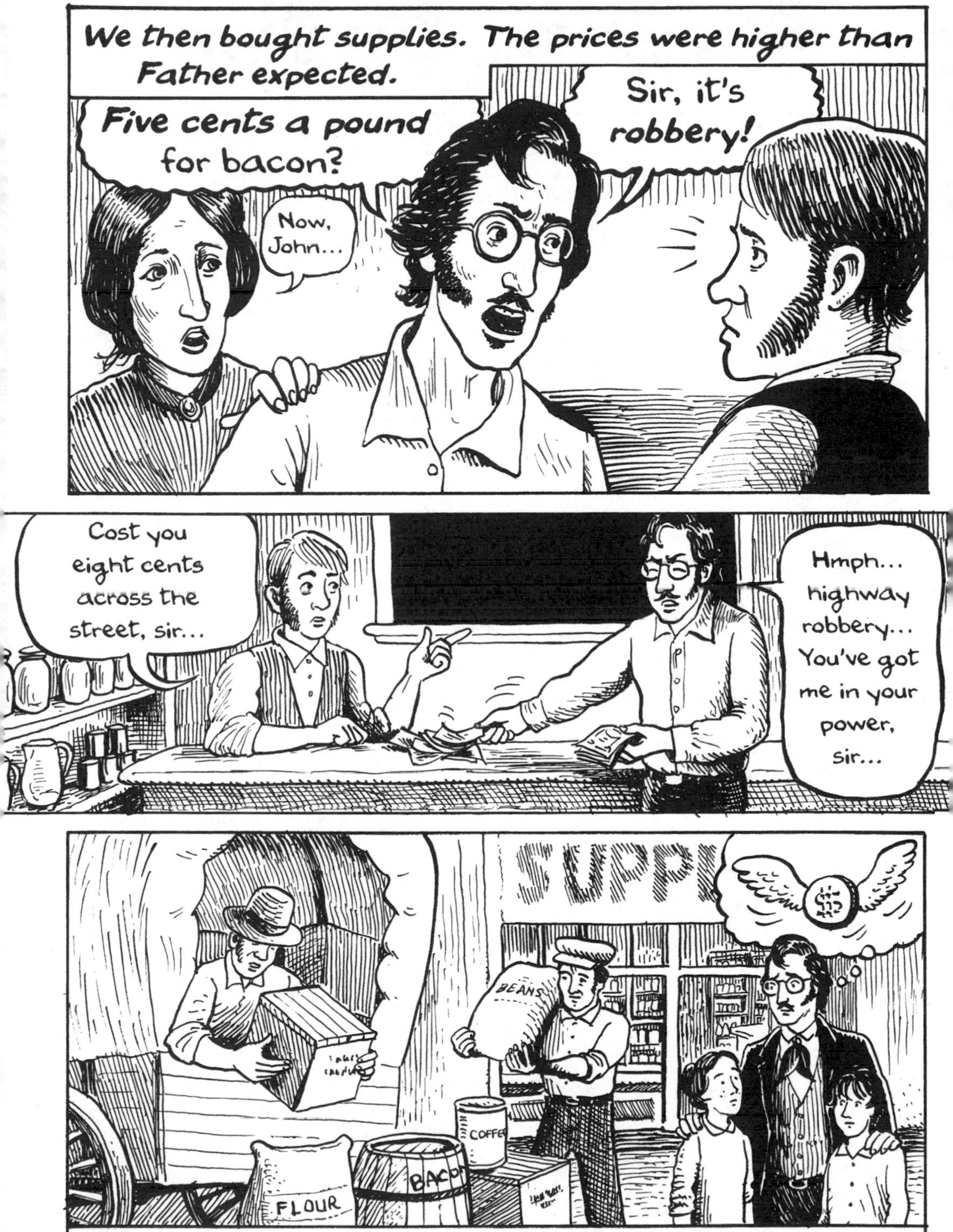
We then bought supplies. The prices were higher than Father expected.
Five cents a pound for bacon?
Sir, it's robbery!
Now, John...
Cost you eight cents across the street, sir...
Hmph... highway robbery... You've got me in your power, sir...
BEANS
FLOUR
We needed these things to stay the course to Oregon. This is what we bought for the trip...

Stocking Up For

COVERED WAGONS

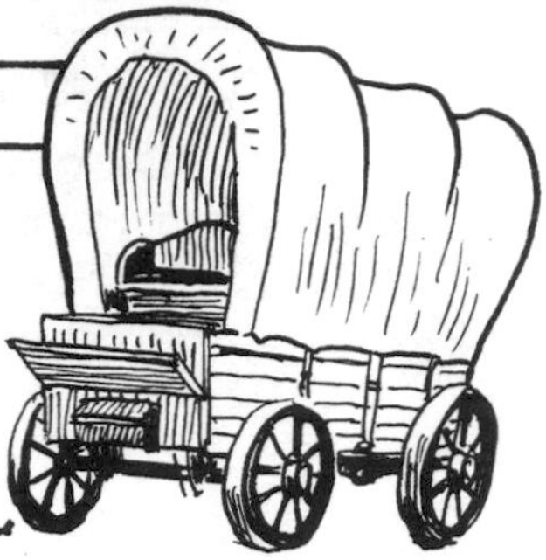

$100 for BASIC WAGON

$75 FOR SPARE AXLE

$25 FOR SPARE WAGON WHEEL

$15 00 for YOKES, CANVAS COVER & CHAINS

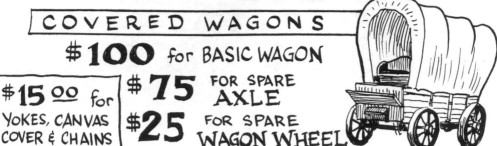

Assorted LIVESTOCK

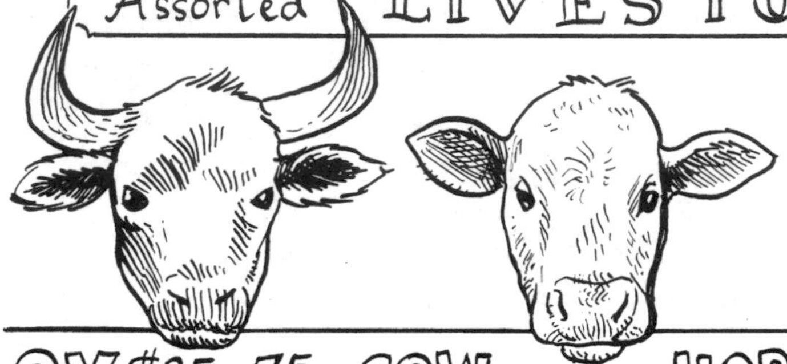

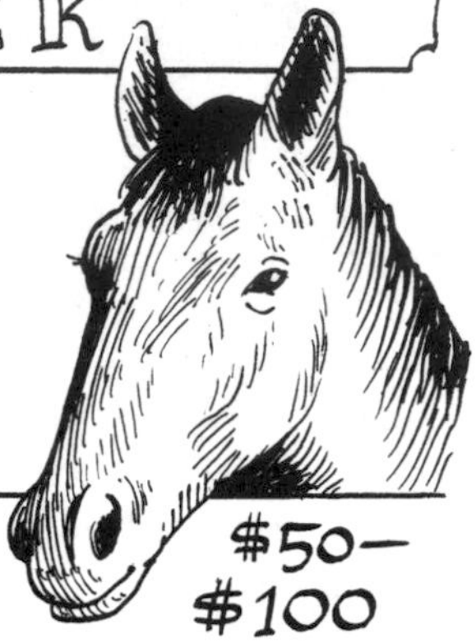

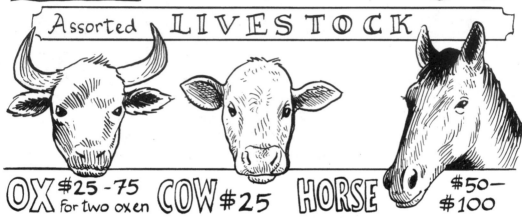

OX $25 - 75 for two oxen

COW $25

HORSE $50– $100

TOOLS

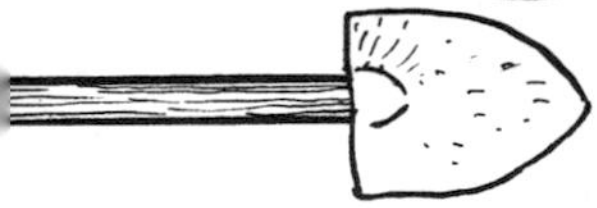

SHOVEL $1 25

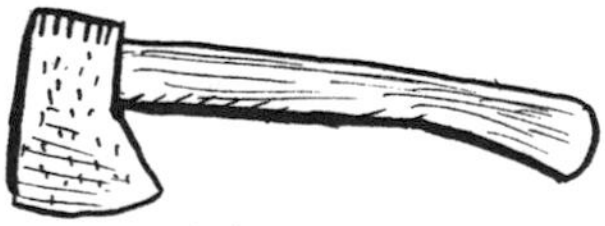

AXE $1 50

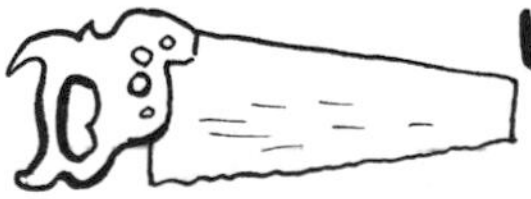

HANDSAW $1 50

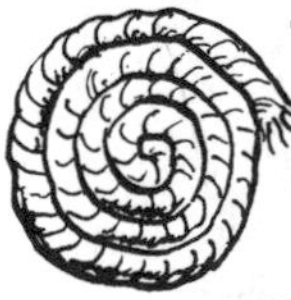

ROPE 100 ft. $2 25

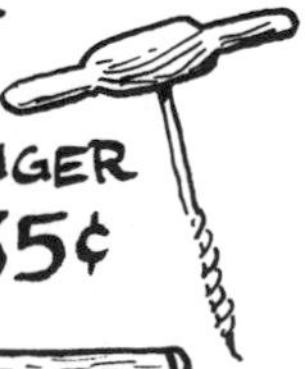

AUGER 35¢

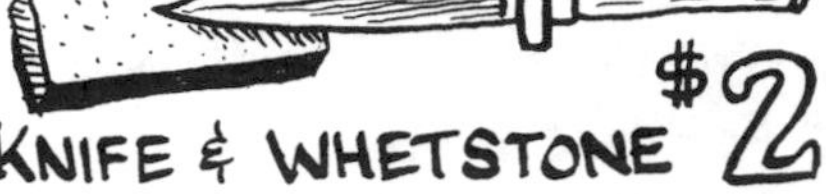

KNIFE & WHETSTONE $2 50

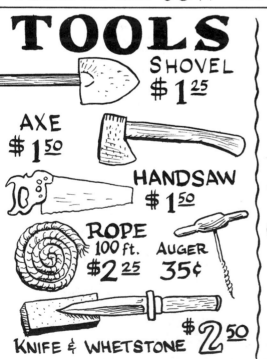

SUNDRIES

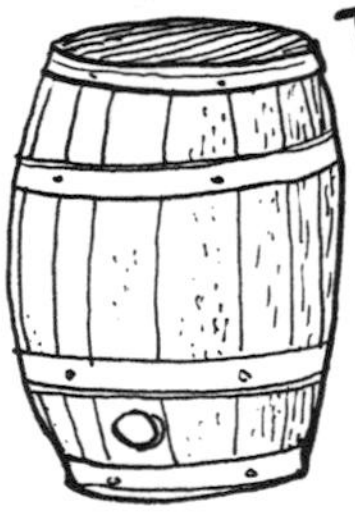

Water Keg $2 50

10 GALLONS

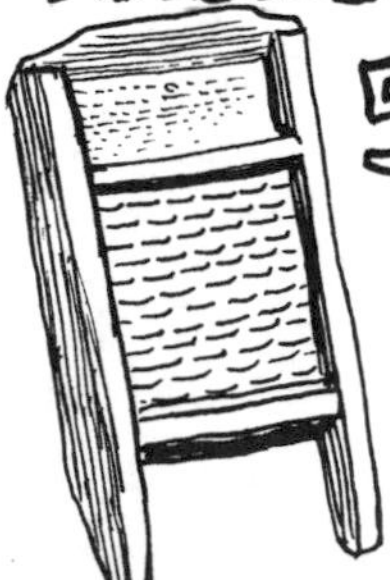

WASHBOARD 50¢

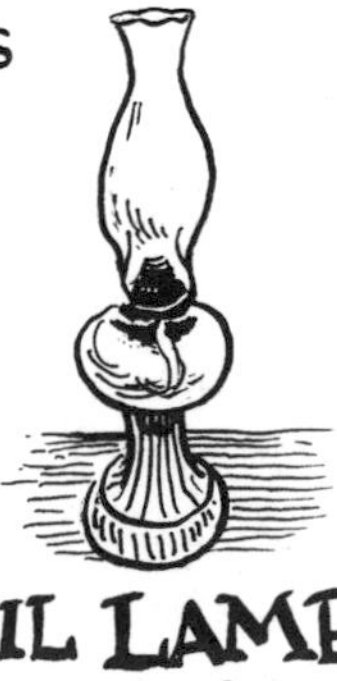

OIL LAMP {& OIL} $3 50

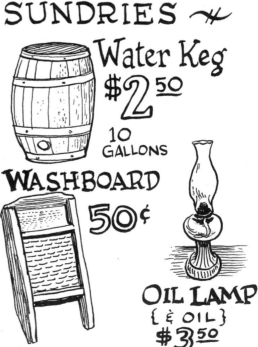

The Oregon Trail

DRY GOODS and COOKWARE

bacon (.05/lb), baking soda (.03/lb), beans (.03/lb), beef jerky (.06/lb), coffee (.08/lb), corn meal (.01/lb), dried fruit (.06/lb), flour (.02/lb), lard (.05/lb), molasses (.06/lb), pepper ($1.20/6 lbs), rice (.05/lb), salt (.06/lb), sugar (.04/lb), tea (.55/lb),pickles (.10/lb) matches ($1.00/2 dozen boxes), candles (.11/lb), soap (.11/lb), butter churn (2.00), Dutch oven (1.25), iron skillet (.75), tin plates and cups (1.00 for set of six), coffee pot (1.00), coffee mill (.50), iron utensils (1.25 per set), mixing pan for bread (.75)

CLOTHING

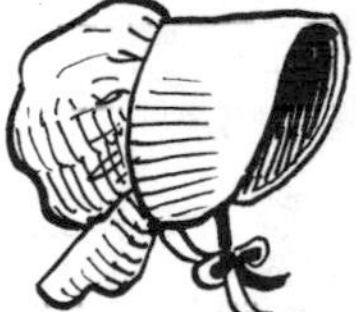

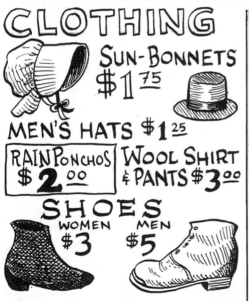

SUN-BONNETS $1.75

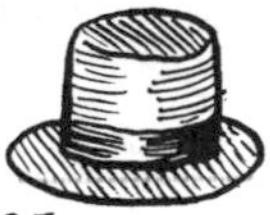

MEN'S HATS $1.25

RAIN PONCHOS $2.00

WOOL SHIRT & PANTS $3.00

SHOES

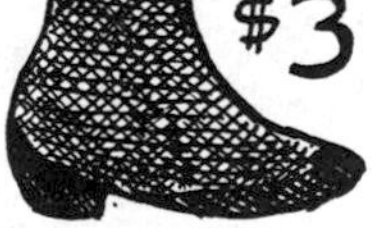

WOMEN $3

MEN $5

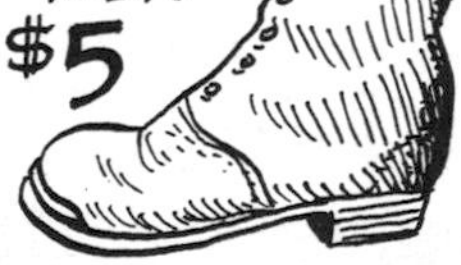

SELF-DEFENSE

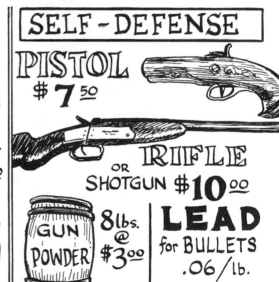

PISTOL $7.50

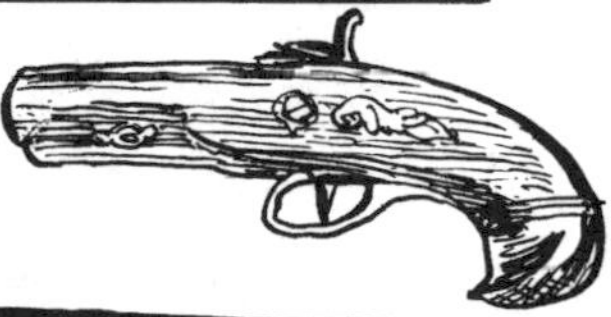

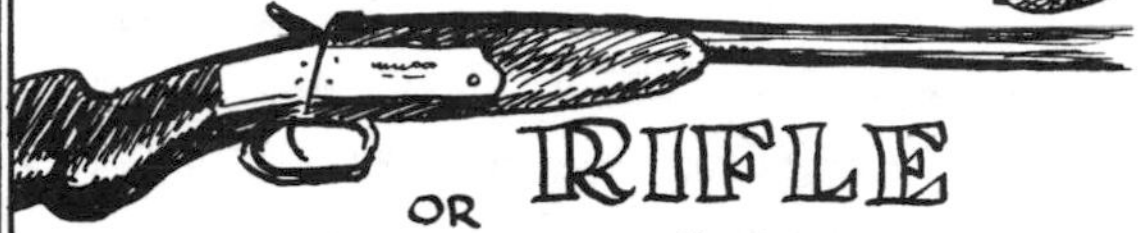

RIFLE OR SHOTGUN $10.00

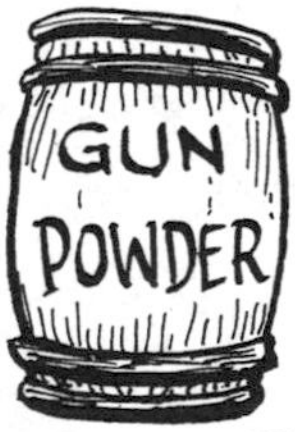
GUN
POWDER

8 lbs. @ $3.00

LEAD for BULLETS .06/lb.

MEDICINE CABINET

BRANDY $12/3 gal QUININE $.05/lb

CITRIC ACID $.25/vial

LAUDANUM $.25/vial

TINCTURE of OPIUM $.25/vial

MORPHINE $.25/vial

FUN FACT: IN 1848, $1.00 HAD THE BUYING POWER OF ABOUT $25.00 IN 2012.

CHAPTER 2
We Find Our Traveling Party

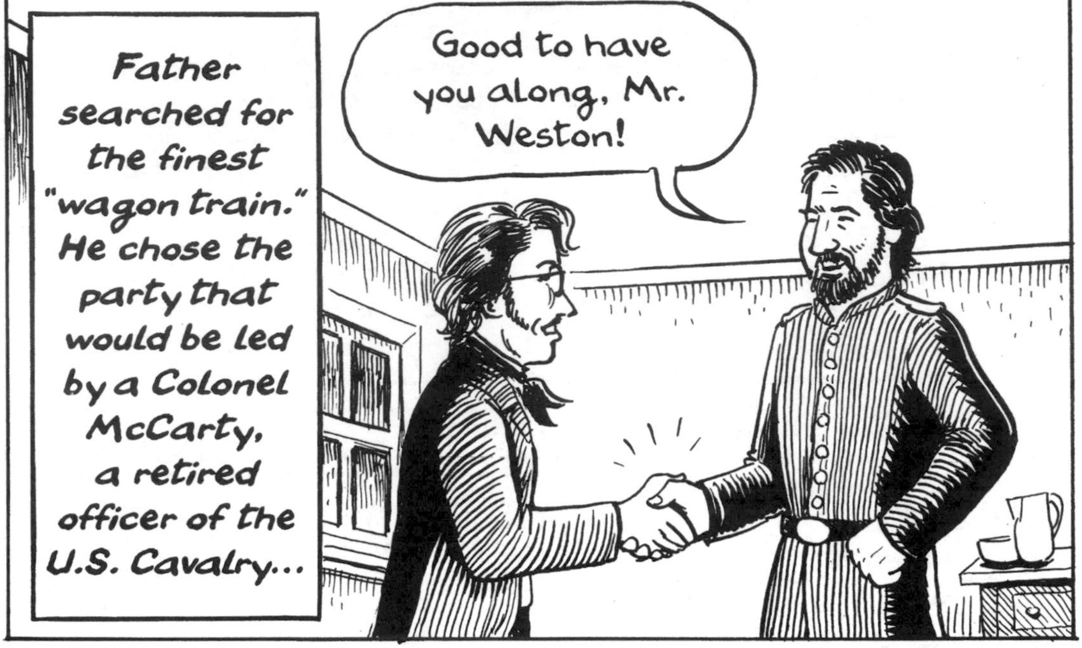
Father searched for the finest "wagon train." He chose the party that would be led by a Colonel McCarty, a retired officer of the U.S. Cavalry...
Good to have you along, Mr. Weston!

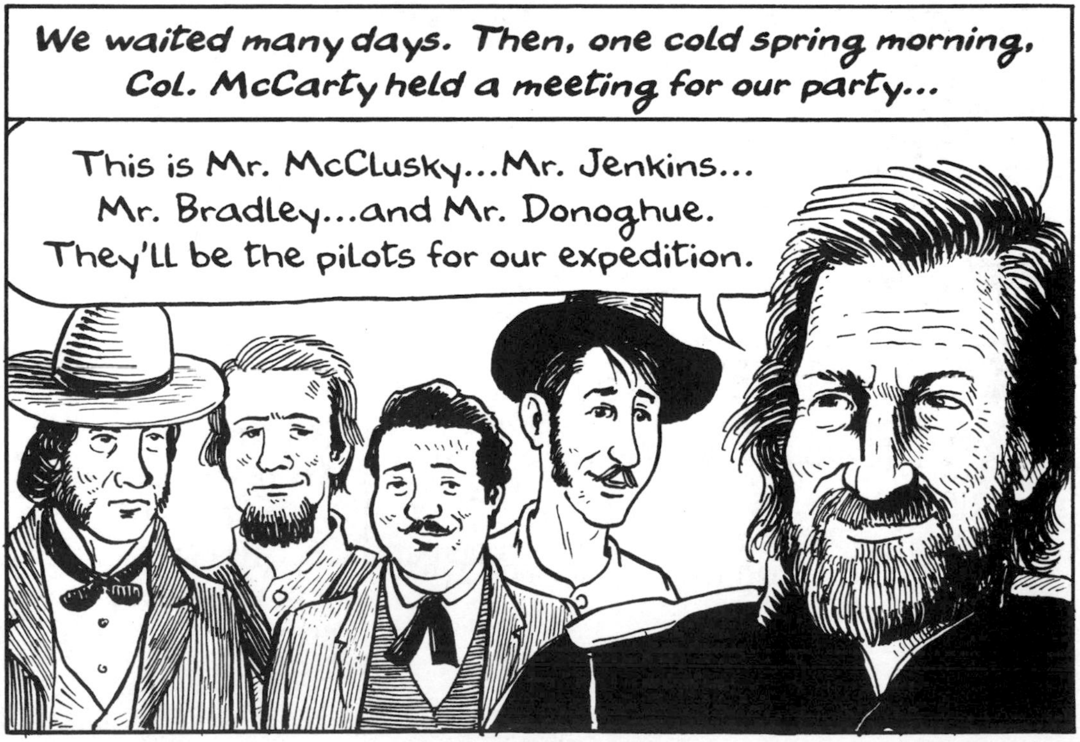
We waited many days. Then, one cold spring morning, Col. McCarty held a meeting for our party...
This is Mr. McClusky...Mr. Jenkins... Mr. Bradley...and Mr. Donoghue. They'll be the pilots for our expedition.

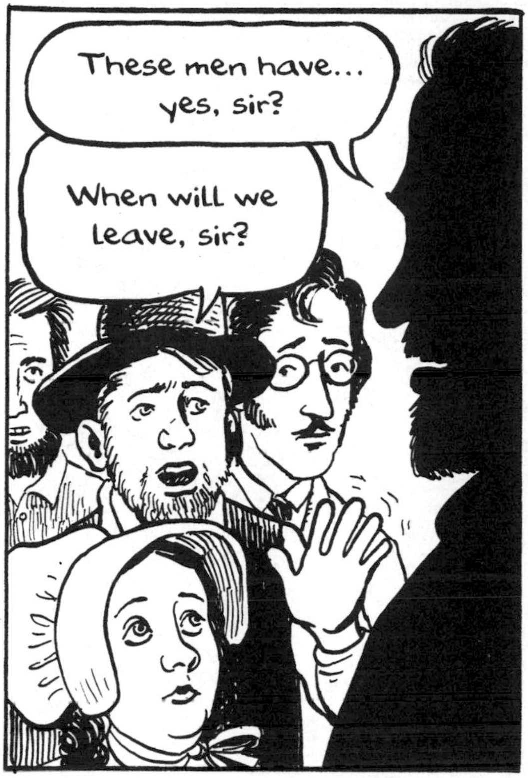
These men have... yes, sir?
When will we leave, sir?

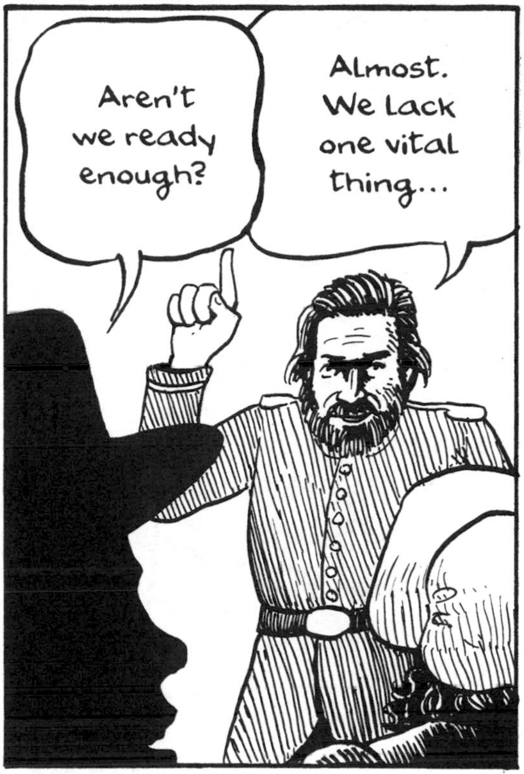
Aren't we ready enough?
Almost. We lack one vital thing...

"Grass for our oxen! Otherwise, our beasts of burden will starve! We must wait..."

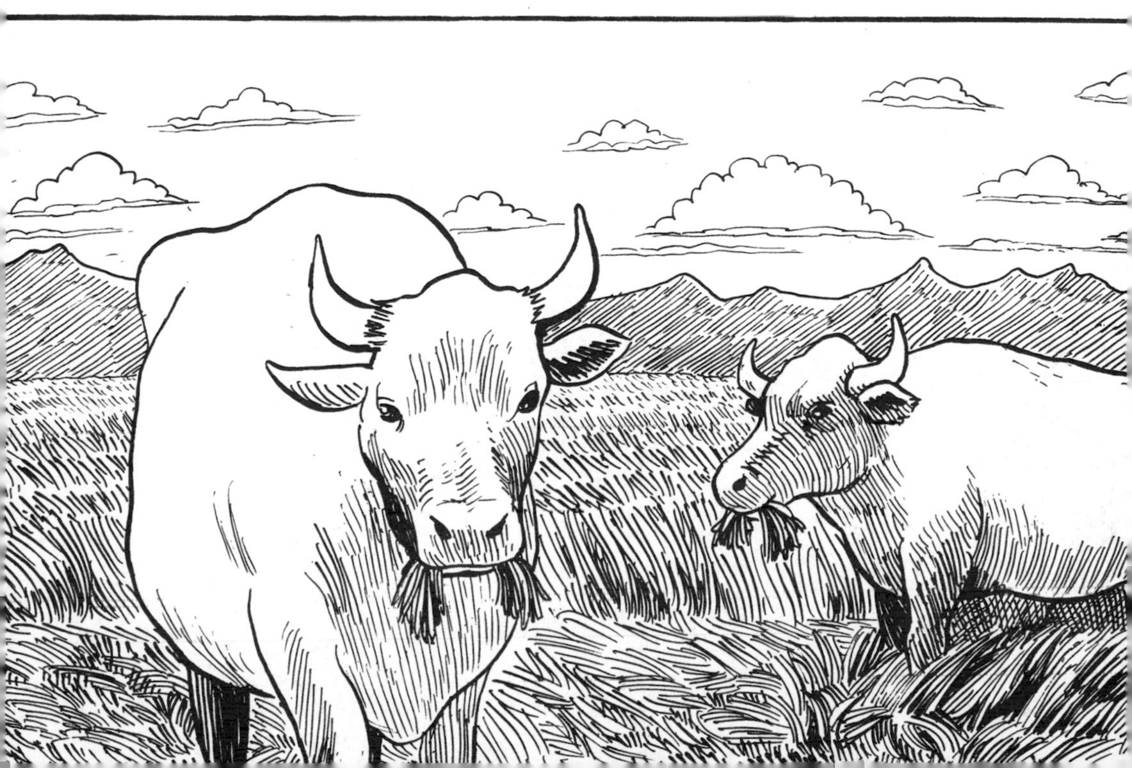

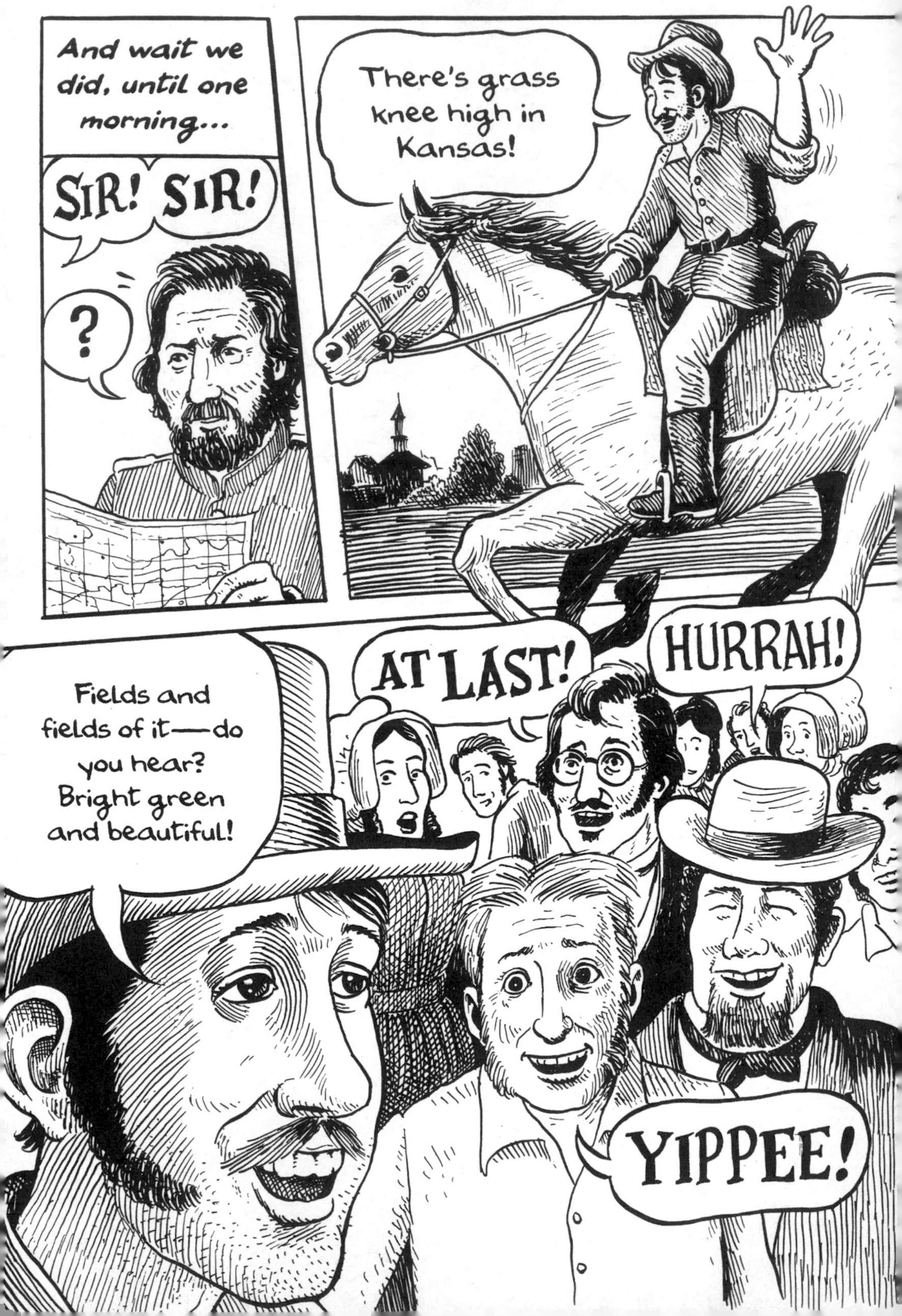
And wait we did, until one morning...
SIR! SIR!
?
There's grass knee high in Kansas!
Fields and fields of it—do you hear? Bright green and beautiful!
AT LAST!
HURRAH!
YIPPEE!

And at dawn, the next day...our wagon train began its trek down the Oregon Trail!

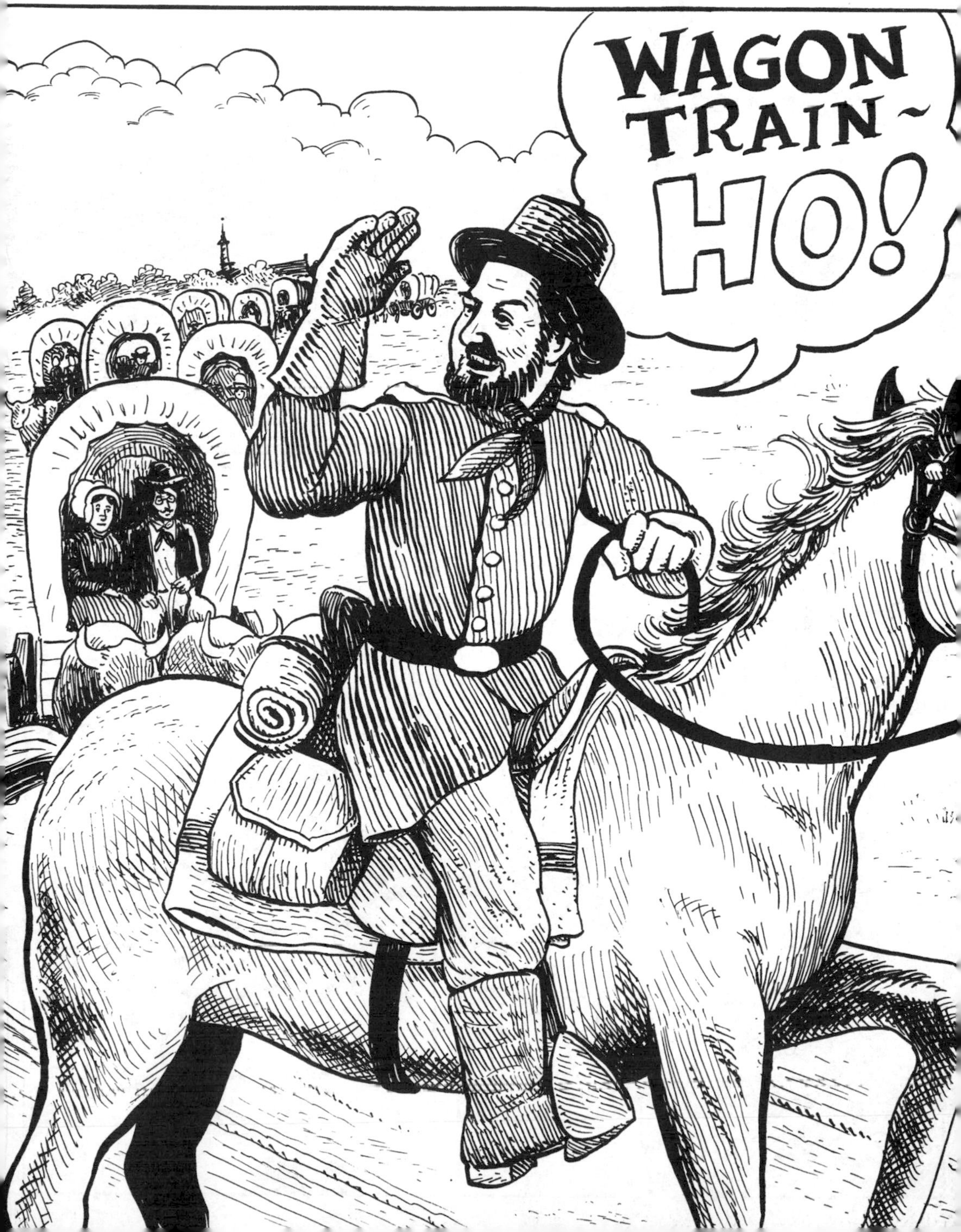
WAGON TRAIN~ HO!

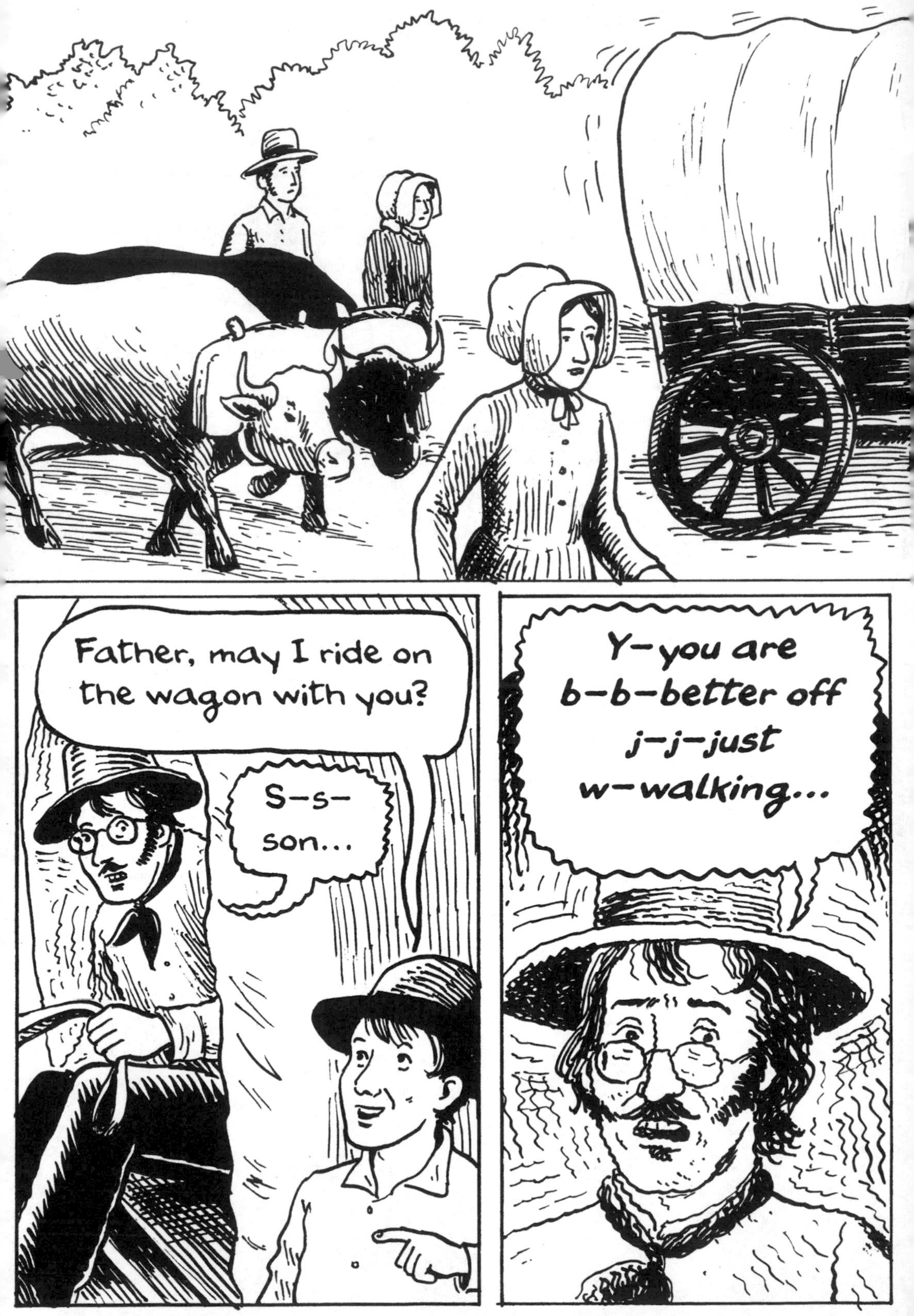
Father, may I ride on the wagon with you?
S-s- son...
Y-you are b-b-better off j-j-just w-walking...

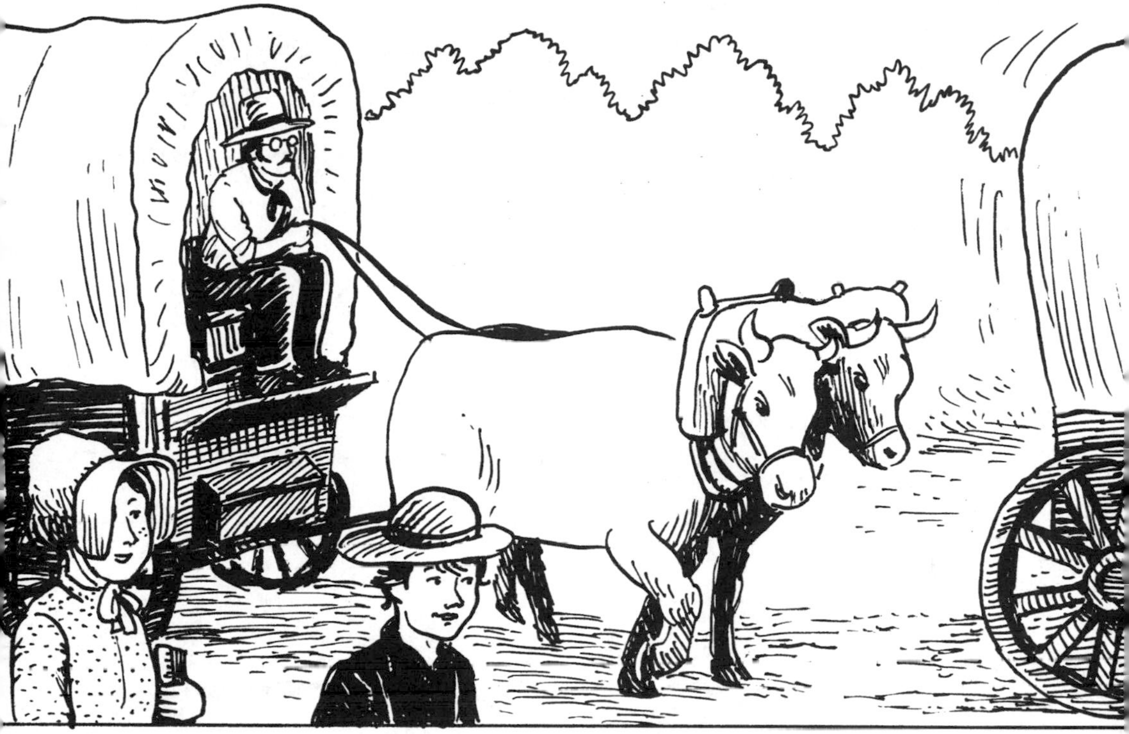

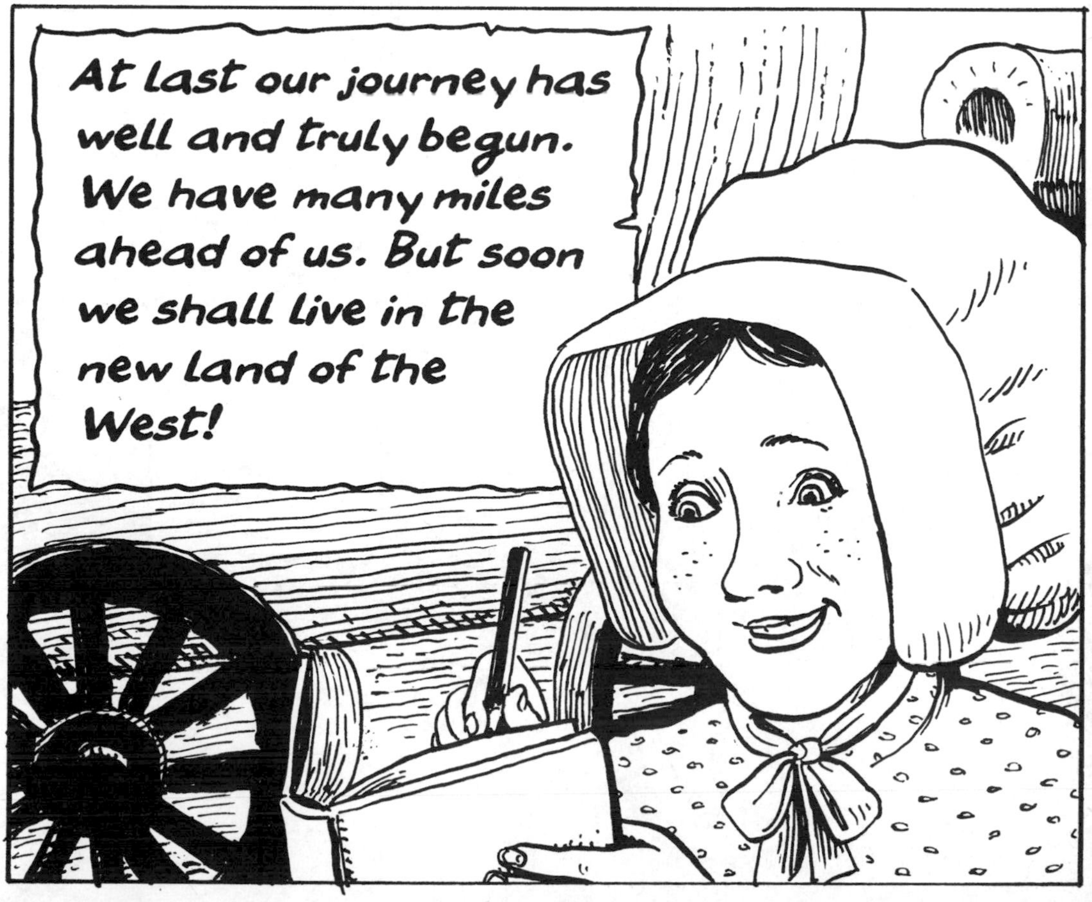
At last our journey has well and truly begun. We have many miles ahead of us. But soon we shall live in the new land of the West!

The Uncovered

To Oregon Trail travelers, the covered wagon was home on wheels. What was under its canvas cover? What did it carry?

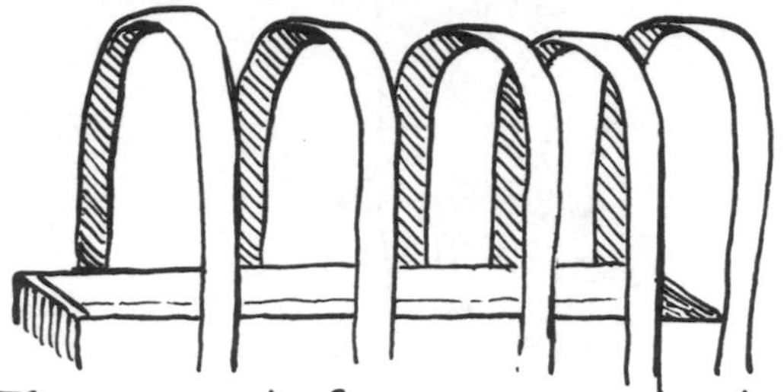

The cover's frame was made of long pieces of wood bent over and fastened together.

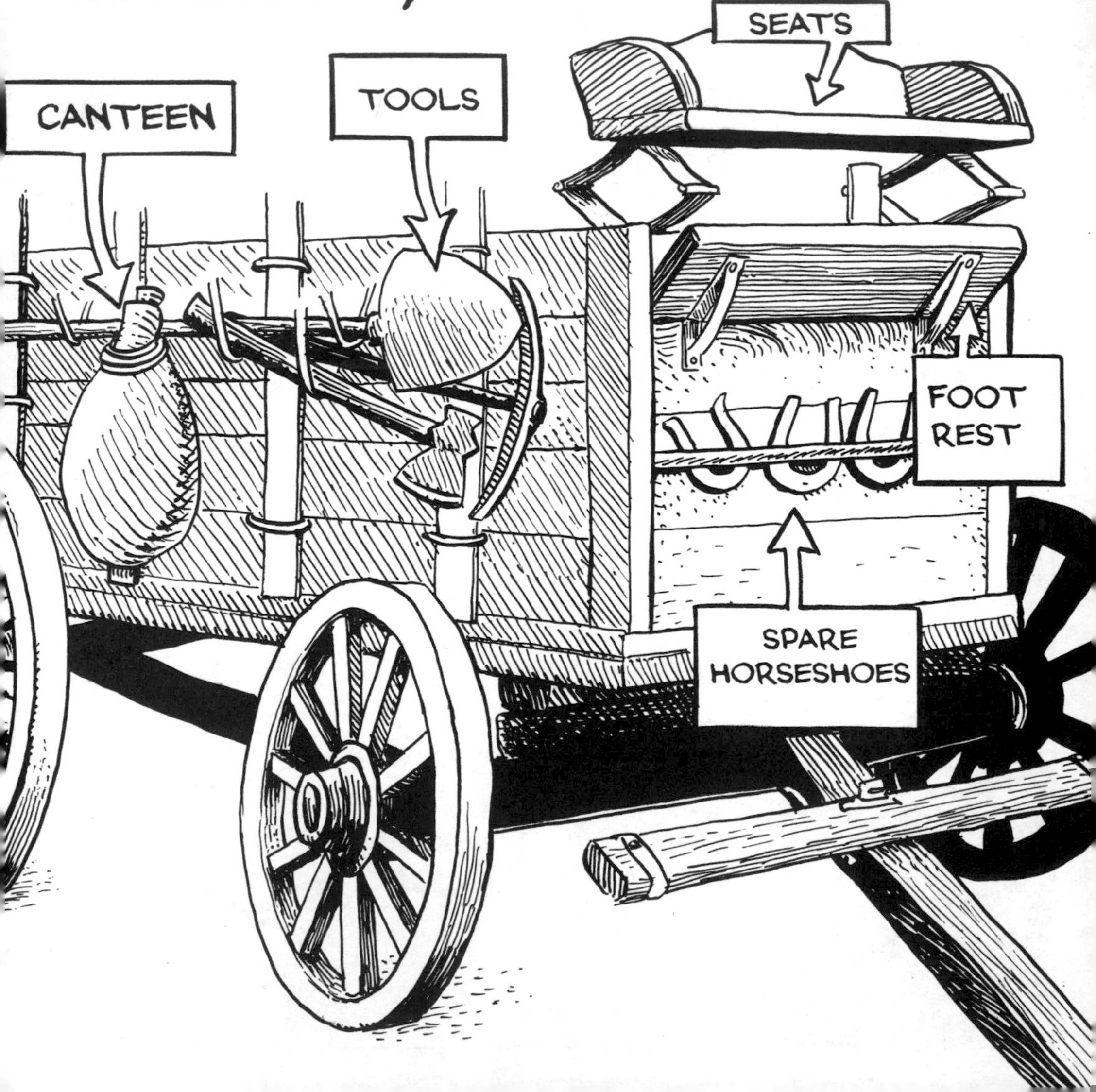
SEATS
CANTEEN
TOOLS
FOOT REST
SPARE HORSESHOES

Wagon

The wagon was packed with food, clothes, tools, and other essential supplies for this rugged journey.

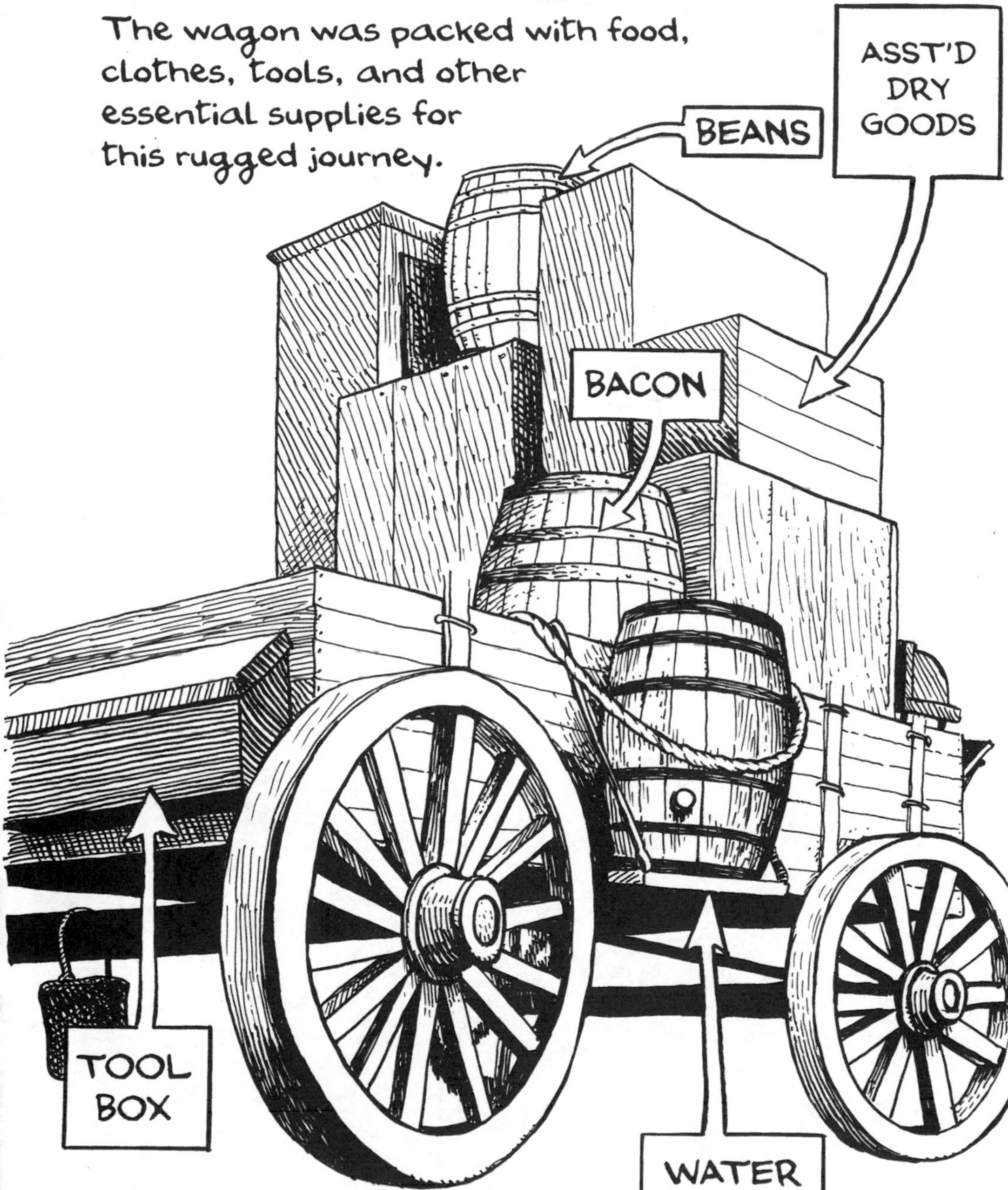
ASST'D DRY GOODS
BEANS
BACON
TOOL BOX
WATER BARREL

Spare wheels were stored under the wagon, along with other tools, weapons, etc.

Every inch of space counted!

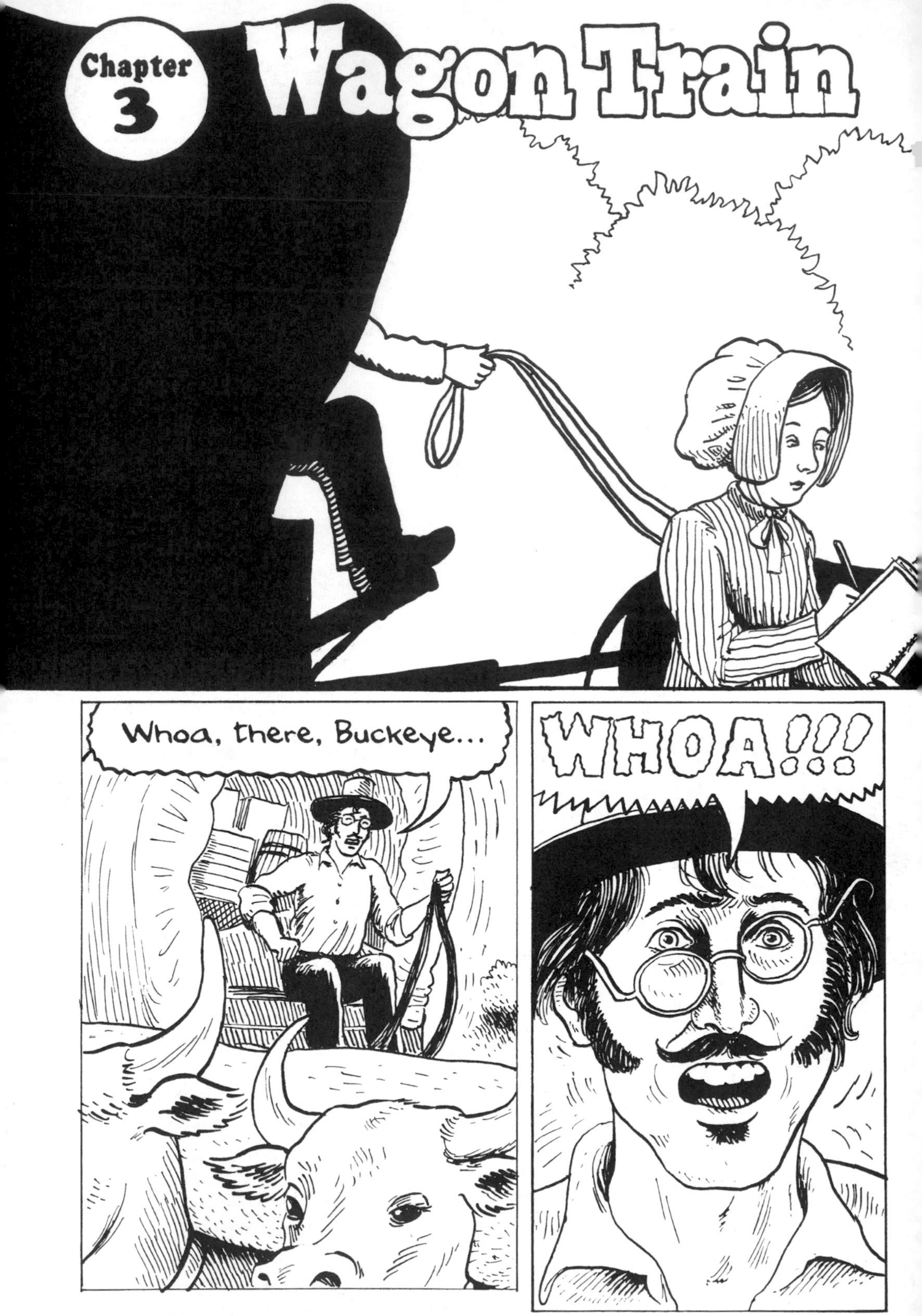
Chapter 3
Wagon Train
Whoa, there, Buckeye...
WHOA!!!

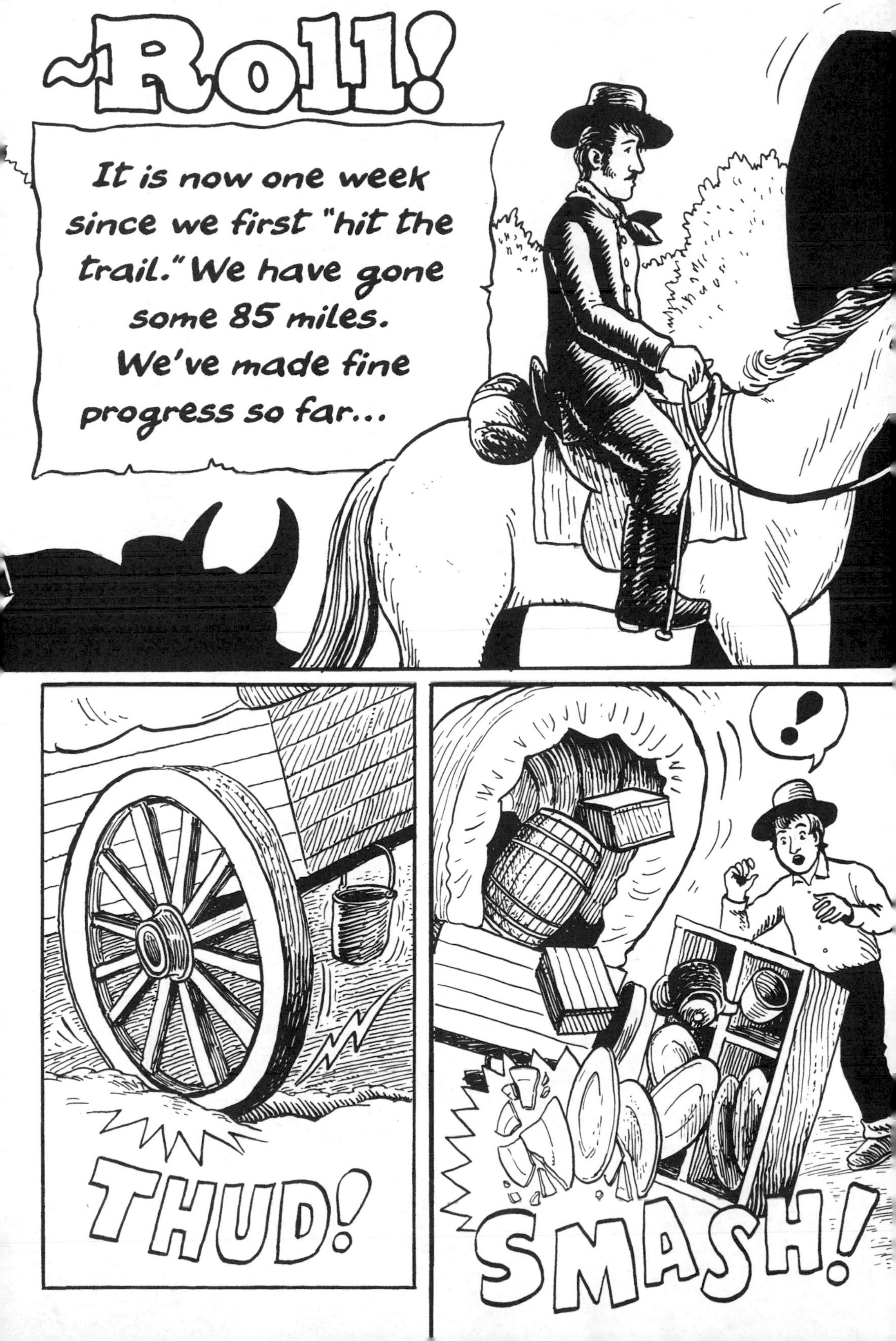
~Roll!
It is now one week since we first "hit the trail." We have gone some 85 miles. We've made fine progress so far...
THUD!
!
SMASH!

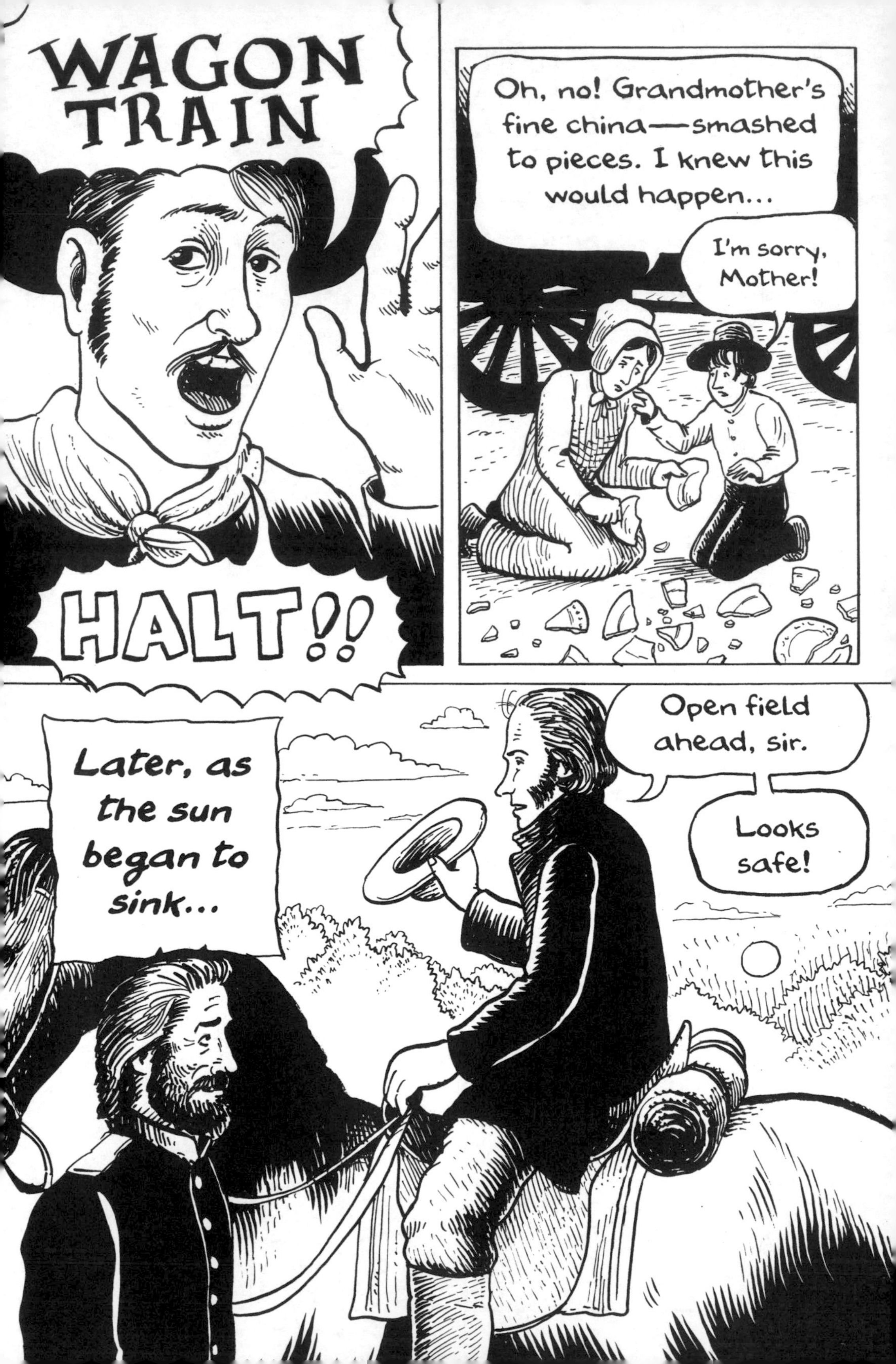
WAGON TRAIN
HALT!!
Oh, no! Grandmother's fine china—smashed to pieces. I knew this would happen...
I'm sorry, Mother!
Later, as the sun began to sink...
Open field ahead, sir.
Looks safe!

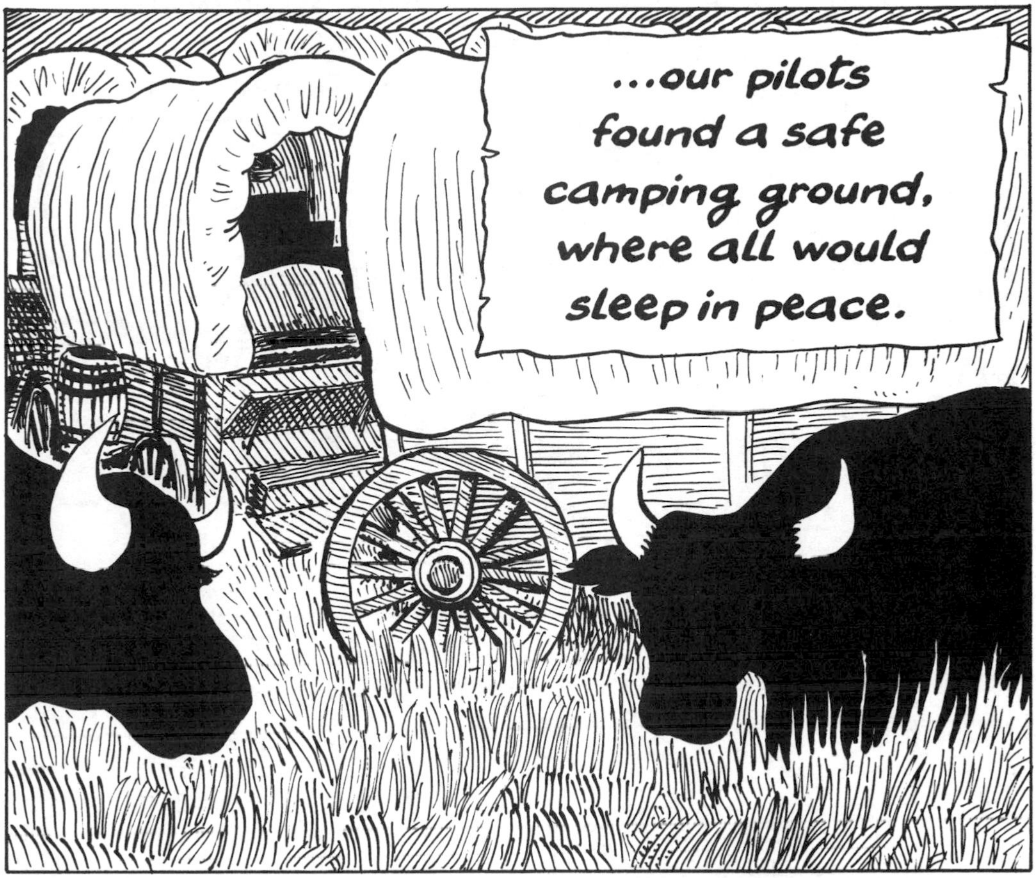
...our pilots found a safe camping ground, where all would sleep in peace.

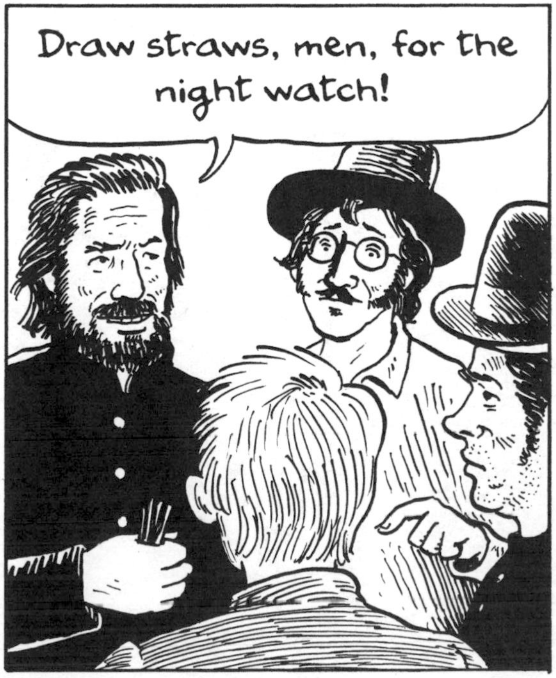
Draw straws, men, for the night watch!

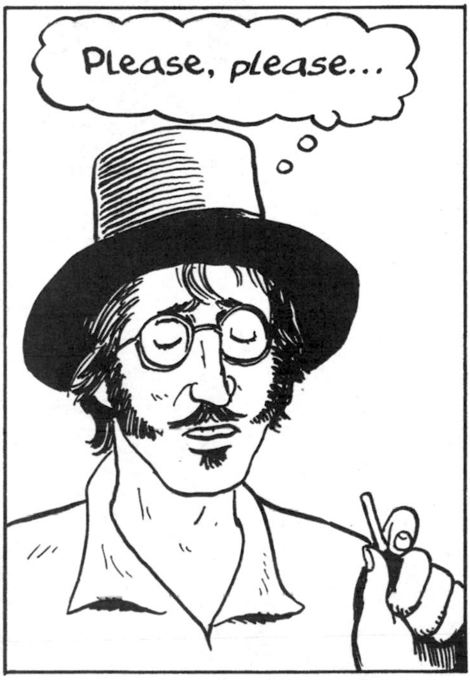
Please, please...

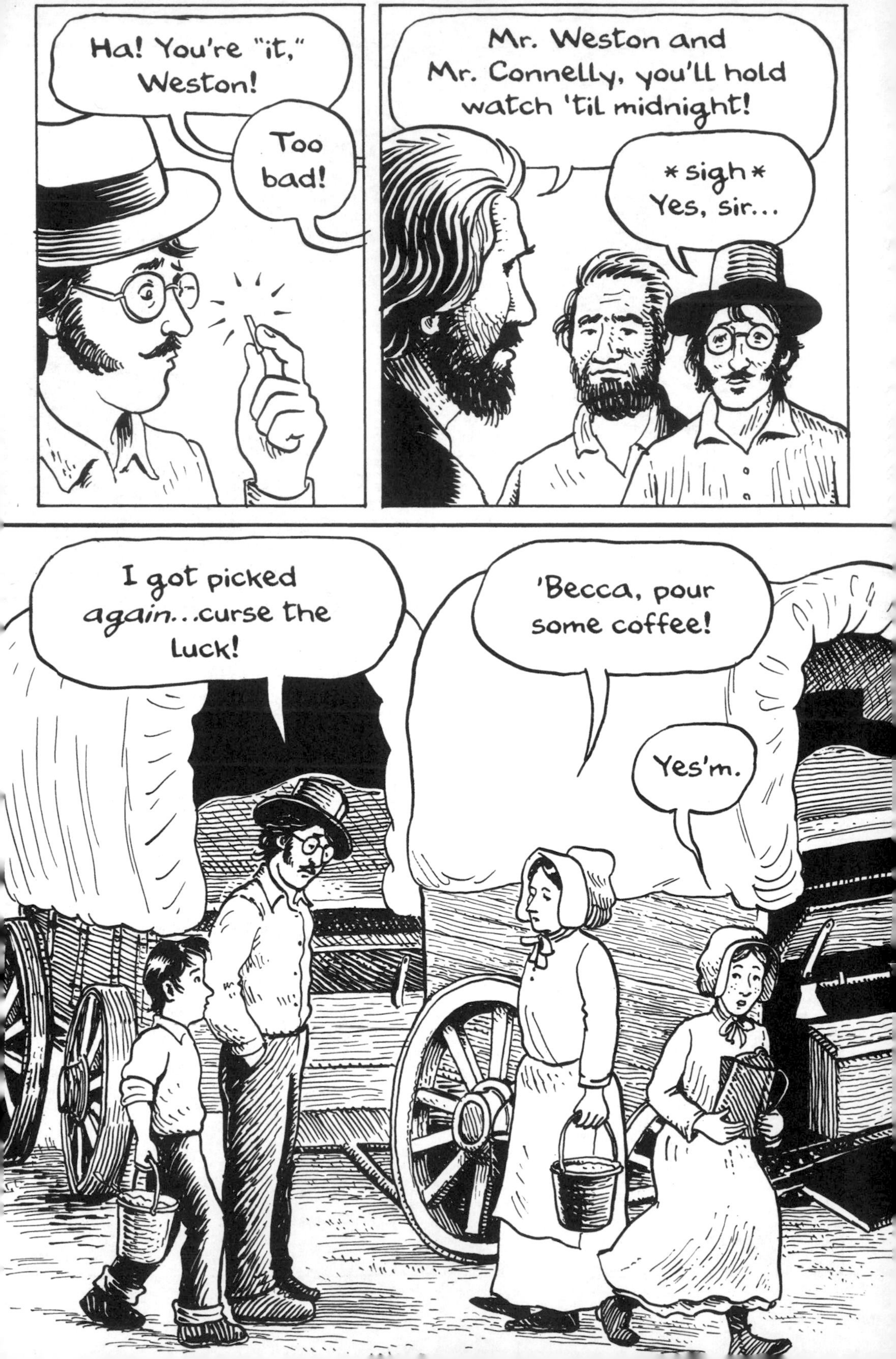
Ha! You're "it," Weston!
Too bad!
Mr. Weston and Mr. Connelly, you'll hold watch 'til midnight!
sigh Yes, sir...
I got picked *again*...curse the luck!
'Becca, pour some coffee!
Yes'm.

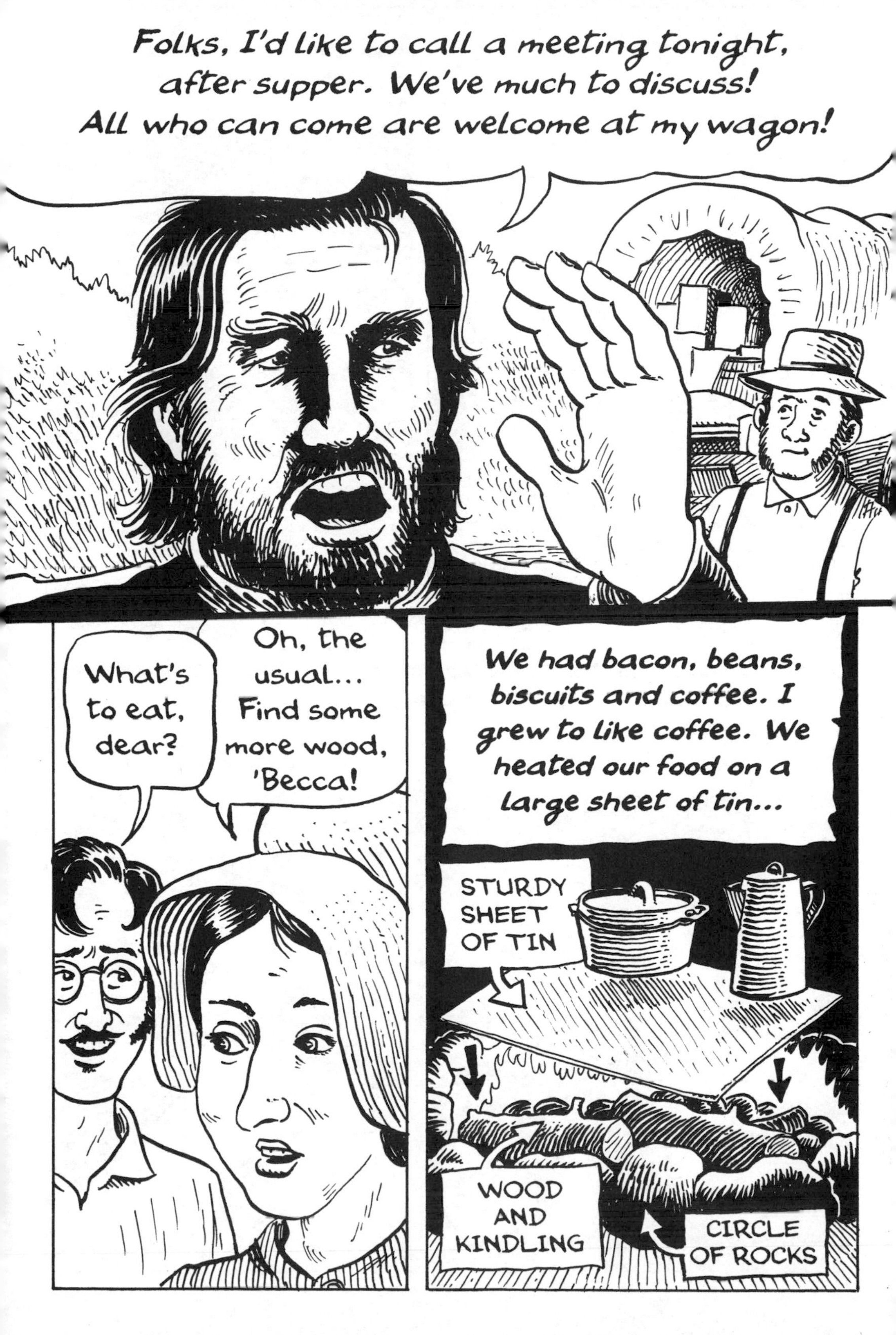

Folks, I'd like to call a meeting tonight, after supper. We've much to discuss! All who can come are welcome at my wagon!
What's to eat, dear?
Oh, the usual... Find some more wood, 'Becca!
We had bacon, beans, biscuits and coffee. I grew to like coffee. We heated our food on a large sheet of tin...
STURDY SHEET OF TIN
WOOD AND KINDLING
CIRCLE OF ROCKS

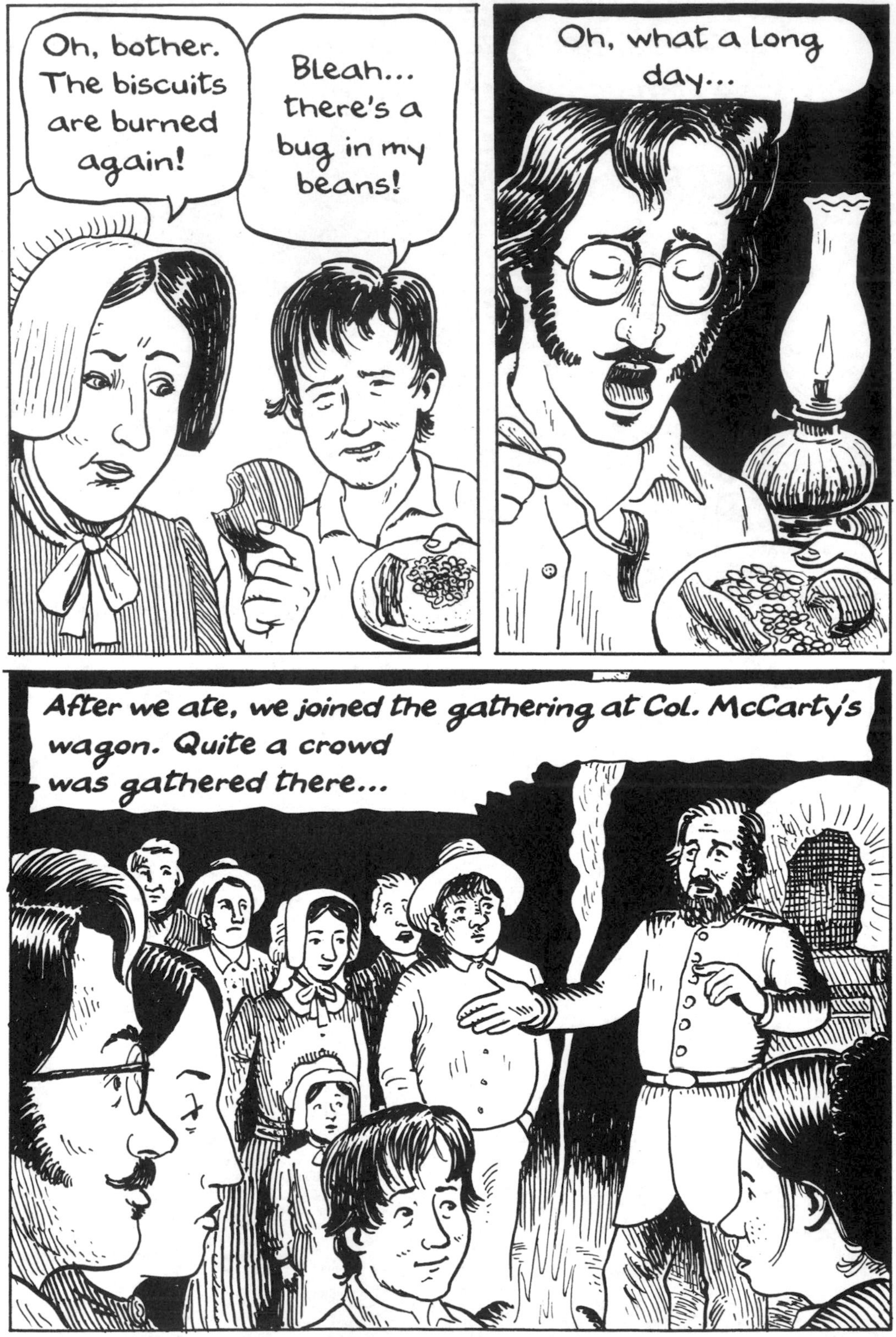
Oh, bother. The biscuits are burned again!
Bleah... there's a bug in my beans!
Oh, what a long day...
After we ate, we joined the gathering at Col. McCarty's wagon. Quite a crowd was gathered there...

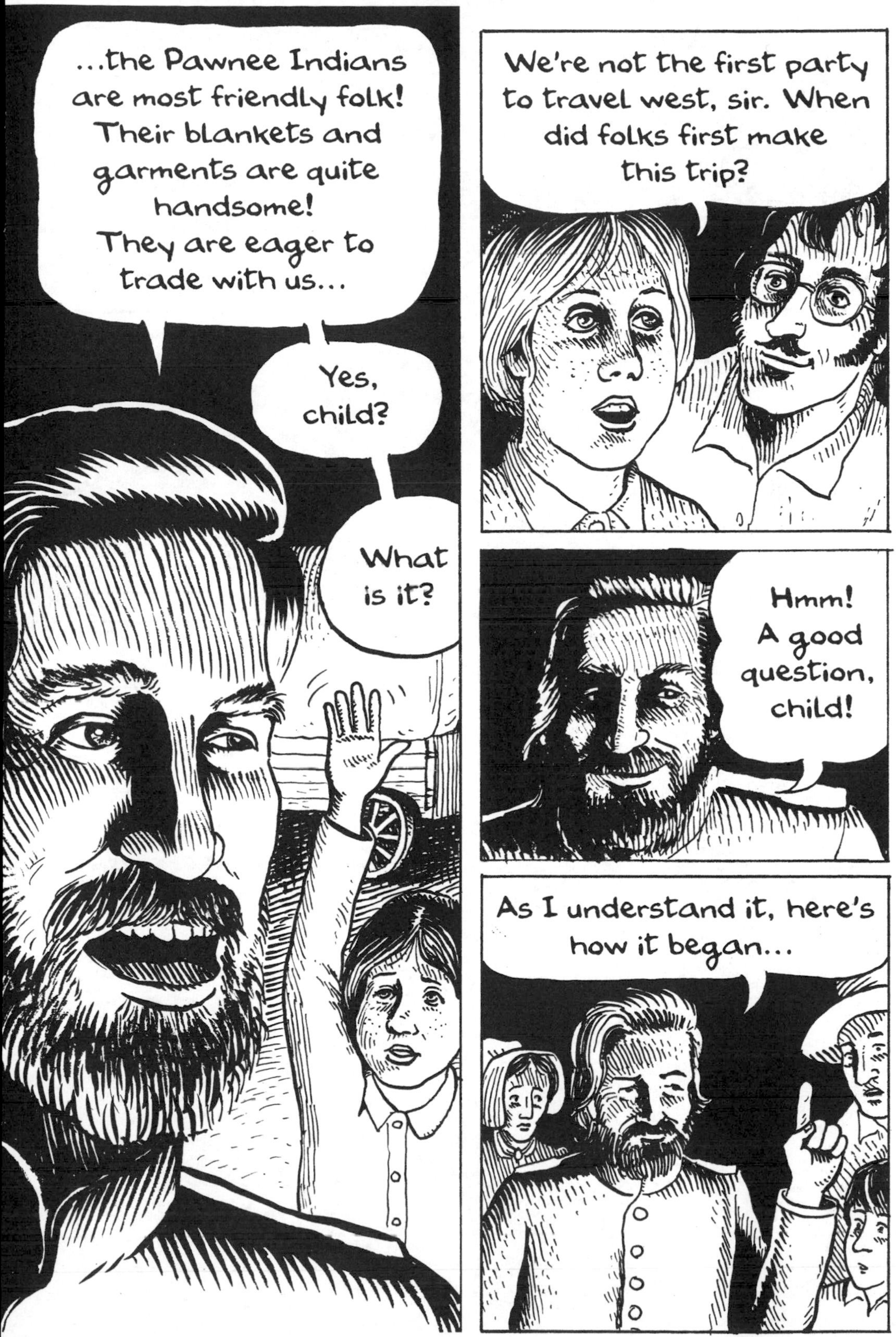
...the Pawnee Indians are most friendly folk! Their blankets and garments are quite handsome! They are eager to trade with us...
Yes, child?
What is it?
We're not the first party to travel west, sir. When did folks first make this trip?
Hmm! A good question, child!
As I understand it, here's how it began...

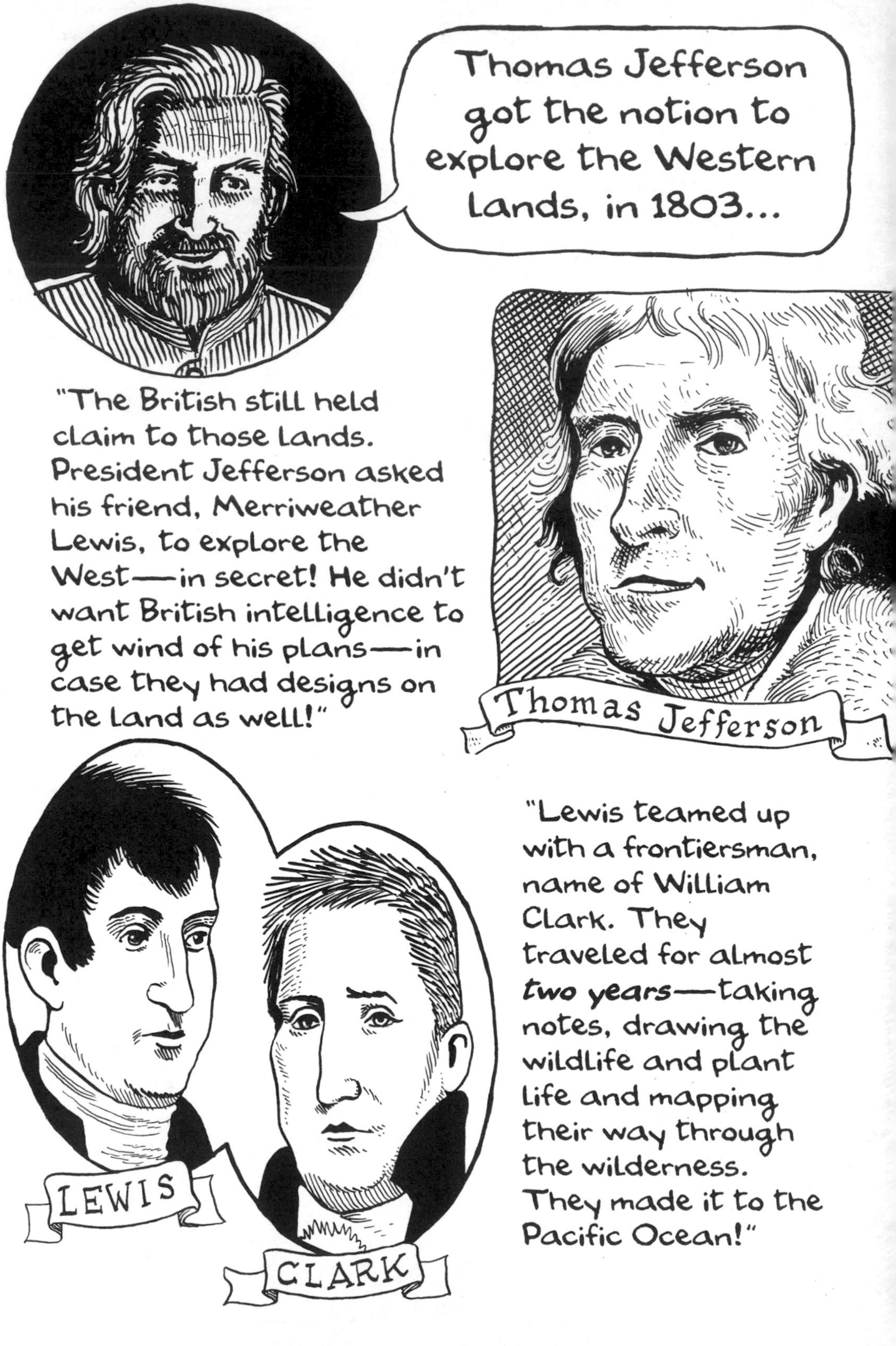
Thomas Jefferson got the notion to explore the Western lands, in 1803...
"The British still held claim to those lands. President Jefferson asked his friend, Merriweather Lewis, to explore the West—in secret! He didn't want British intelligence to get wind of his plans—in case they had designs on the land as well!"
Thomas Jefferson
LEWIS
CLARK
"Lewis teamed up with a frontiersman, name of William Clark. They traveled for almost *two years*—taking notes, drawing the wildlife and plant life and mapping their way through the wilderness. They made it to the Pacific Ocean!"

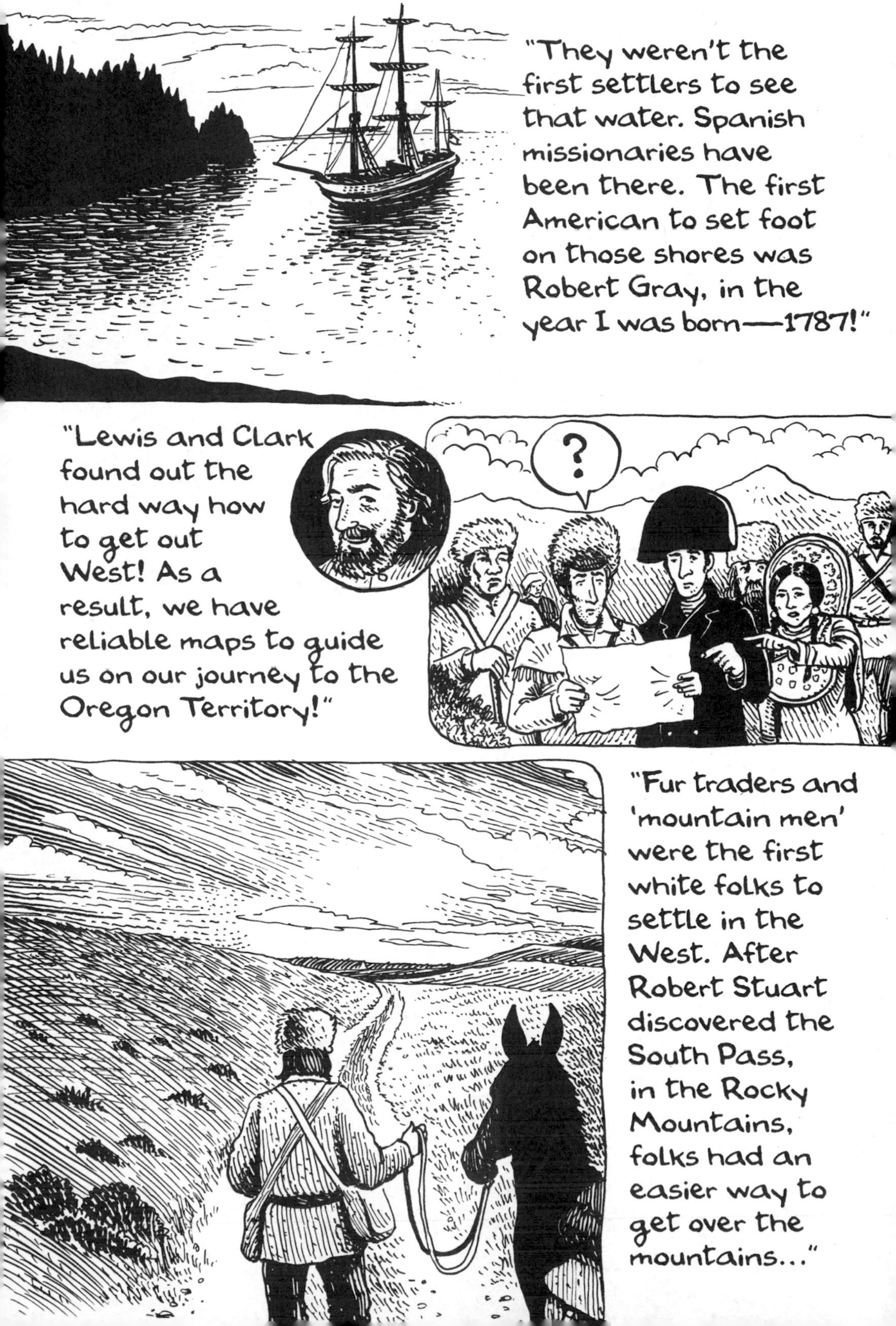
"They weren't the first settlers to see that water. Spanish missionaries have been there. The first American to set foot on those shores was Robert Gray, in the year I was born—1787!"
"Lewis and Clark found out the hard way how to get out West! As a result, we have reliable maps to guide us on our journey to the Oregon Territory!"
?
"Fur traders and 'mountain men' were the first white folks to settle in the West. After Robert Stuart discovered the South Pass, in the Rocky Mountains, folks had an easier way to get over the mountains..."

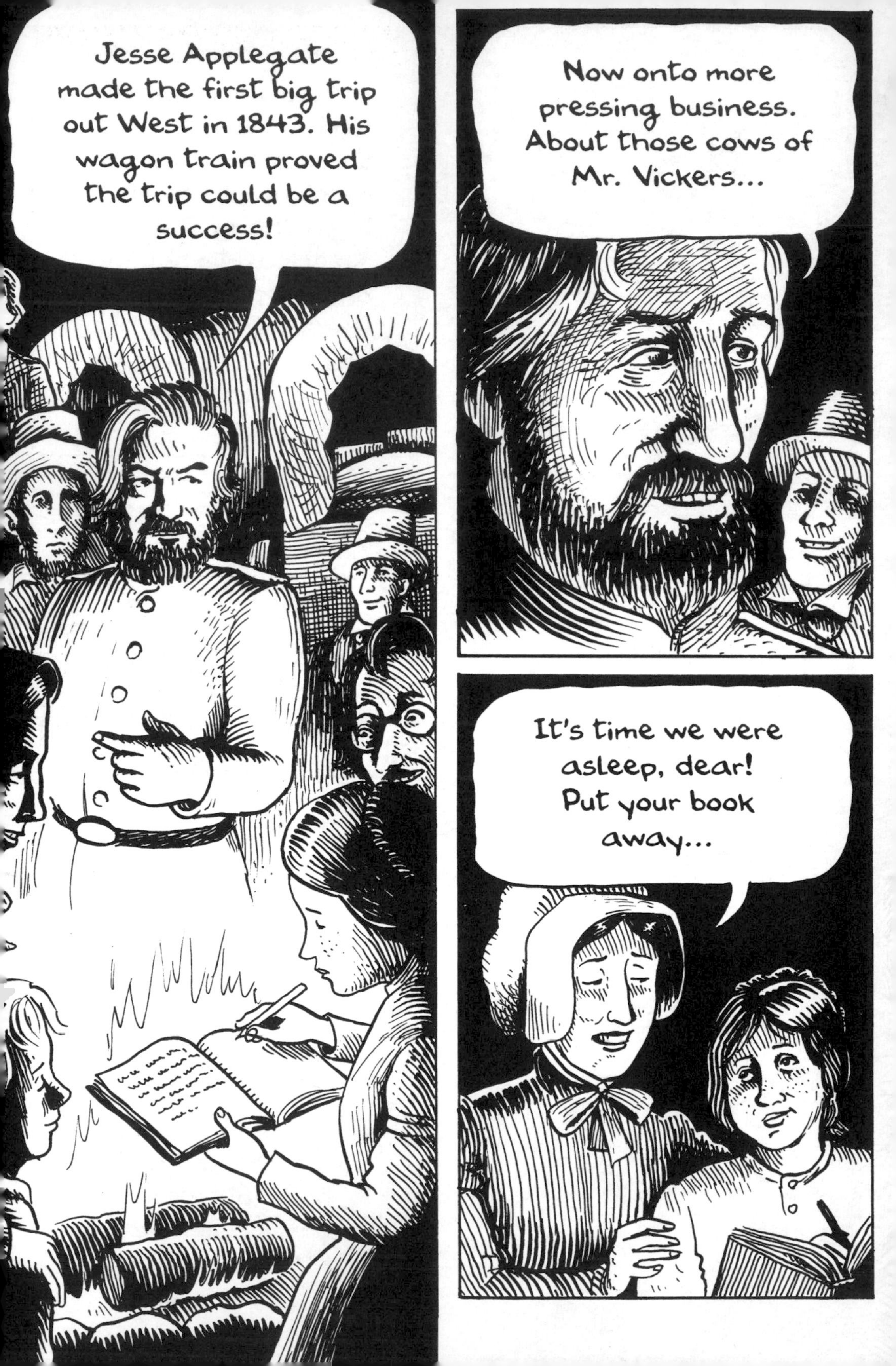
Jesse Applegate made the first big trip out West in 1843. His wagon train proved the trip could be a success!
Now onto more pressing business. About those cows of Mr. Vickers...
It's time we were asleep, dear! Put your book away...

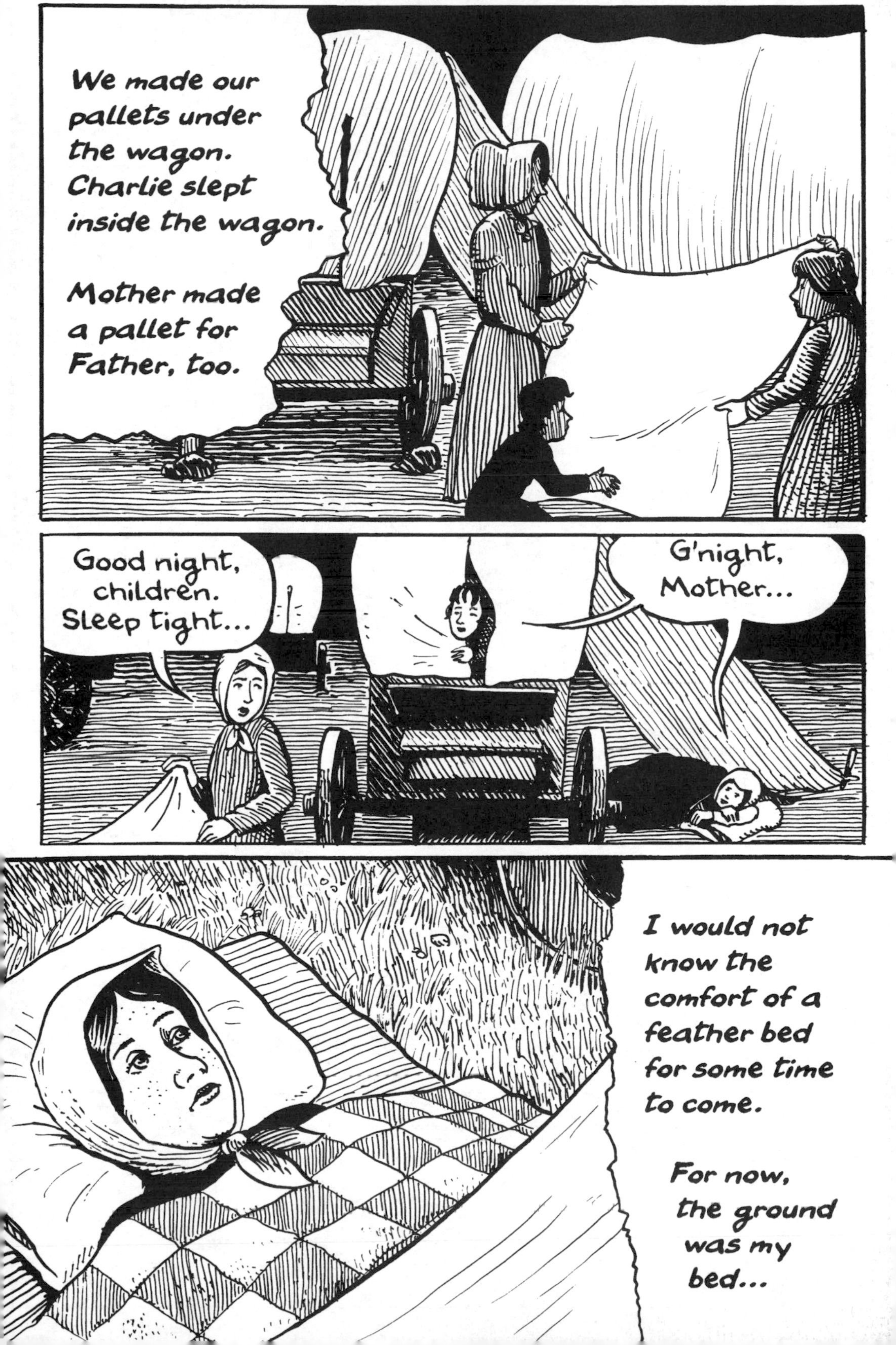
We made our pallets under the wagon. Charlie slept inside the wagon.
Mother made a pallet for Father, too.
Good night, children. Sleep tight...
G'night, Mother...
I would not know the comfort of a feather bed for some time to come.
For now, the ground was my bed...

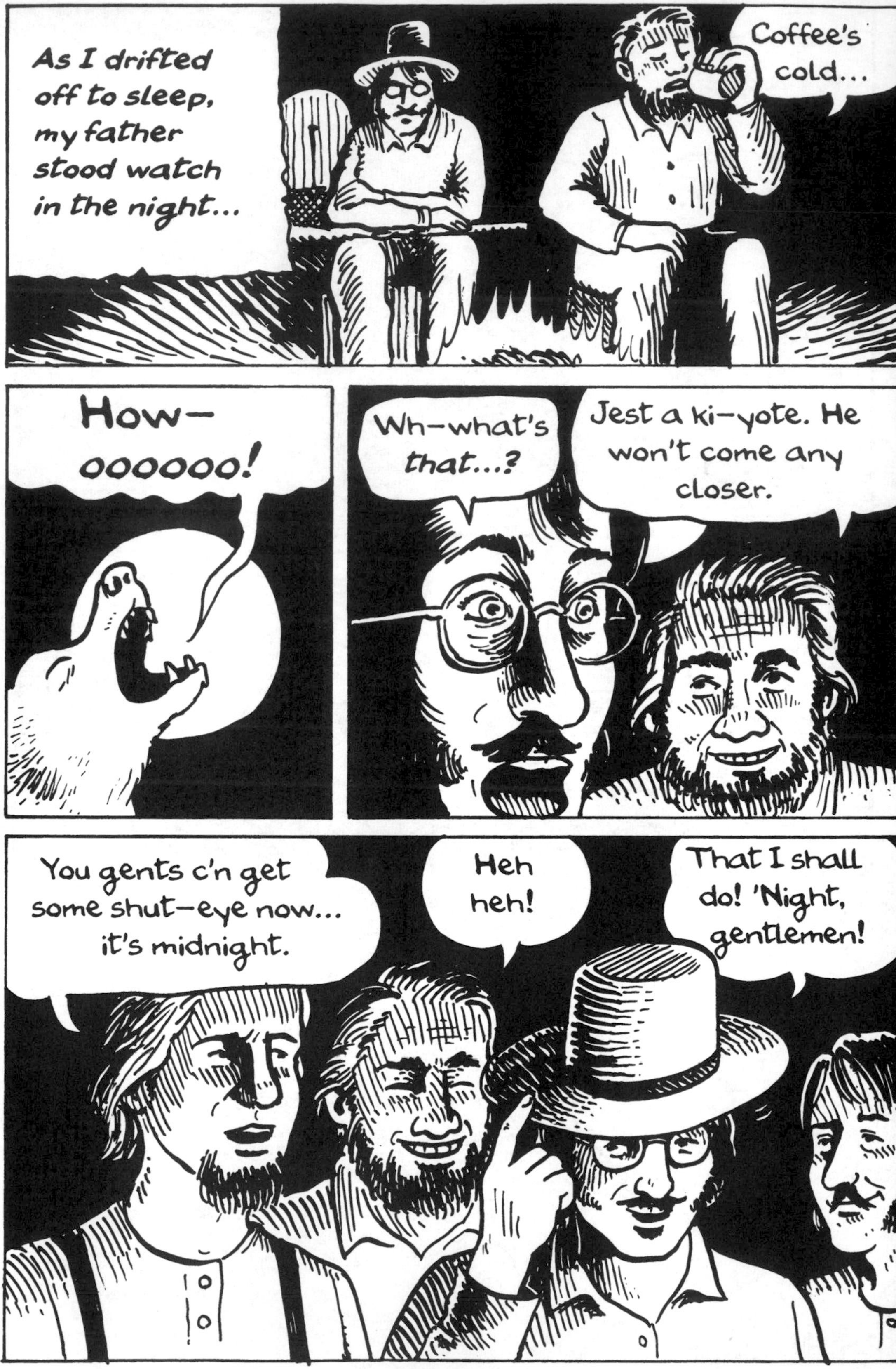
As I drifted off to sleep, my father stood watch in the night...
Coffee's cold...
How-oooooo!
Wh-what's *that*...?
Jest a ki-yote. He won't come any closer.
You gents c'n get some shut-eye now... it's midnight.
Heh heh!
That I shall do! 'Night, gentlemen!

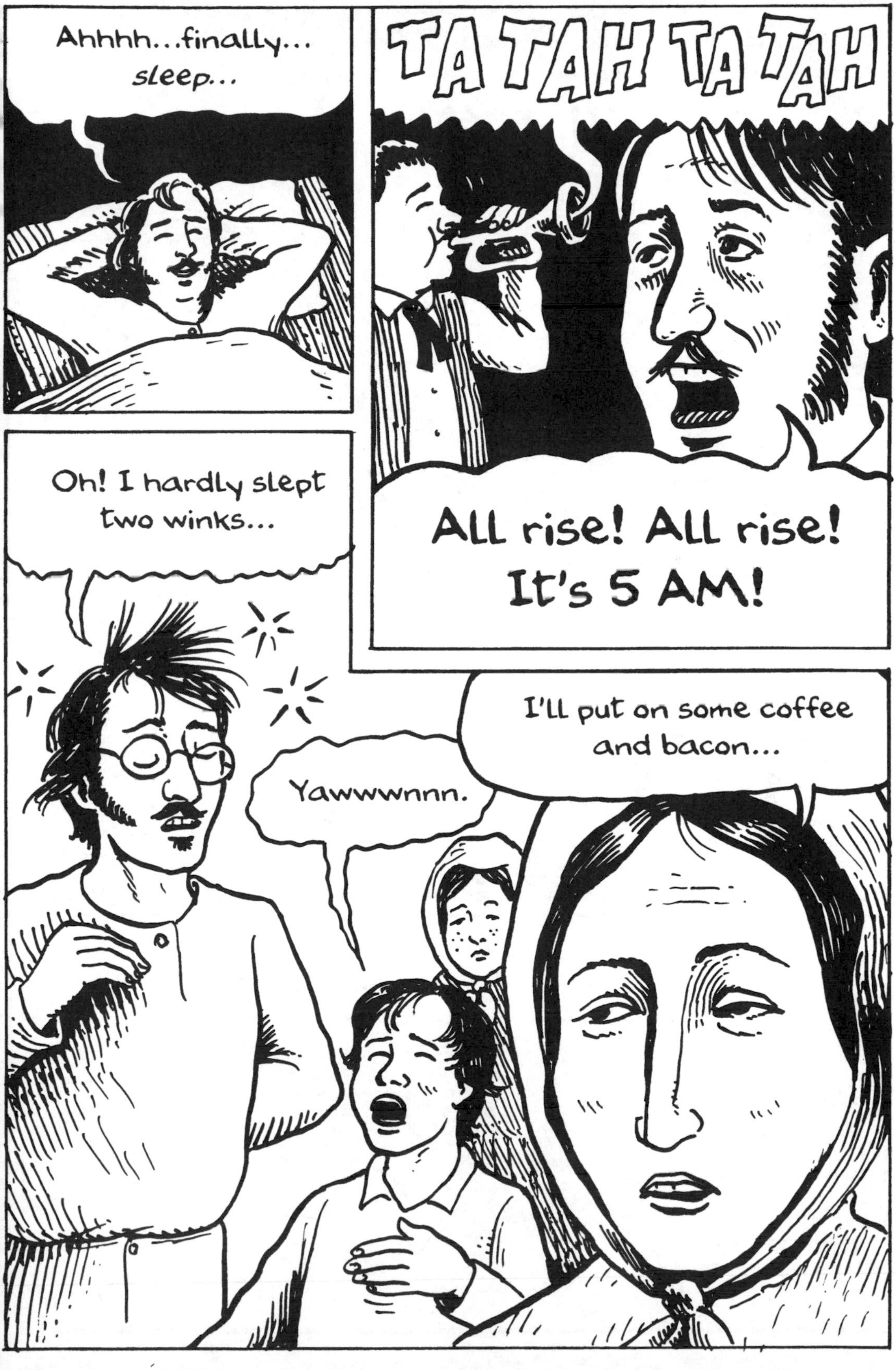
Ahhhh...finally... sleep...
TA TAH TA TAH
All rise! All rise! It's 5 AM!
Oh! I hardly slept two winks...
Yawwwnnn.
I'll put on some coffee and bacon...

All too soon, it was 7 AM...time to go!

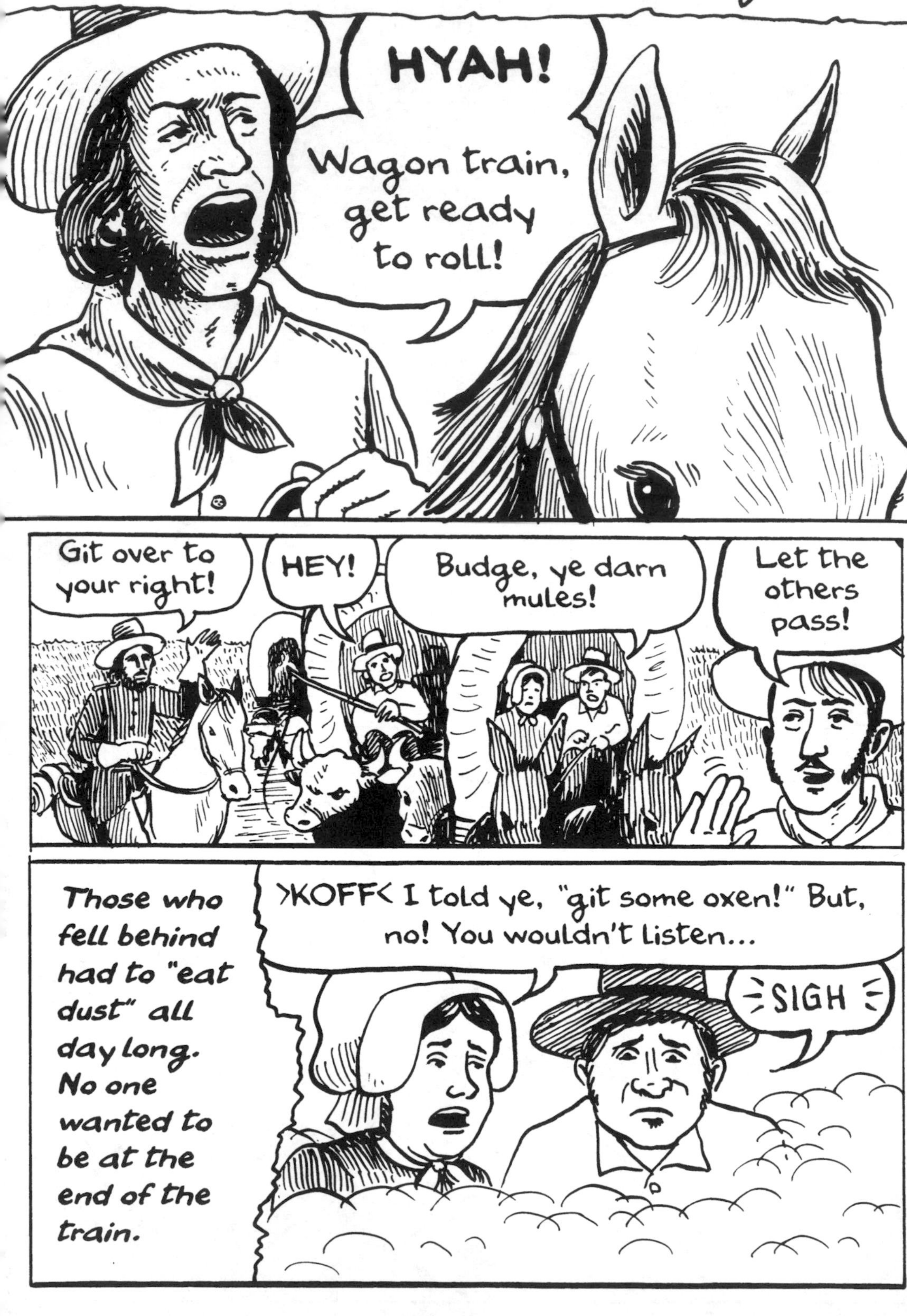
HYAH!
Wagon train, get ready to roll!
Git over to your right!
HEY!
Budge, ye darn mules!
Let the others pass!
Those who fell behind had to "eat dust" all day long. No one wanted to be at the end of the train.
>KOFF< I told ye, "git some oxen!" But, no! You wouldn't listen...
SIGH

Chapter Four

Home on the Range

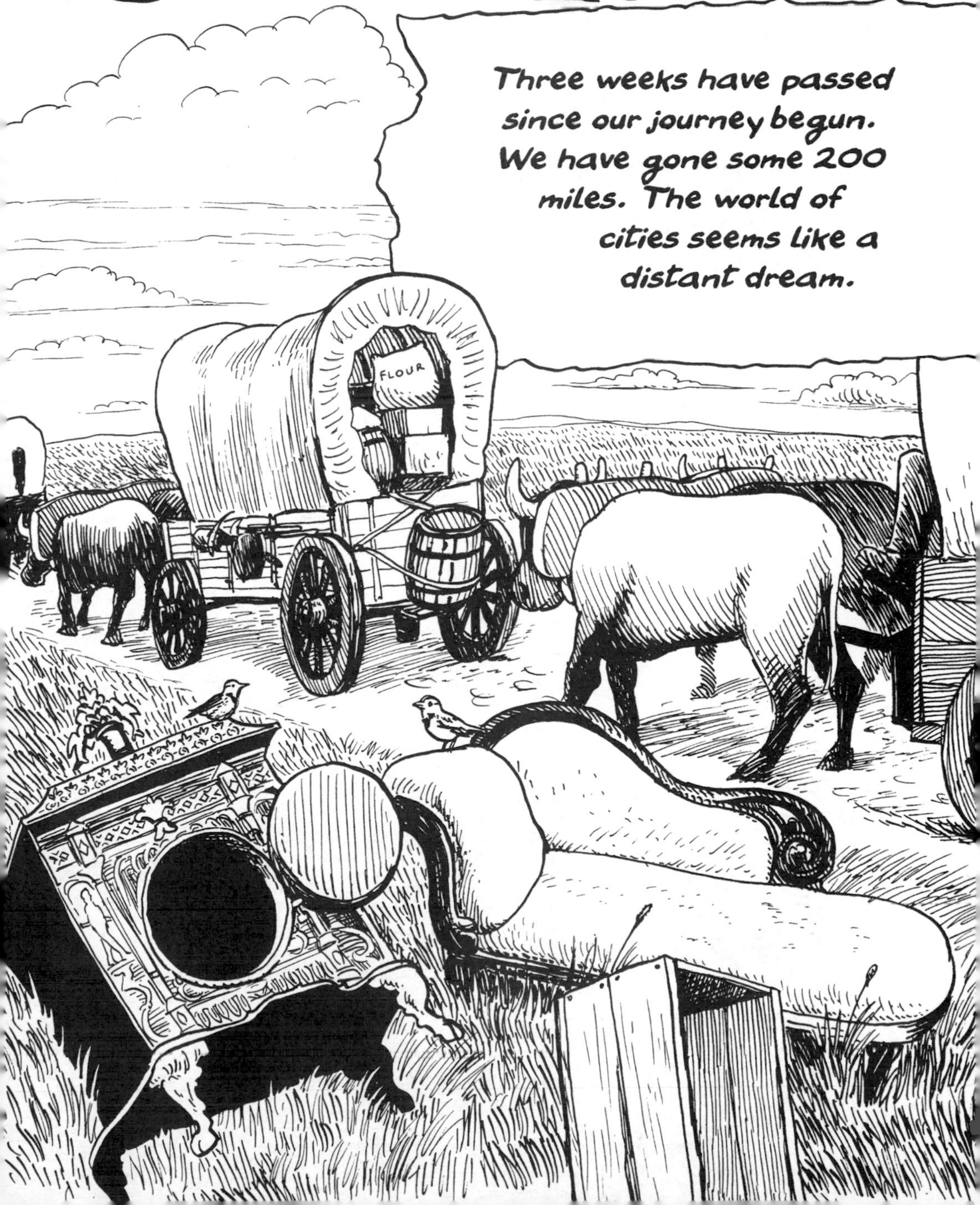
Three weeks have passed since our journey begun. We have gone some 200 miles. The world of cities seems like a distant dream.
FLOUR

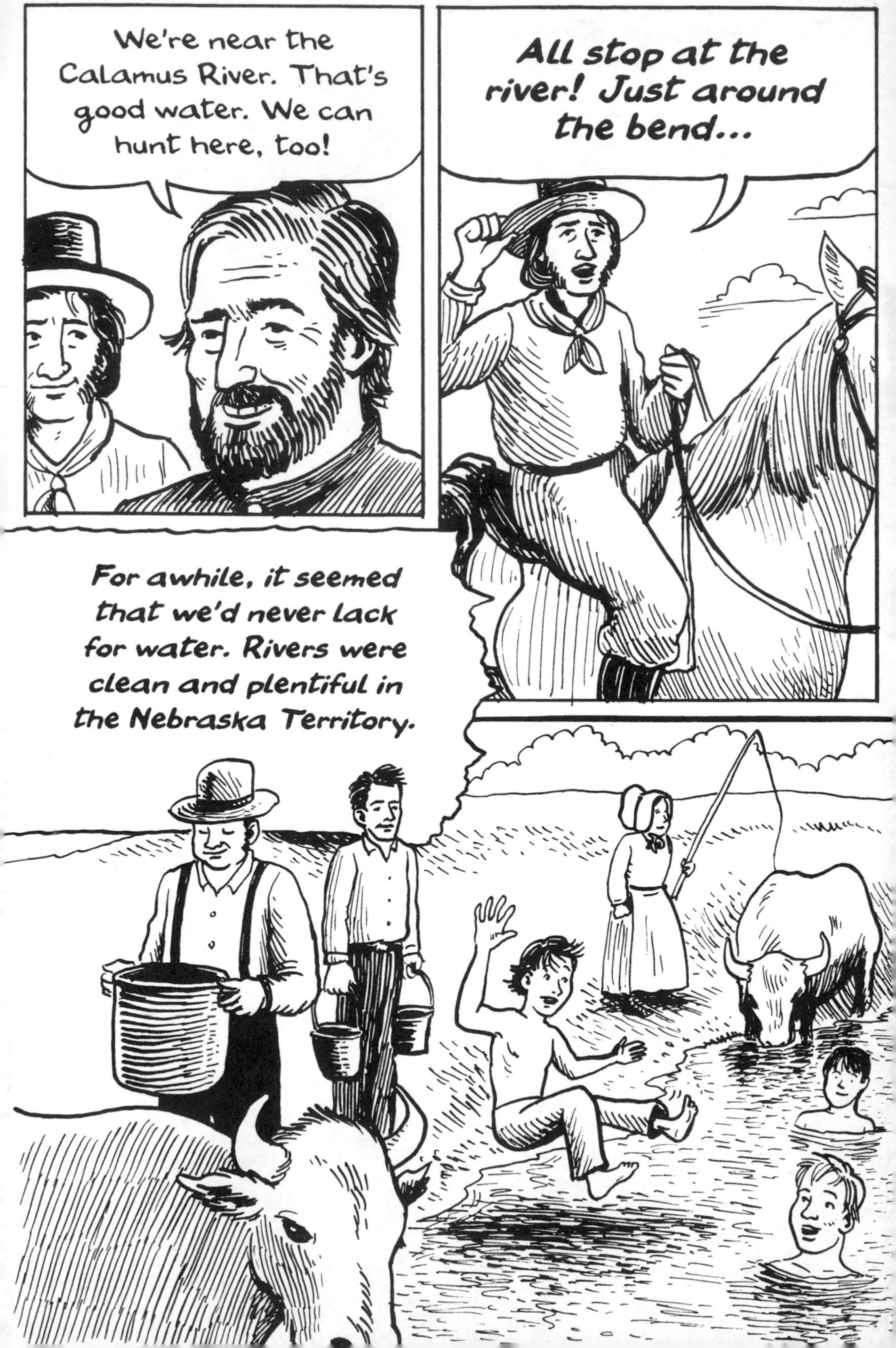
We're near the Calamus River. That's good water. We can hunt here, too!
All stop at the river! Just around the bend...
For awhile, it seemed that we'd never lack for water. Rivers were clean and plentiful in the Nebraska Territory.

The next morning, the men in the party organized a buffalo hunt. Col. McCarty led the expedition from his horse. They shot and killed a gigantic beast...

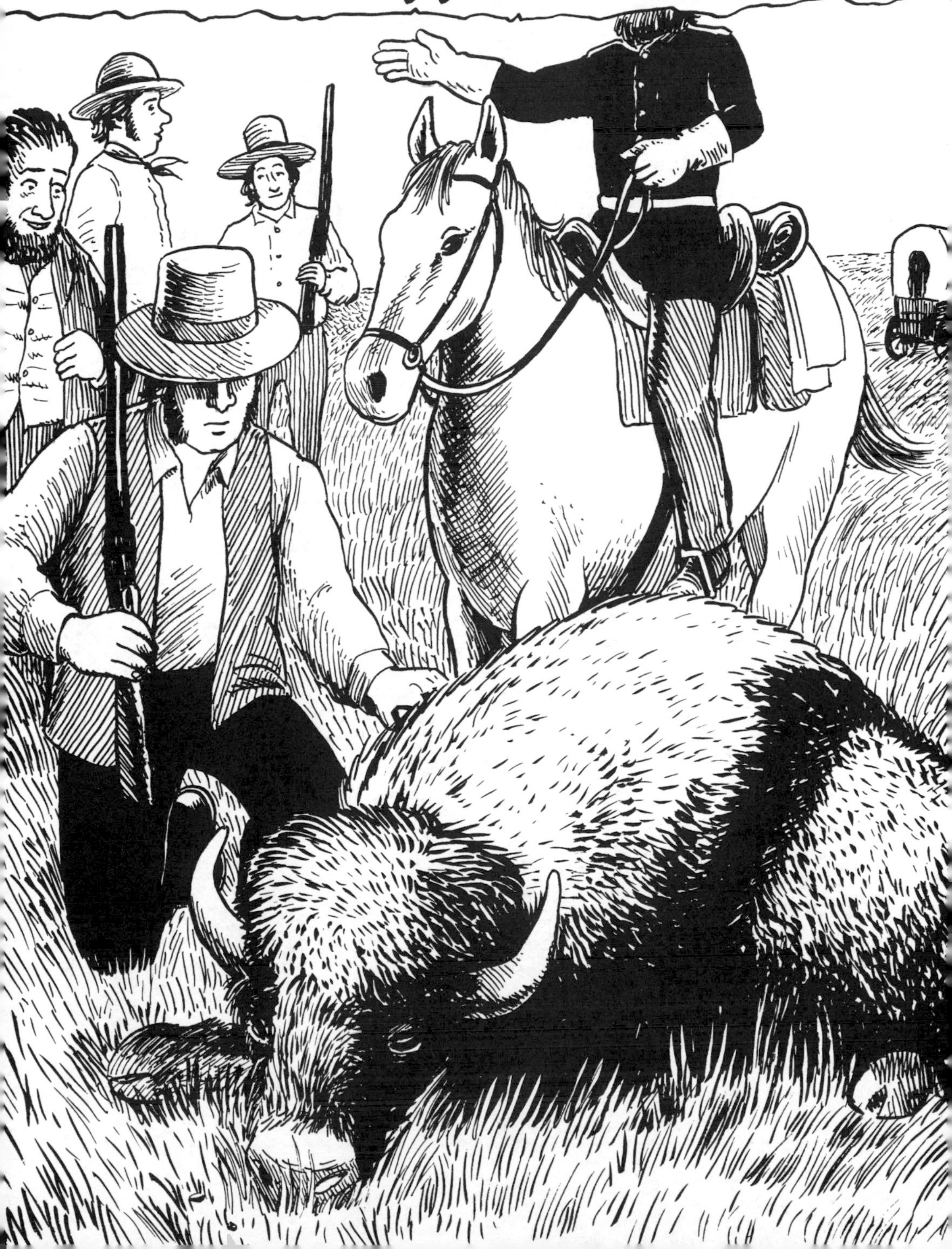

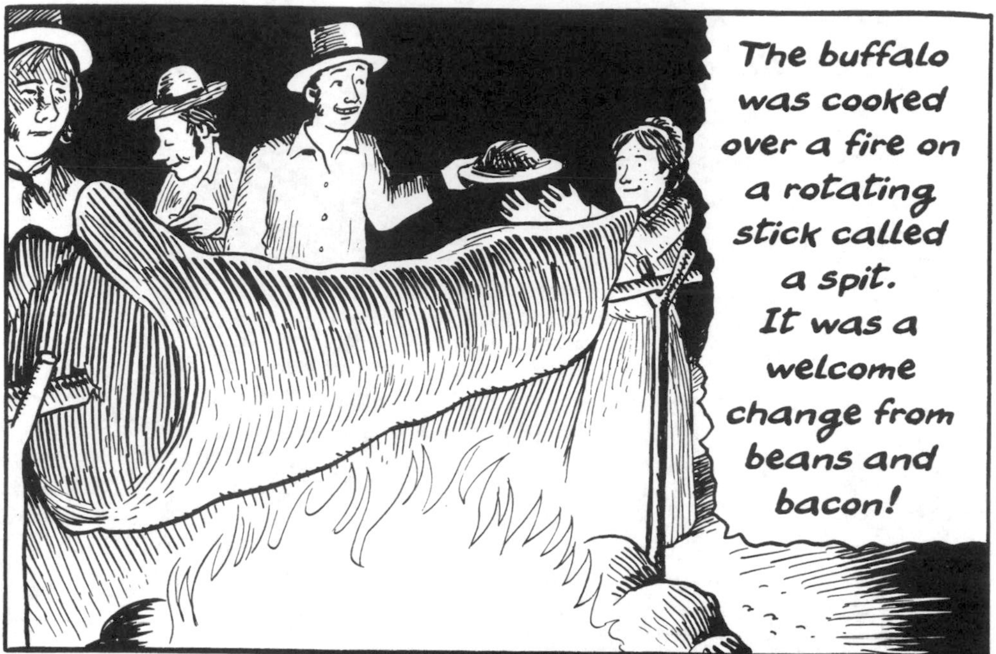
The buffalo was cooked over a fire on a rotating stick called a spit. It was a welcome change from beans and bacon!

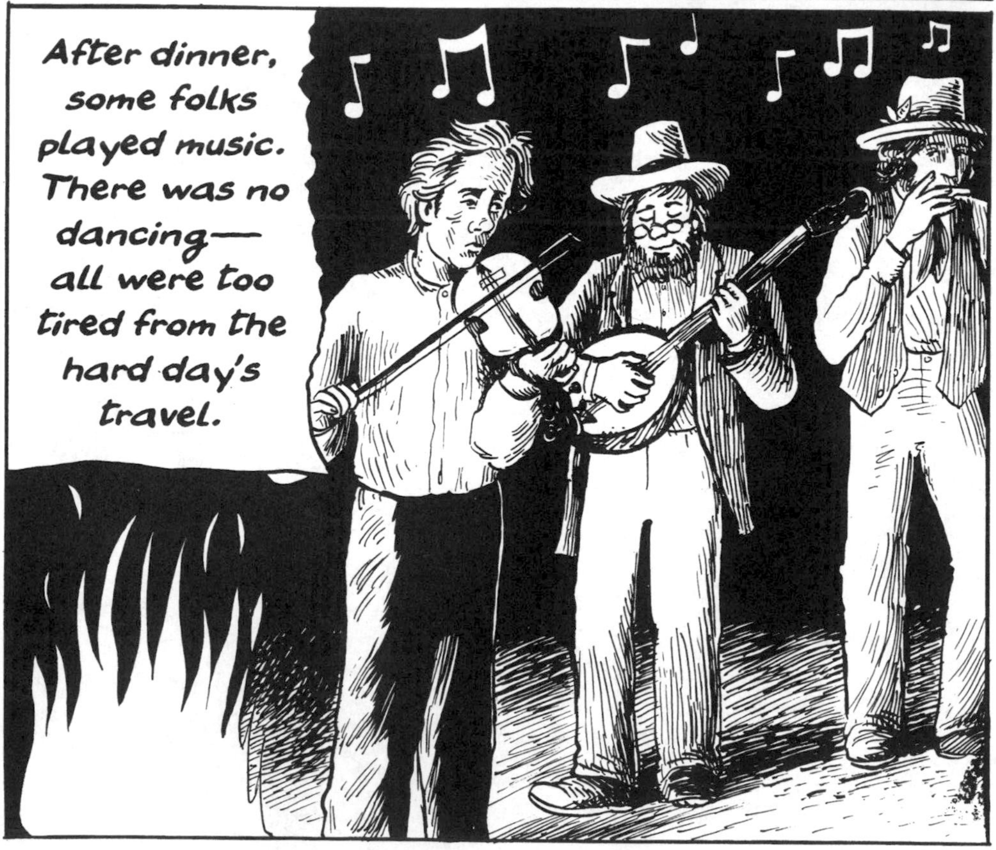
After dinner, some folks played music. There was no dancing— all were too tired from the hard day's travel.

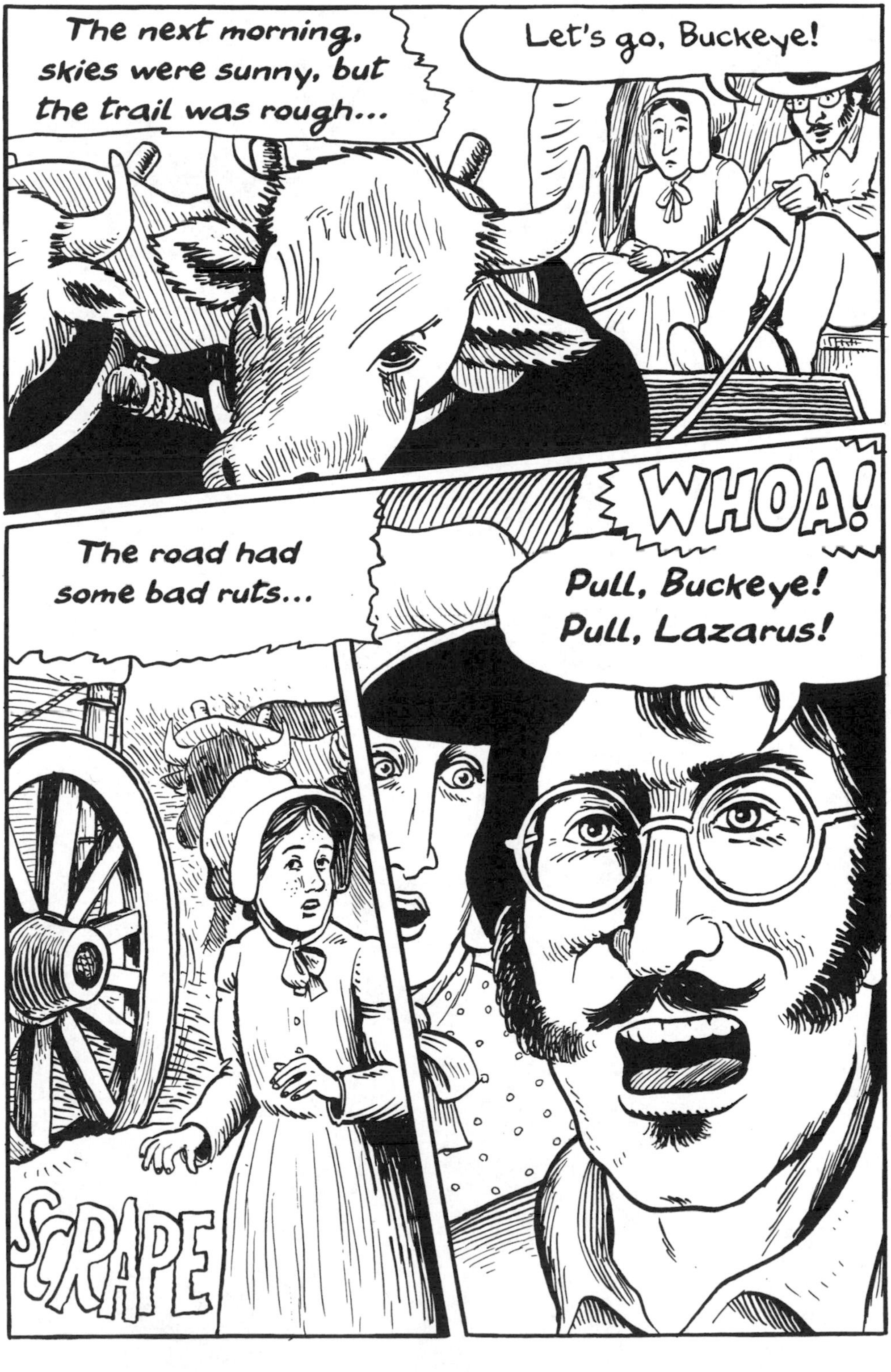
The next morning, skies were sunny, but the trail was rough...
Let's go, Buckeye!
The road had some bad ruts...
WHOA!
Pull, Buckeye! Pull, Lazarus!
SCRAPE

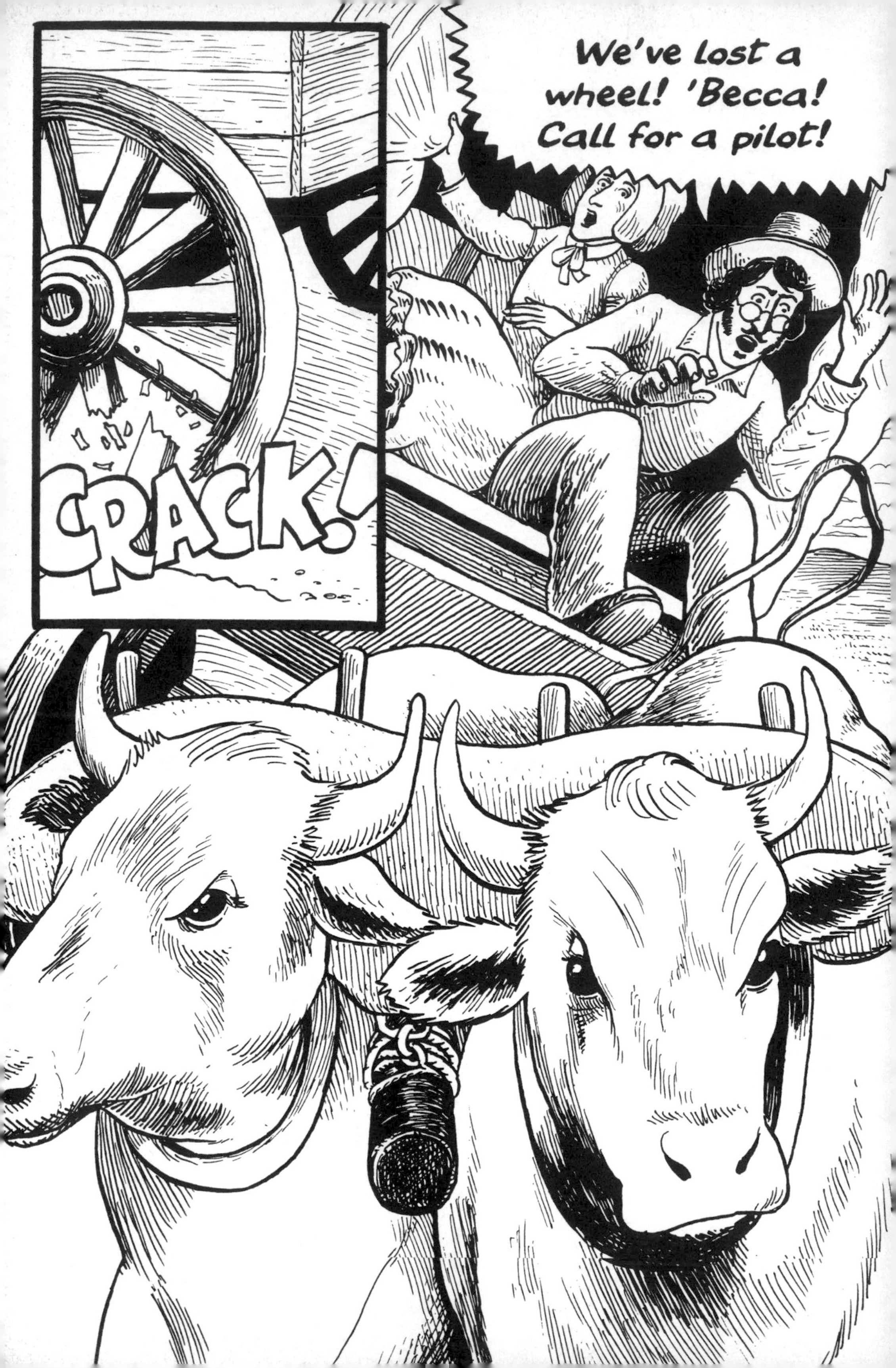
CRACK!
We've lost a wheel! 'Becca! Call for a pilot!

How To Fix A Broken Wagon Wheel

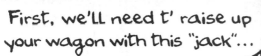

First, we'll need t' raise up your wagon with this "jack"...

This wheel's in bad shape. It's all dried out from the sun.

Can it be fixed?

①

②

I reckon so! Have ye any bacon grease? This axle is dry as dust!

Corinne, do we have...

I was saving this for supper...

③

④

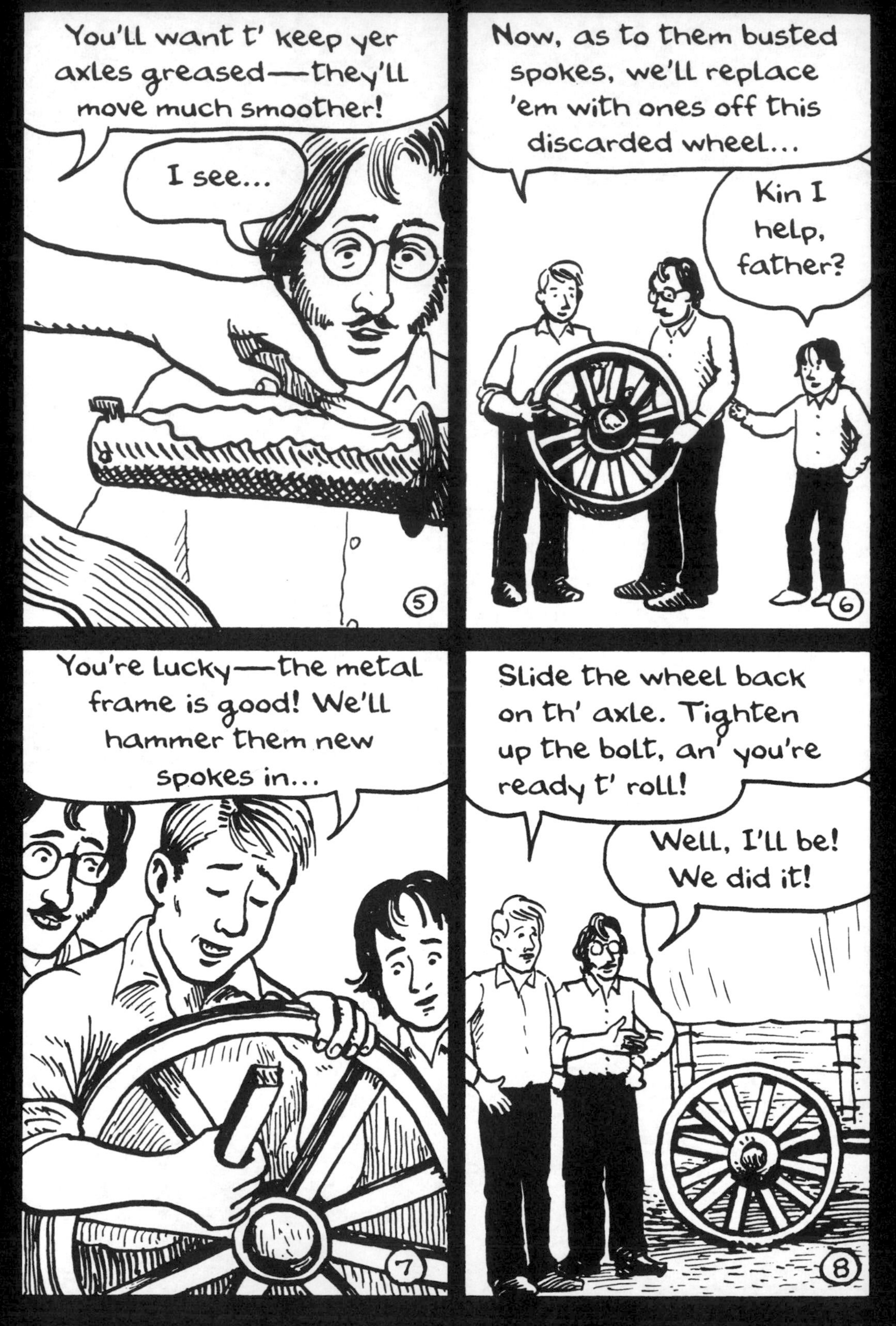
You'll want t' keep yer axles greased—they'll move much smoother!
I see...
5
Now, as to them busted spokes, we'll replace 'em with ones off this discarded wheel...
Kin I help, father?
6
You're lucky—the metal frame is good! We'll hammer them new spokes in...
7
Slide the wheel back on th' axle. Tighten up the bolt, an' you're ready t' roll!
Well, I'll be! We did it!
8

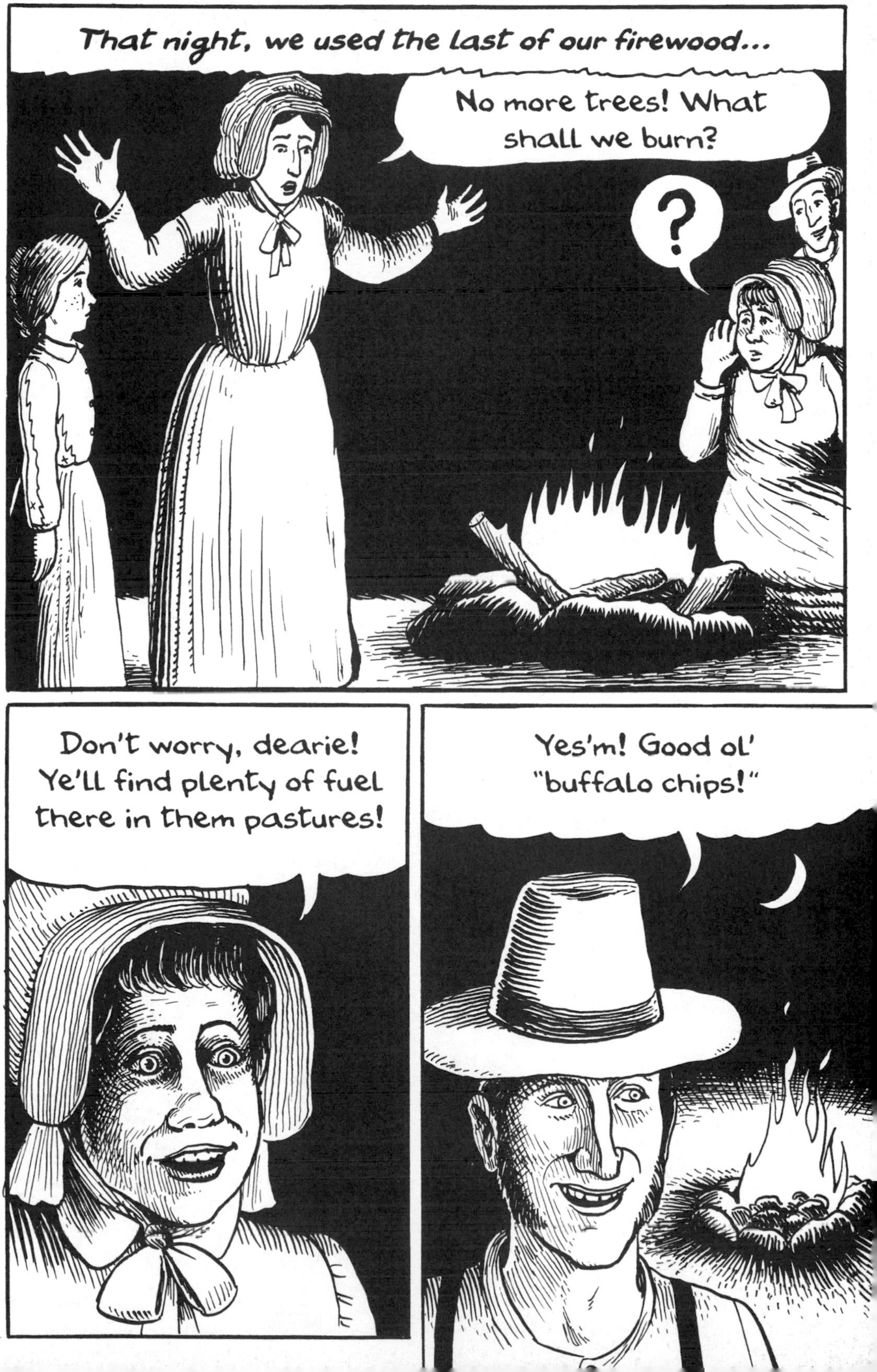
That night, we used the last of our firewood...
No more trees! What shall we burn?
?
Don't worry, dearie! Ye'll find plenty of fuel there in them pastures!
Yes'm! Good ol' "buffalo chips!"

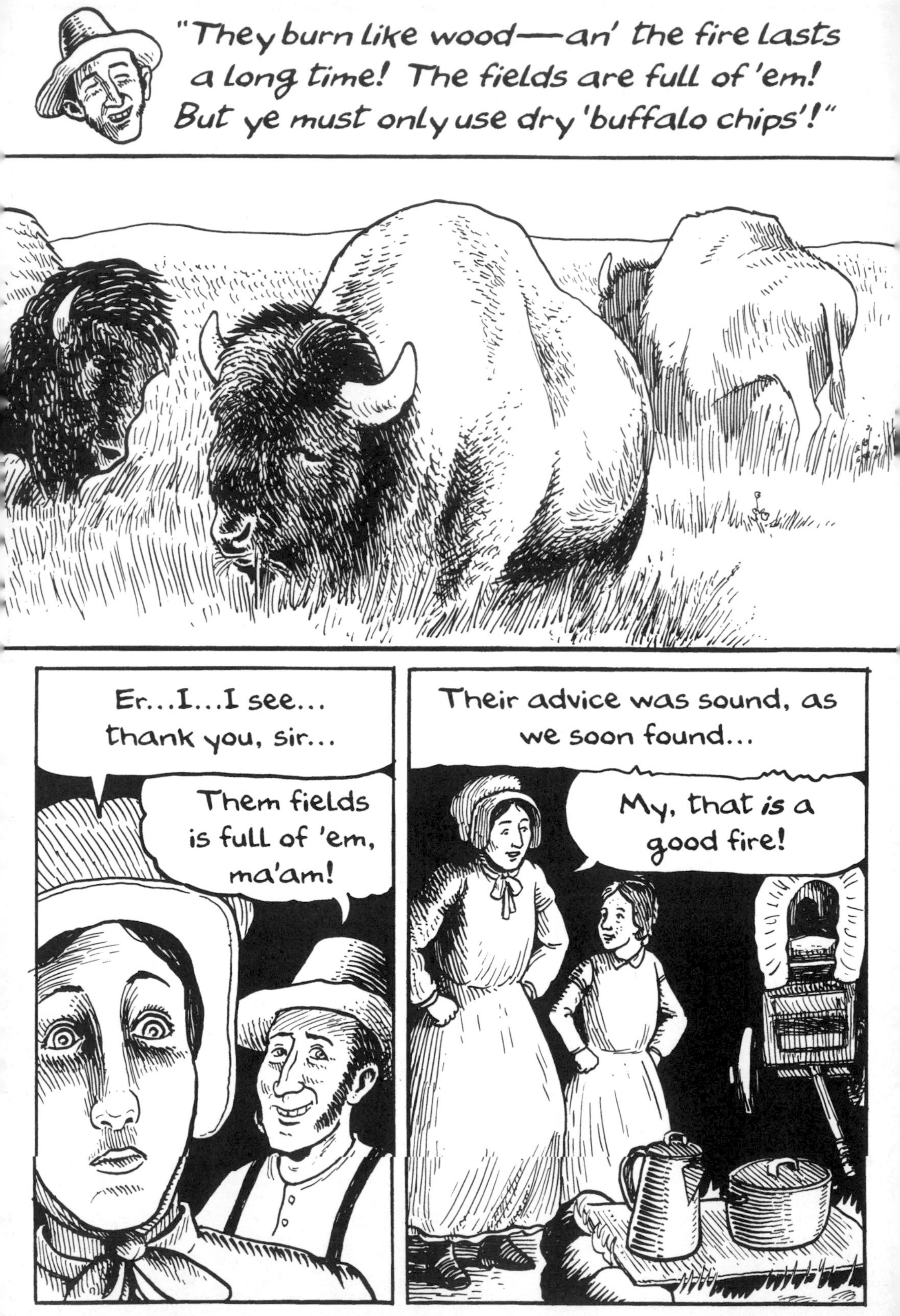
"They burn like wood—an' the fire lasts a long time! The fields are full of 'em! But ye must only use dry 'buffalo chips'!"
Er...I...I see... thank you, sir...
Them fields is full of 'em, ma'am!
Their advice was sound, as we soon found...
My, that *is* a good fire!

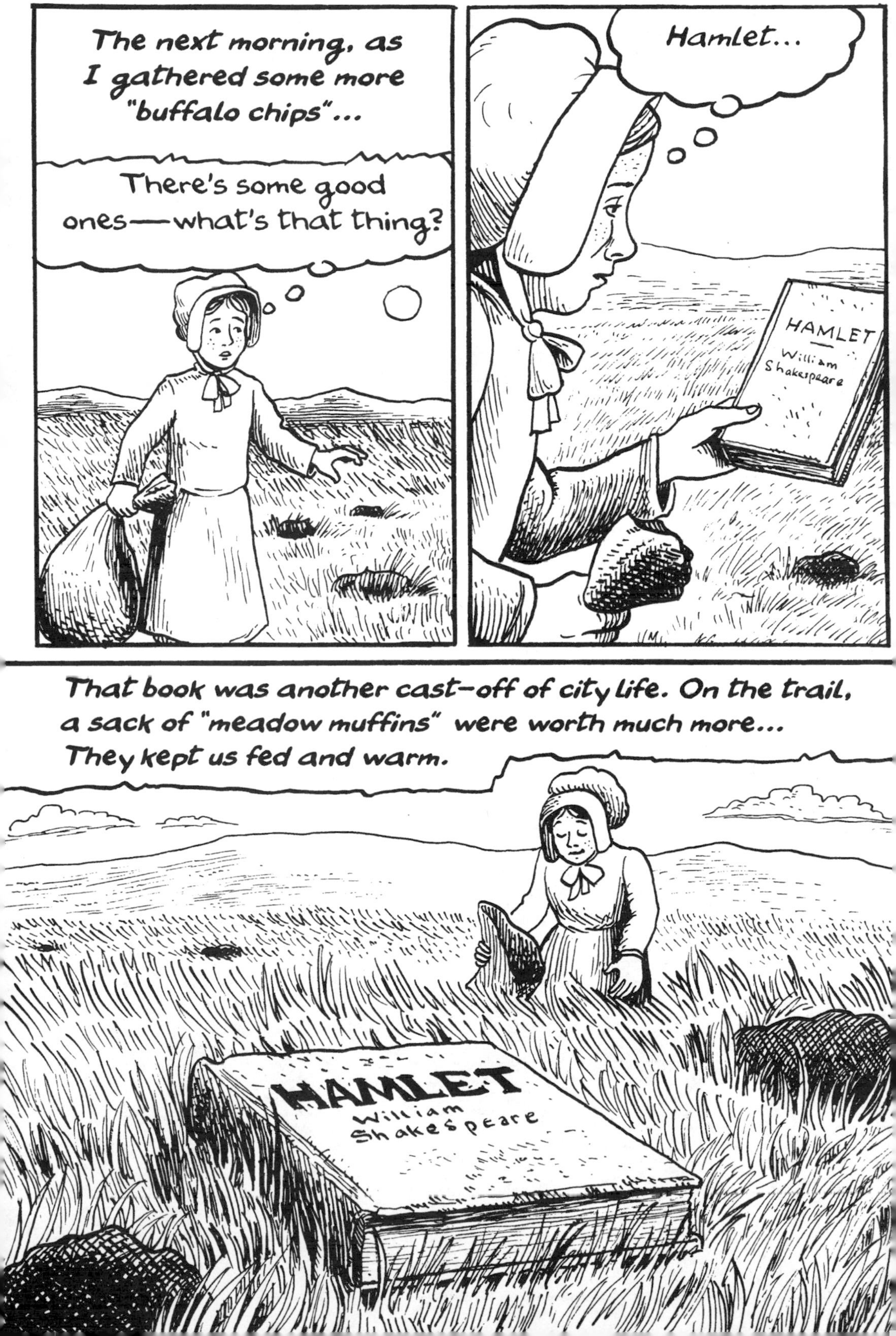
The next morning, as I gathered some more "buffalo chips"...
There's some good ones—what's that thing?
Hamlet...
HAMLET
William Shakespeare
That book was another cast-off of city life. On the trail, a sack of "meadow muffins" were worth much more... They kept us fed and warm.
HAMLET
William Shakespeare

Chapter FIVE Water, Water

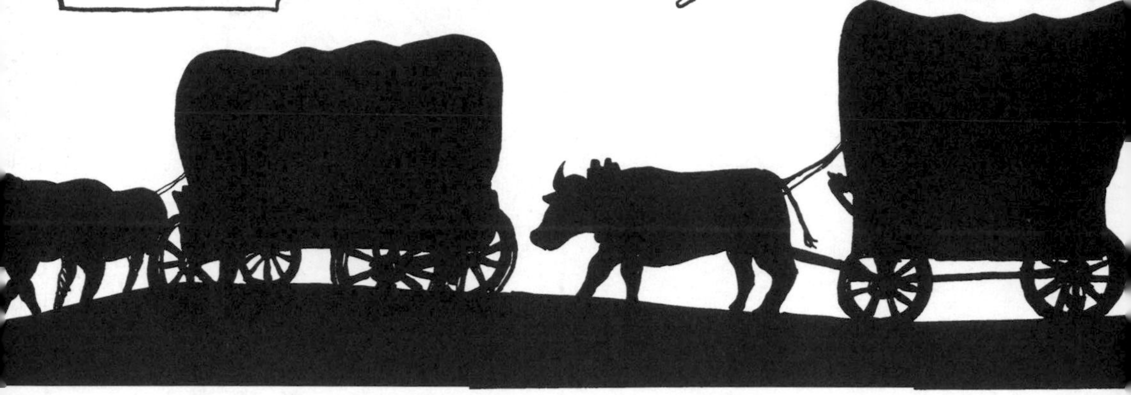

Our first river crossing, at the Platte River,

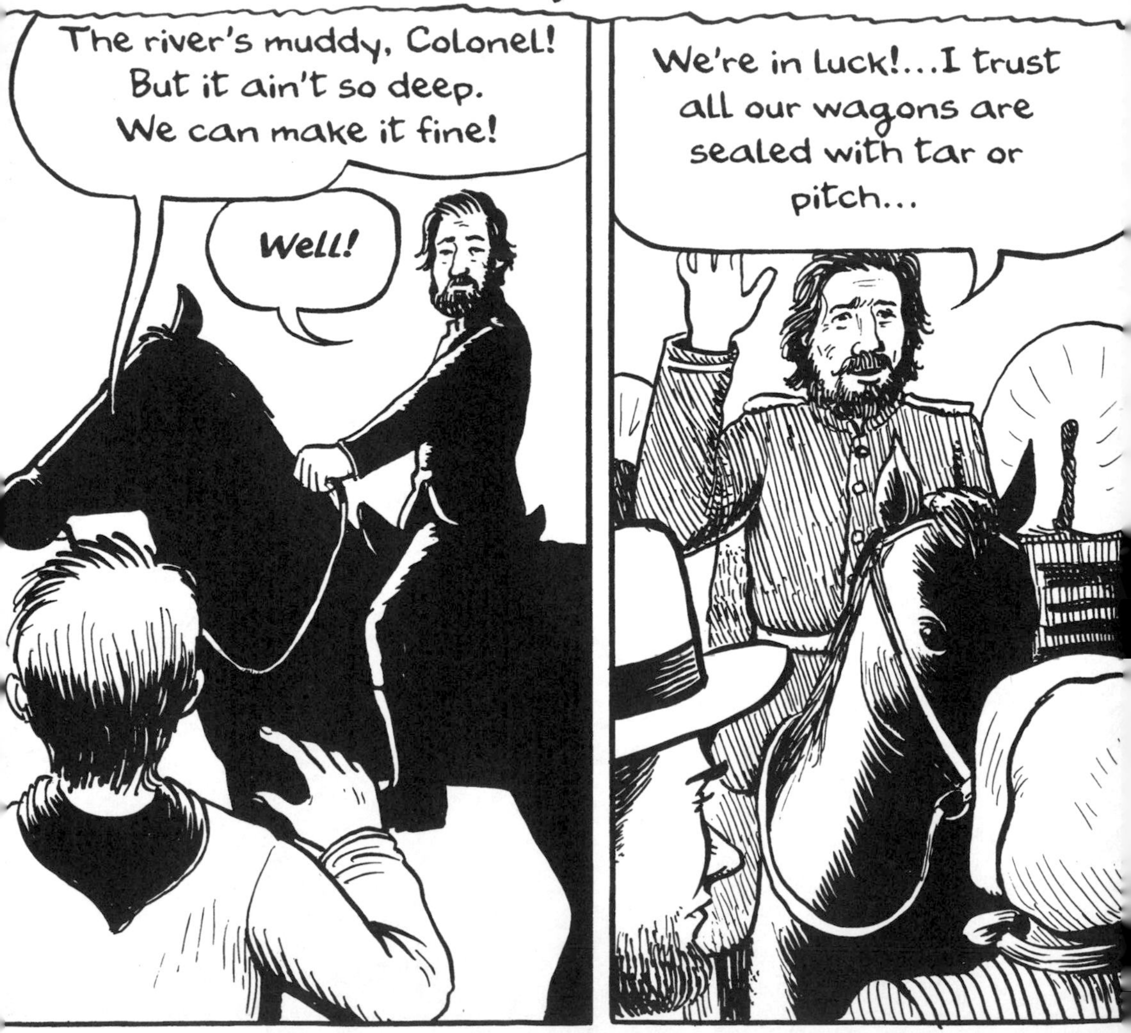
The river's muddy, Colonel! But it ain't so deep. We can make it fine!
Well!
We're in luck!...I trust all our wagons are sealed with tar or pitch...

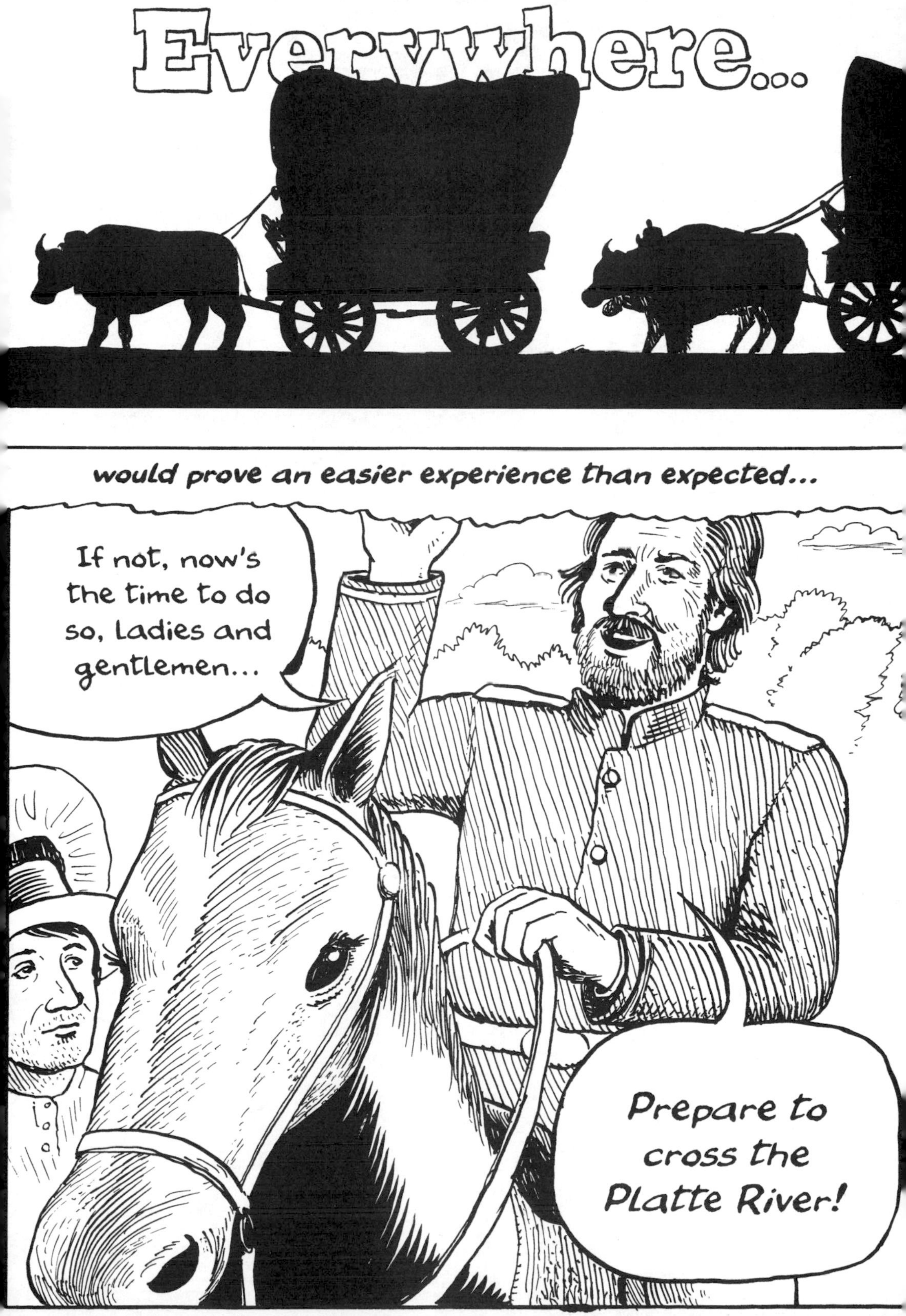
Everywhere...
would prove an easier experience than expected...
If not, now's the time to do so, ladies and gentlemen...
Prepare to cross the Platte River!

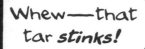 # How To

Whew—that tar **stinks**!

Make sure you fill in every crack!

>KOFF< I am!

STEP ONE: SEAL WAGON WITH TAR OR PITCH

This water don't even come up t' my stomach!

=ULP!=

STEP TWO: TEST WATER DEPTH

I hope we don't sink... Let's go, Buckeye! Ho, Lazarus!

STEP THREE: ENTER

Ford a River

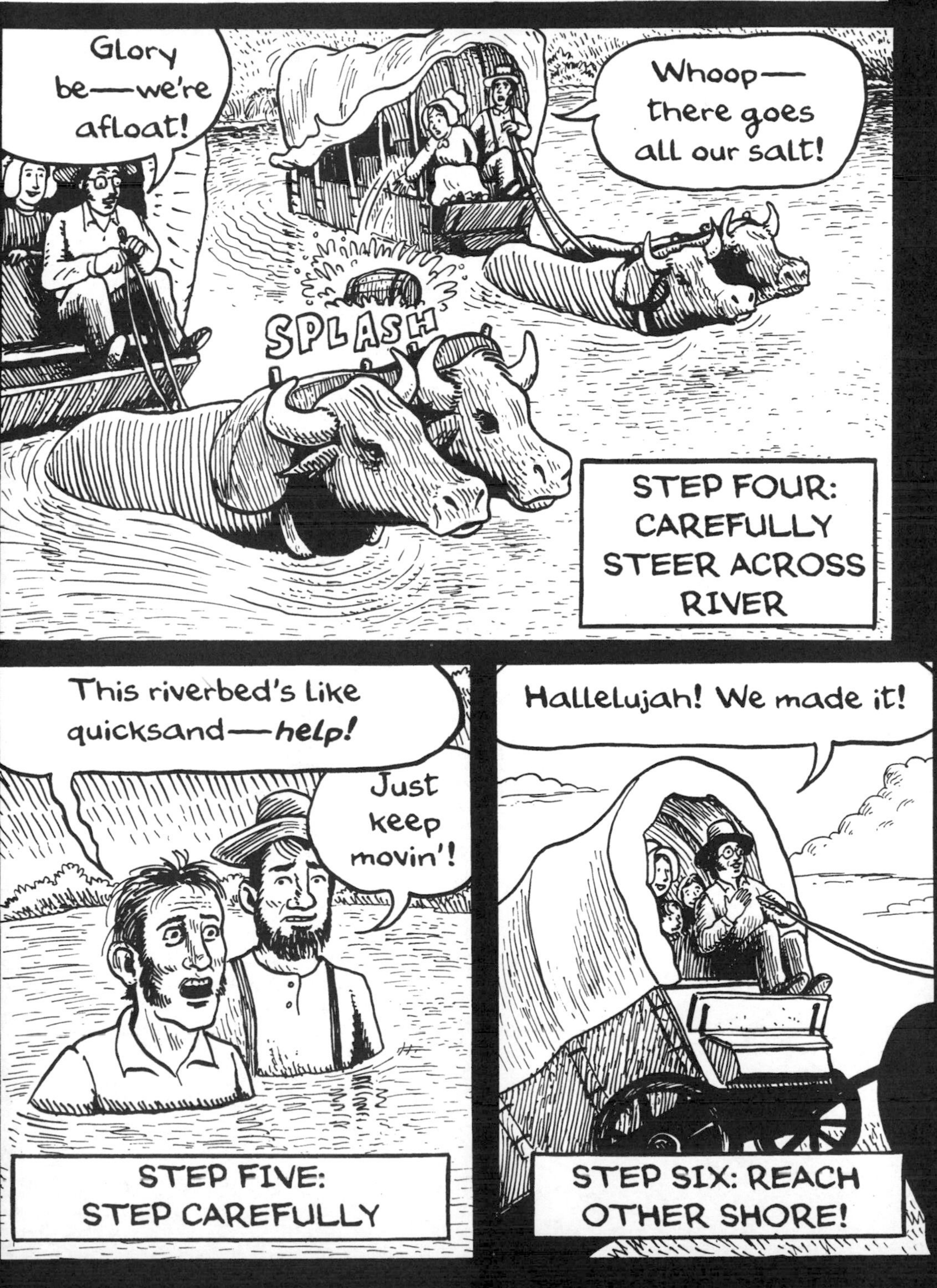
Glory be—we're afloat!
Whoop—there goes all our salt!
SPLASH
STEP FOUR: CAREFULLY STEER ACROSS RIVER
This riverbed's like quicksand—*help!*
Just keep movin'!
STEP FIVE: STEP CAREFULLY
Hallelujah! We made it!
STEP SIX: REACH OTHER SHORE!

Once across the river we were greeted with the welcome sight of trees and bushes. It was tempting to stop here for the night, but we had hours of good daylight remaining...

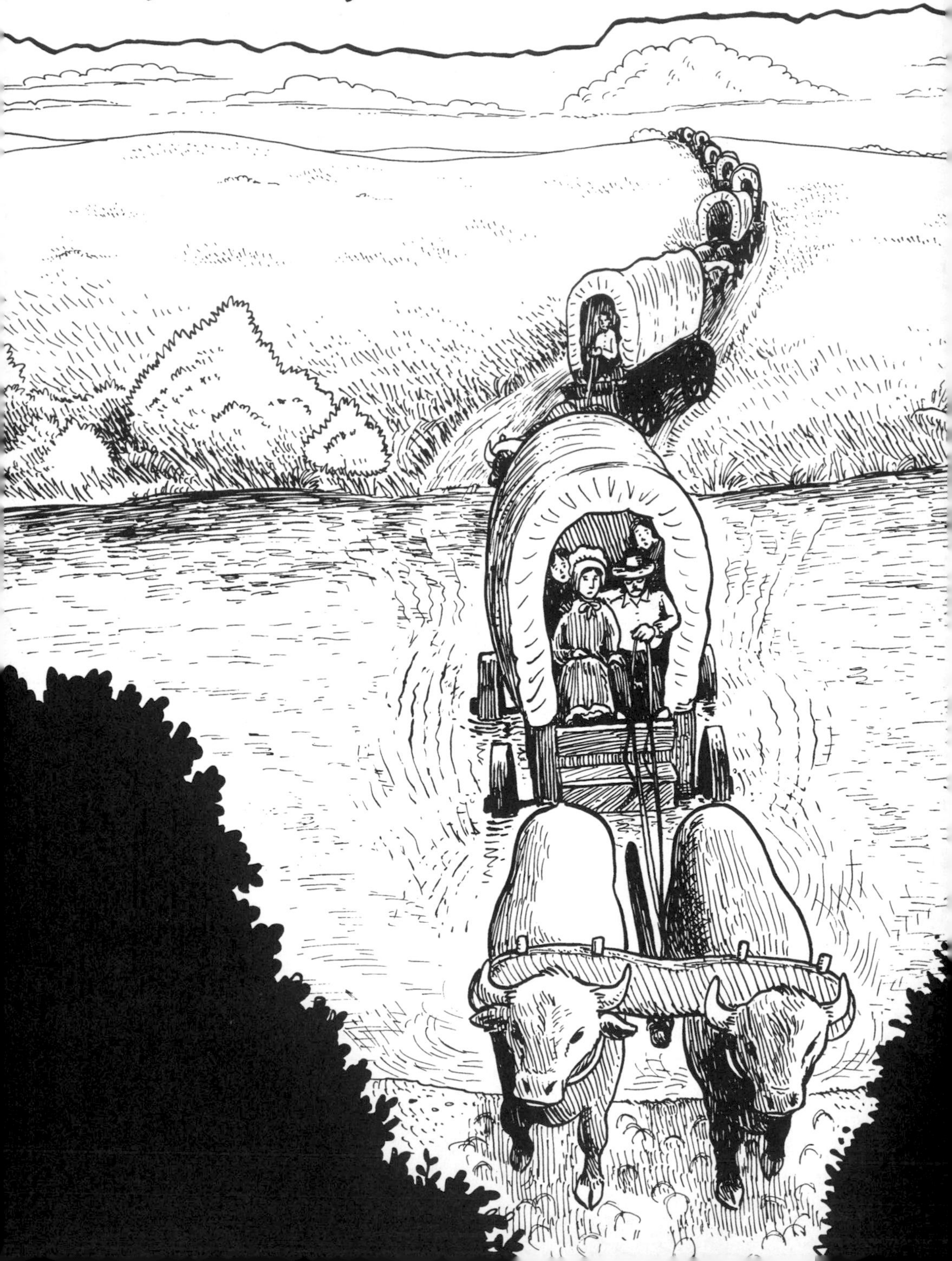

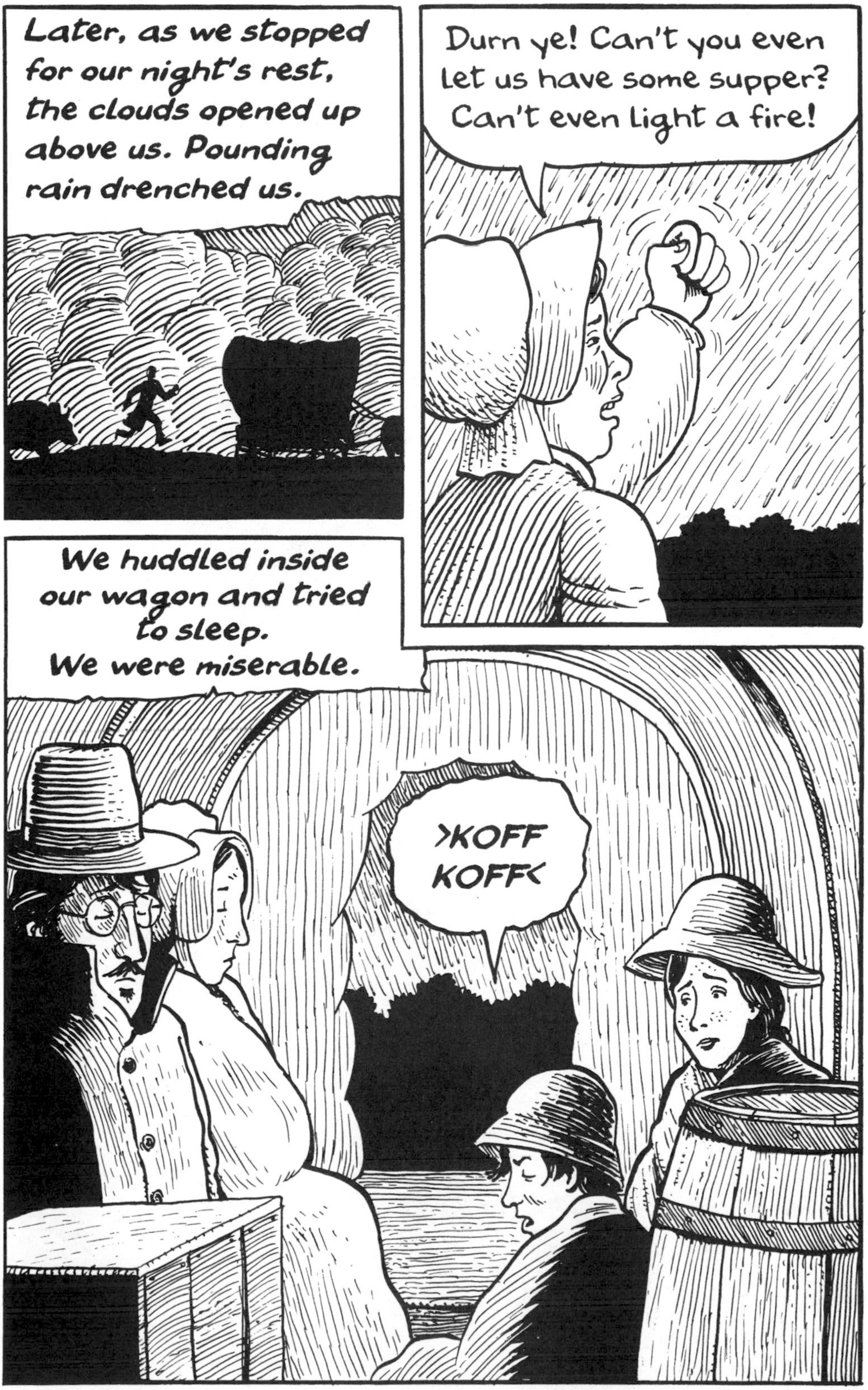
Later, as we stopped for our night's rest, the clouds opened up above us. Pounding rain drenched us.
Durn ye! Can't you even let us have some supper? Can't even light a fire!
We huddled inside our wagon and tried to sleep. We were miserable.
>KOFF KOFF<

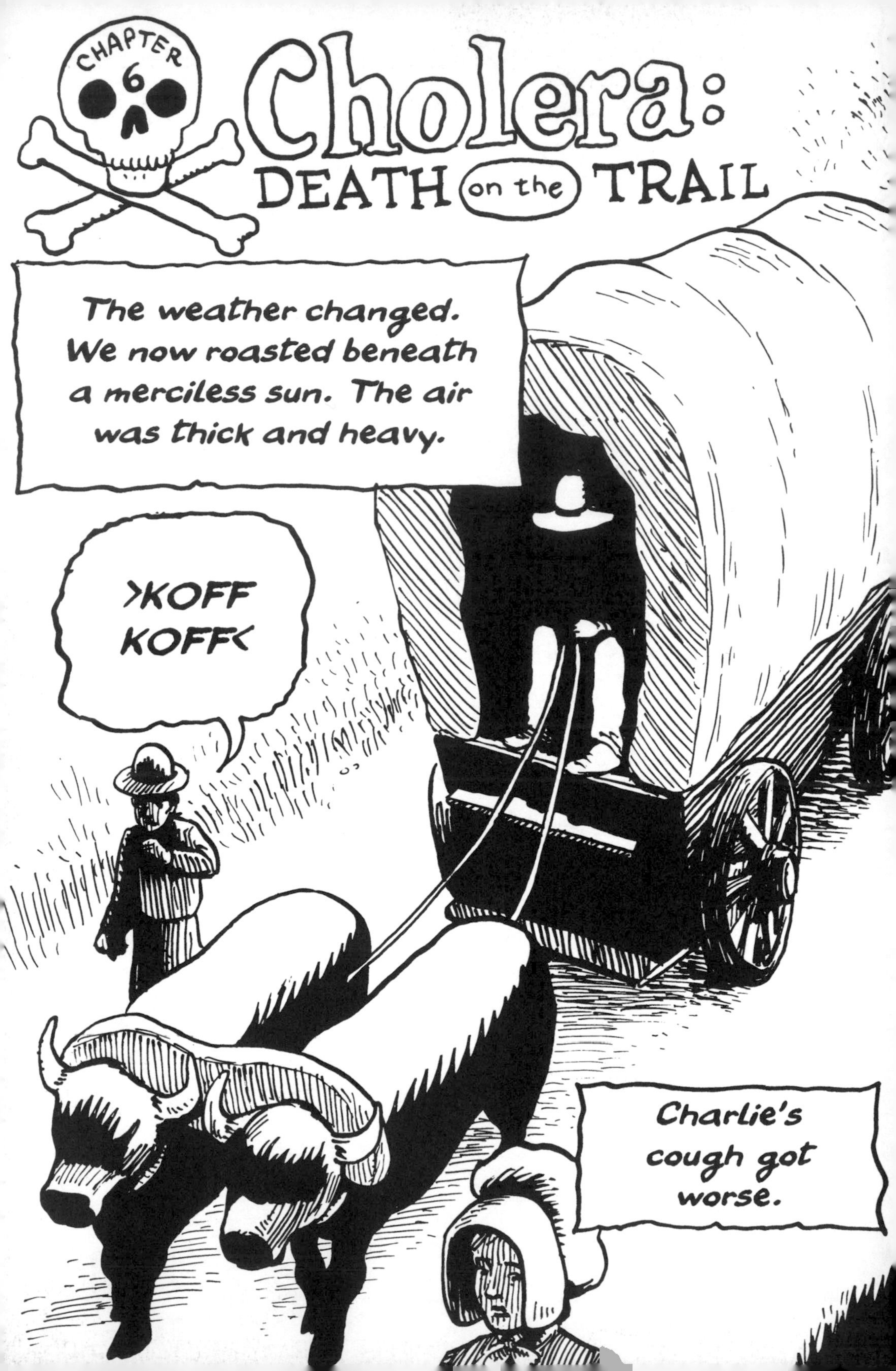
CHAPTER 6
Cholera: DEATH on the TRAIL
The weather changed. We now roasted beneath a merciless sun. The air was thick and heavy.
>KOFF KOFF<
Charlie's cough got worse.

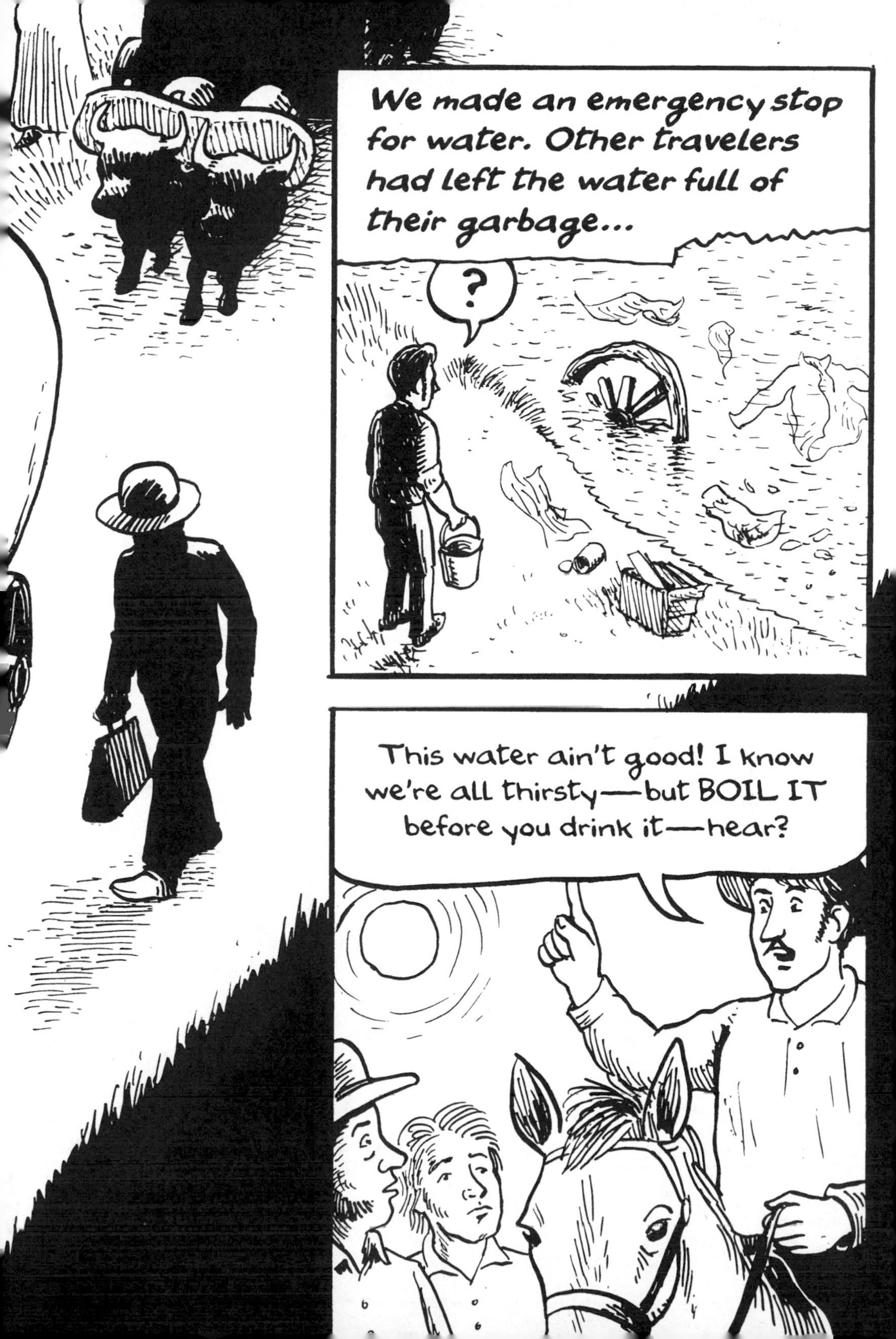
We made an emergency stop for water. Other travelers had left the water full of their garbage...
?
This water ain't good! I know we're all thirsty—but BOIL IT before you drink it—hear?

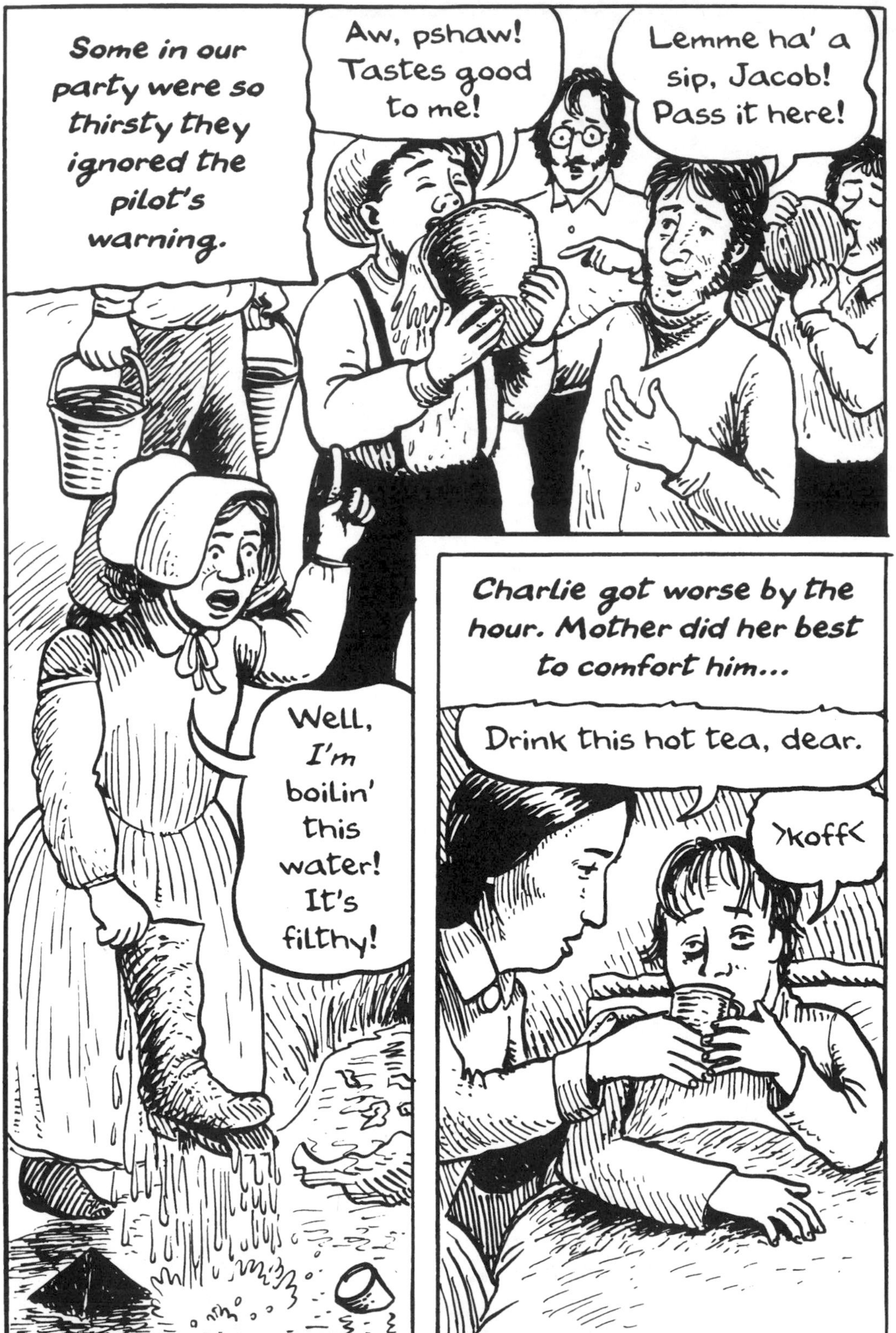
Some in our party were so thirsty they ignored the pilot's warning.
Aw, pshaw! Tastes good to me!
Lemme ha' a sip, Jacob! Pass it here!
Well, I'm boilin' this water! It's filthy!
Charlie got worse by the hour. Mother did her best to comfort him...
Drink this hot tea, dear.
>koff<

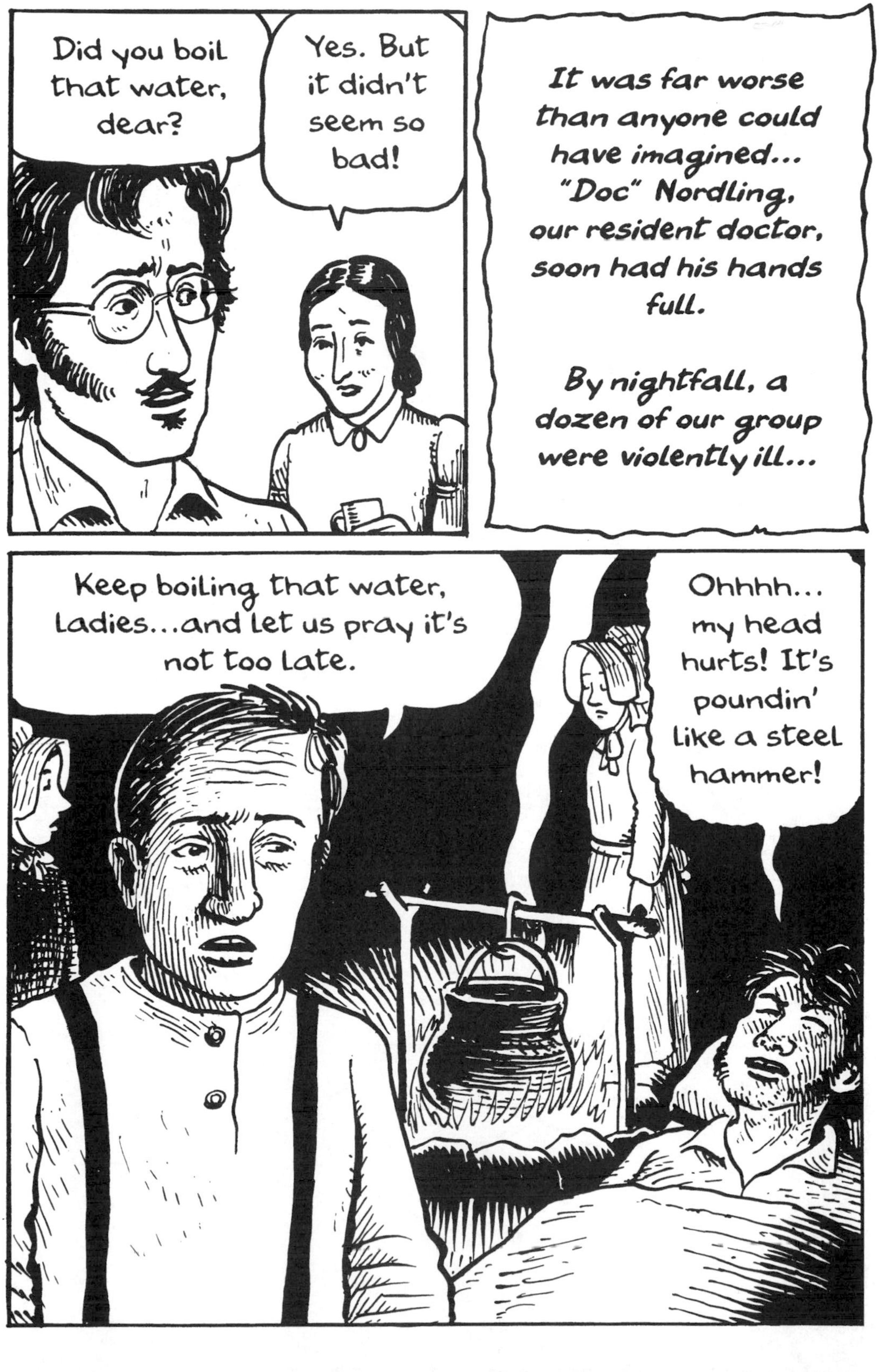
Did you boil that water, dear?
Yes. But it didn't seem so bad!
It was far worse than anyone could have imagined... "Doc" Nordling, our resident doctor, soon had his hands full.
By nightfall, a dozen of our group were violently ill...
Keep boiling that water, ladies...and let us pray it's not too late.
Ohhhh... my head hurts! It's poundin' like a steel hammer!

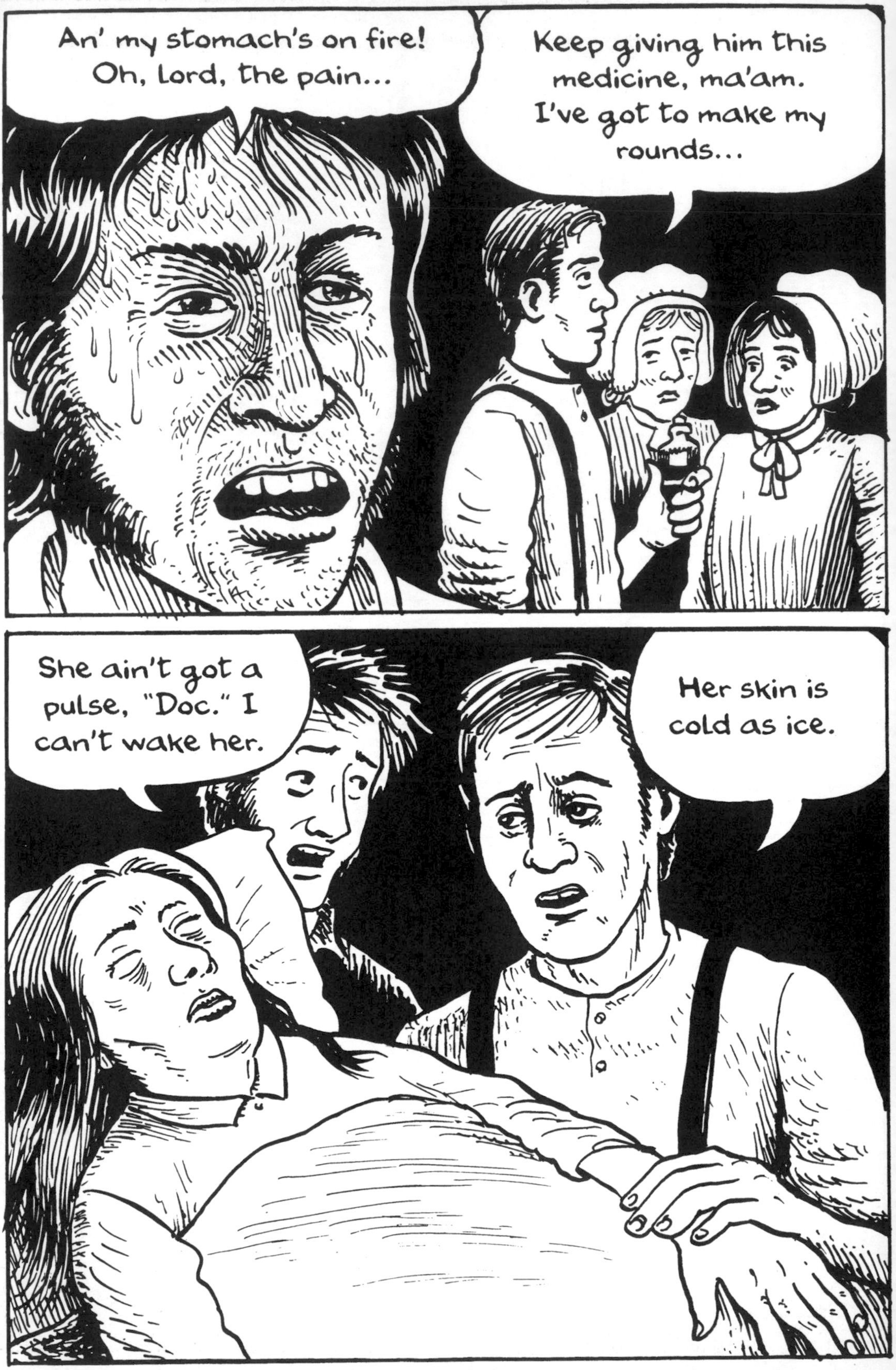
An' my stomach's on fire! Oh, Lord, the pain...
Keep giving him this medicine, ma'am. I've got to make my rounds...
She ain't got a pulse, "Doc." I can't wake her.
Her skin is cold as ice.

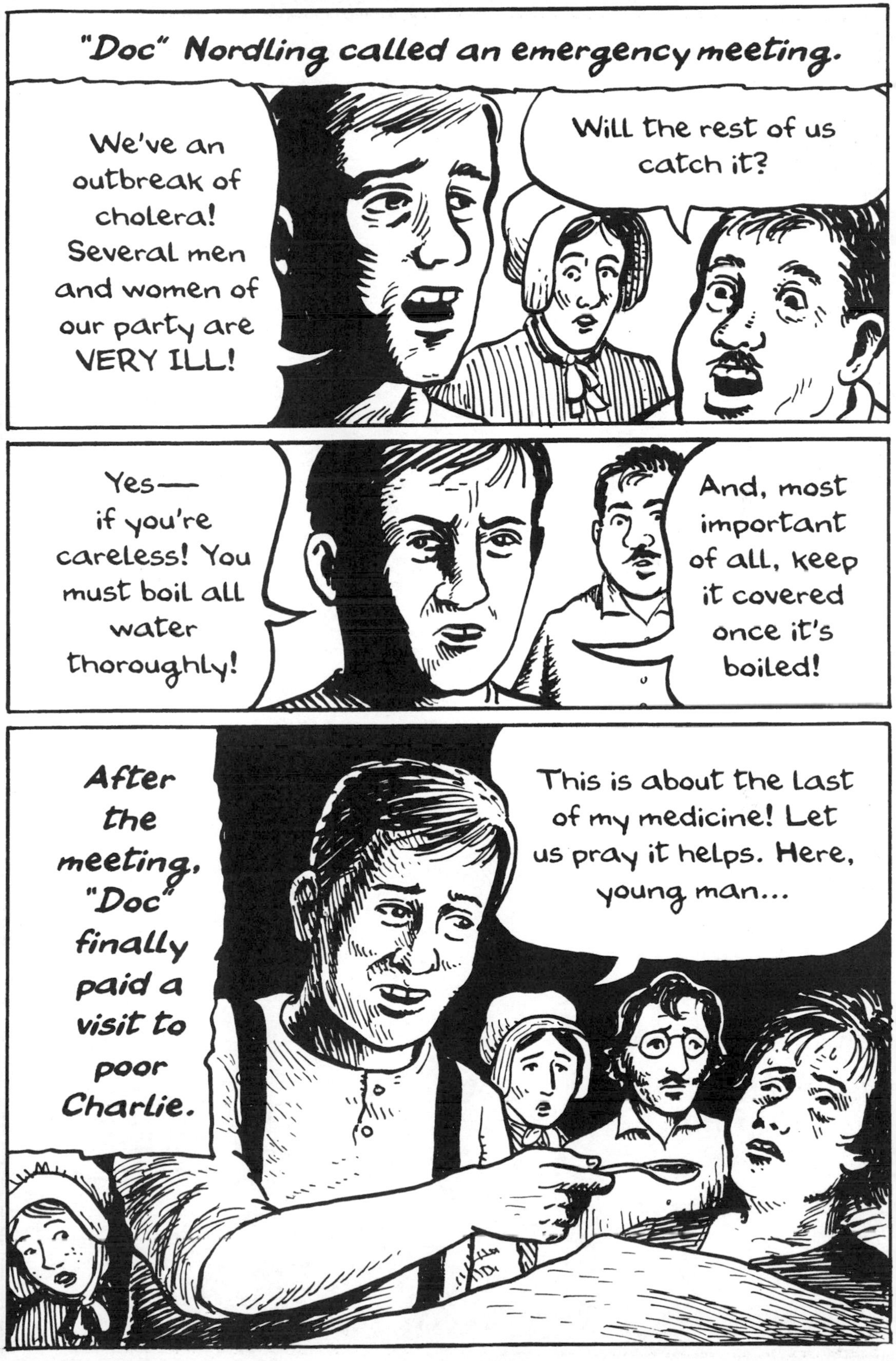
"Doc" Nordling called an emergency meeting.
We've an outbreak of cholera! Several men and women of our party are VERY ILL!
Will the rest of us catch it?
Yes— if you're careless! You must boil all water thoroughly!
And, most important of all, keep it covered once it's boiled!
After the meeting, "Doc" finally paid a visit to poor Charlie.
This is about the last of my medicine! Let us pray it helps. Here, young man...

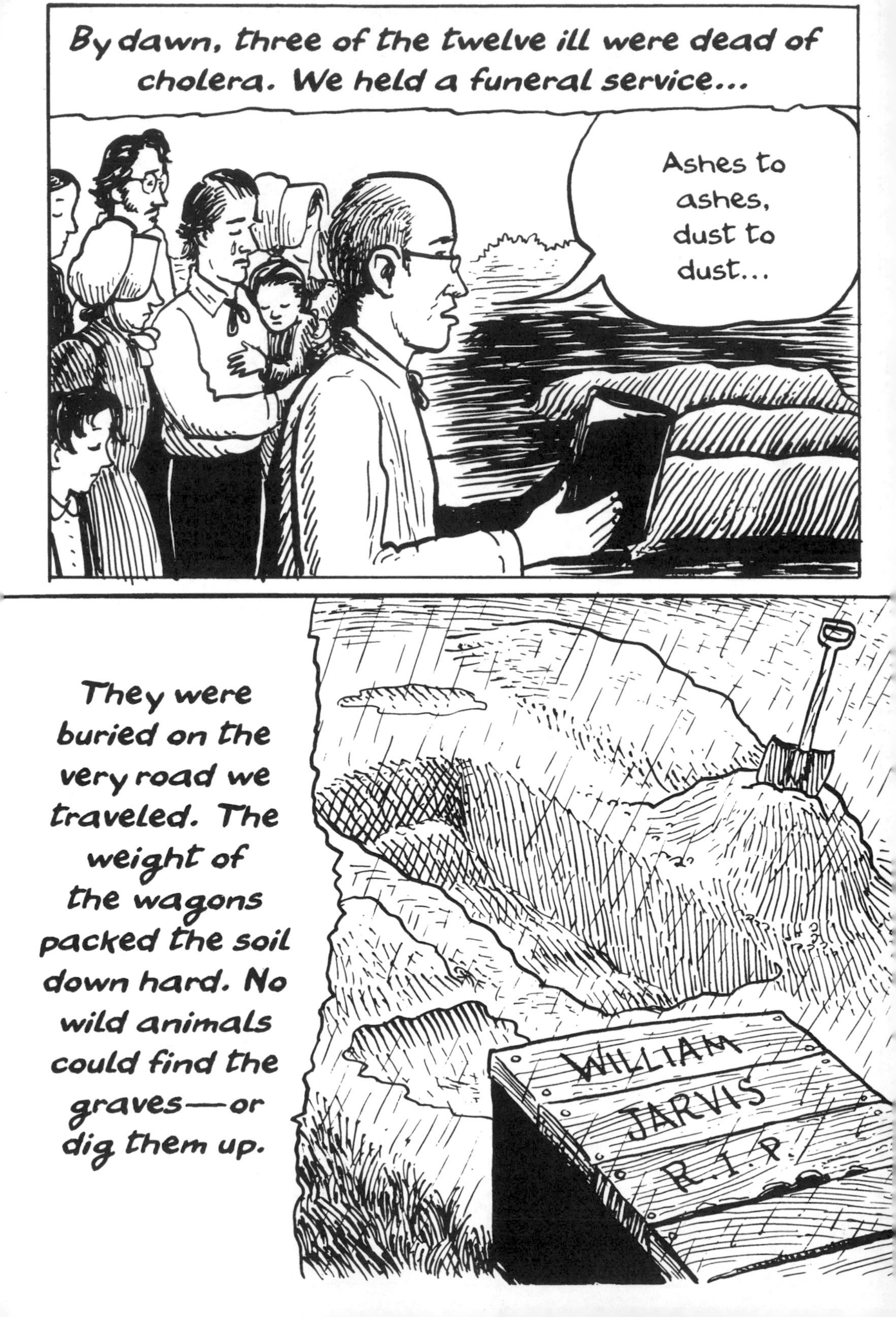
By dawn, three of the twelve ill were dead of cholera. We held a funeral service...
Ashes to ashes, dust to dust...
They were buried on the very road we traveled. The weight of the wagons packed the soil down hard. No wild animals could find the graves—or dig them up.
WILLIAM JARVIS R.I.P.

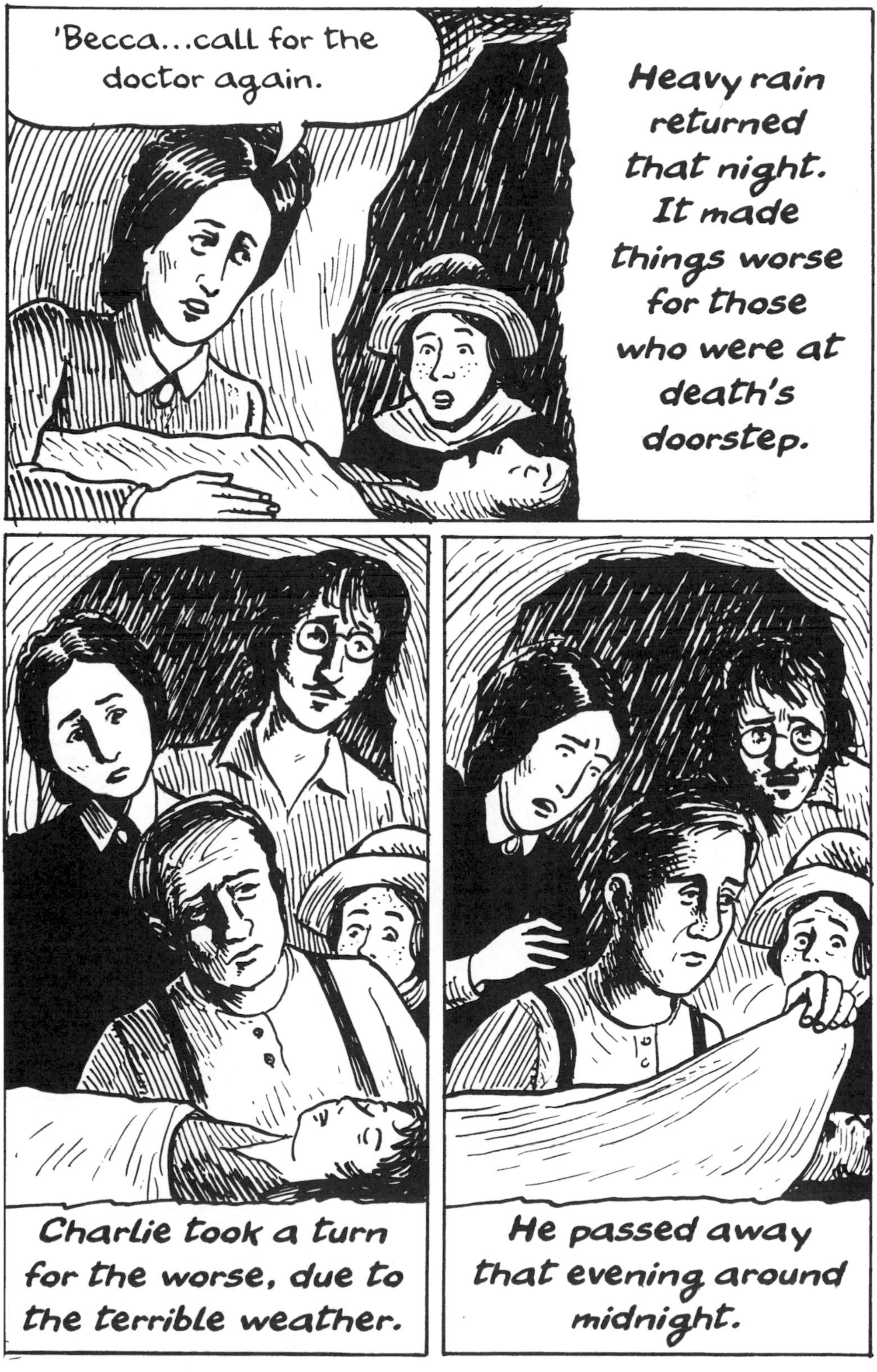

'Becca...call for the doctor again.
Heavy rain returned that night. It made things worse for those who were at death's doorstep.
Charlie took a turn for the worse, due to the terrible weather.
He passed away that evening around midnight.

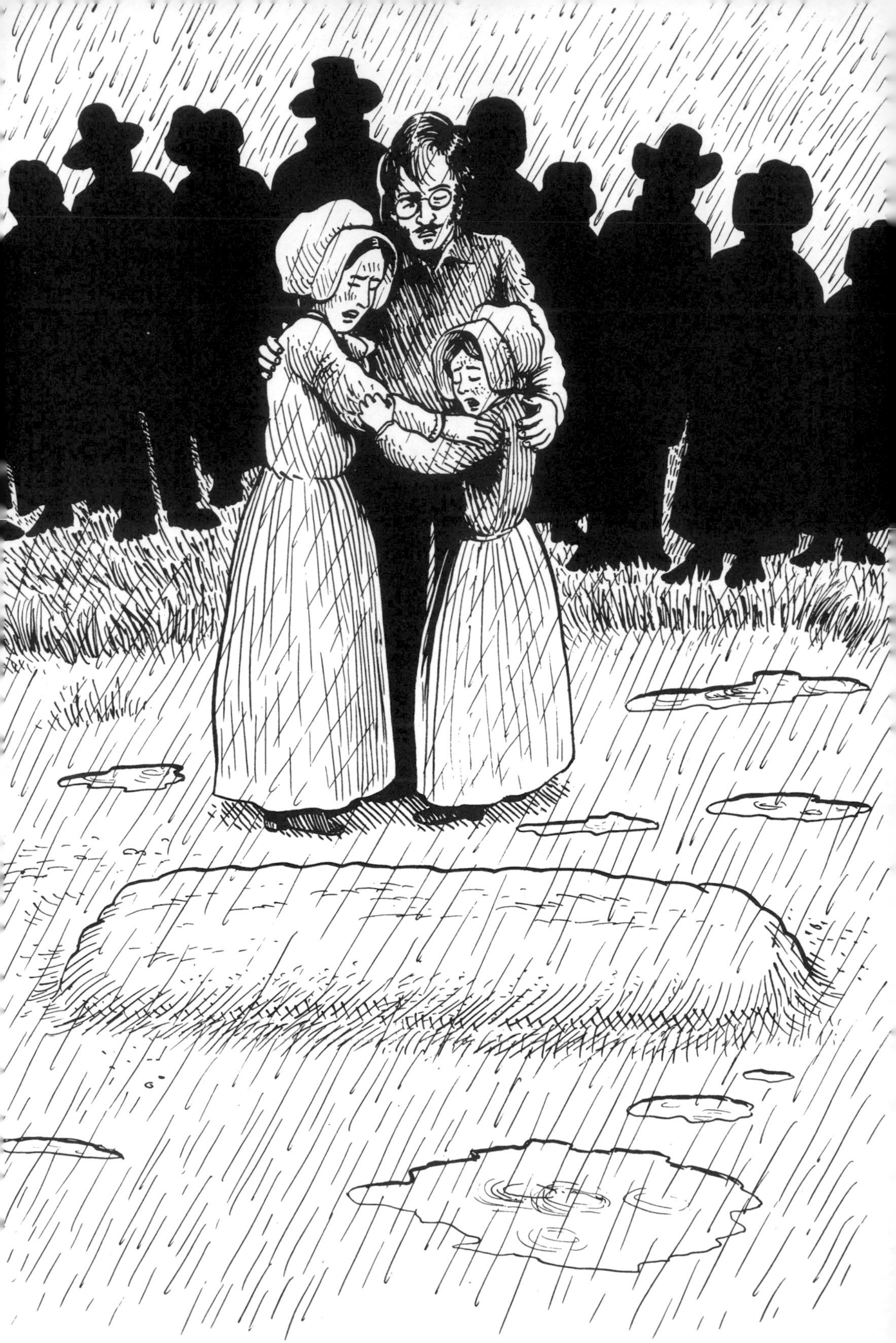

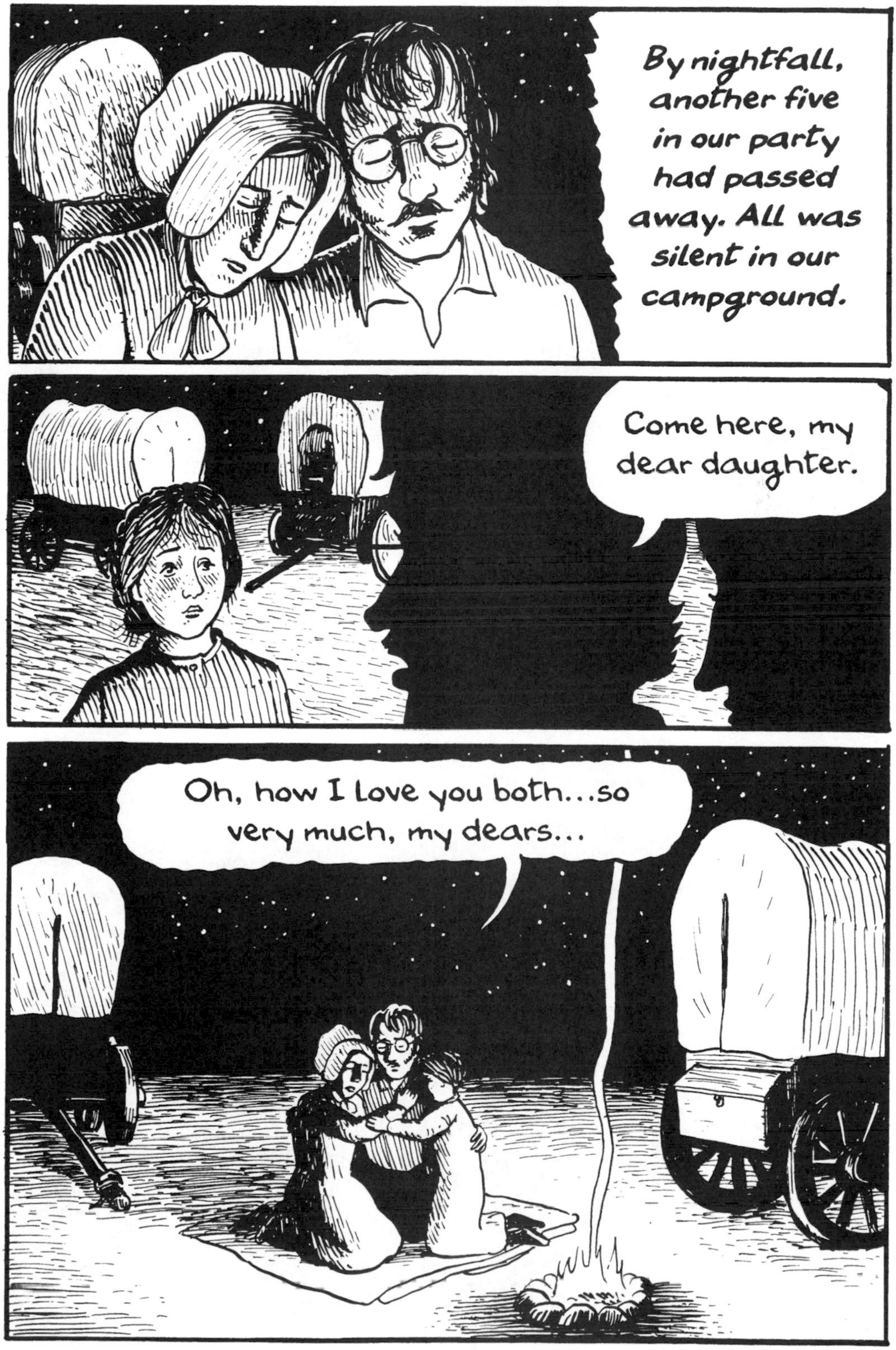
By nightfall, another five in our party had passed away. All was silent in our campground.
Come here, my dear daughter.
Oh, how I love you both...so very much, my dears...

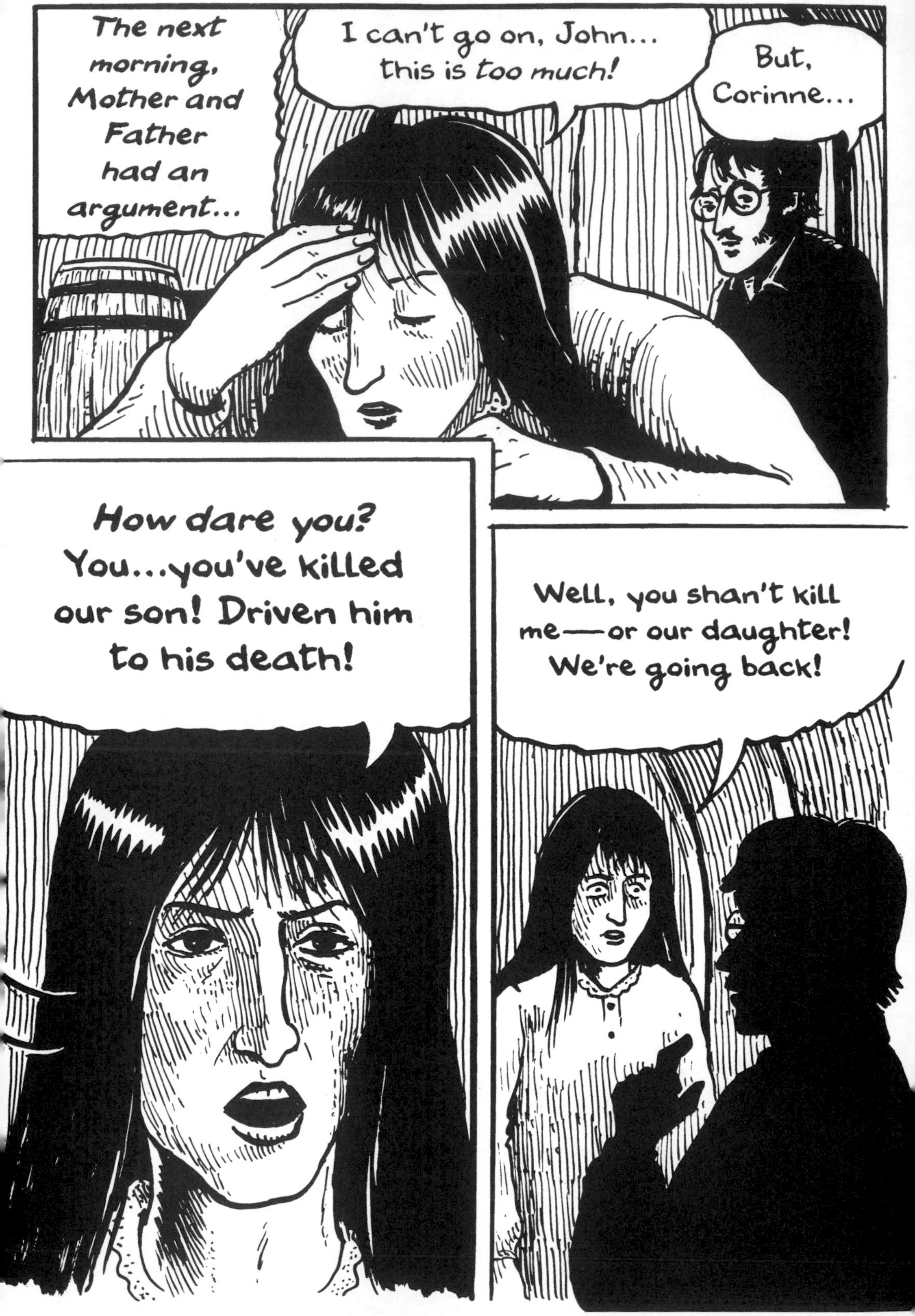
The next morning, Mother and Father had an argument...
I can't go on, John... this is *too much!*
But, Corinne...
How dare you? You...you've killed our son! Driven him to his death!
Well, you shan't kill me—or our daughter! We're going back!

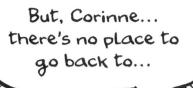

But, Corinne... there's no place to go back to...

We sold it all.

I loved our boy. I took us on this journey for him! So that he'd have clean air!

So that h—he'd get... better...

Mother and Father talked all the day long.

By then, they both understood:

We had to keep going!

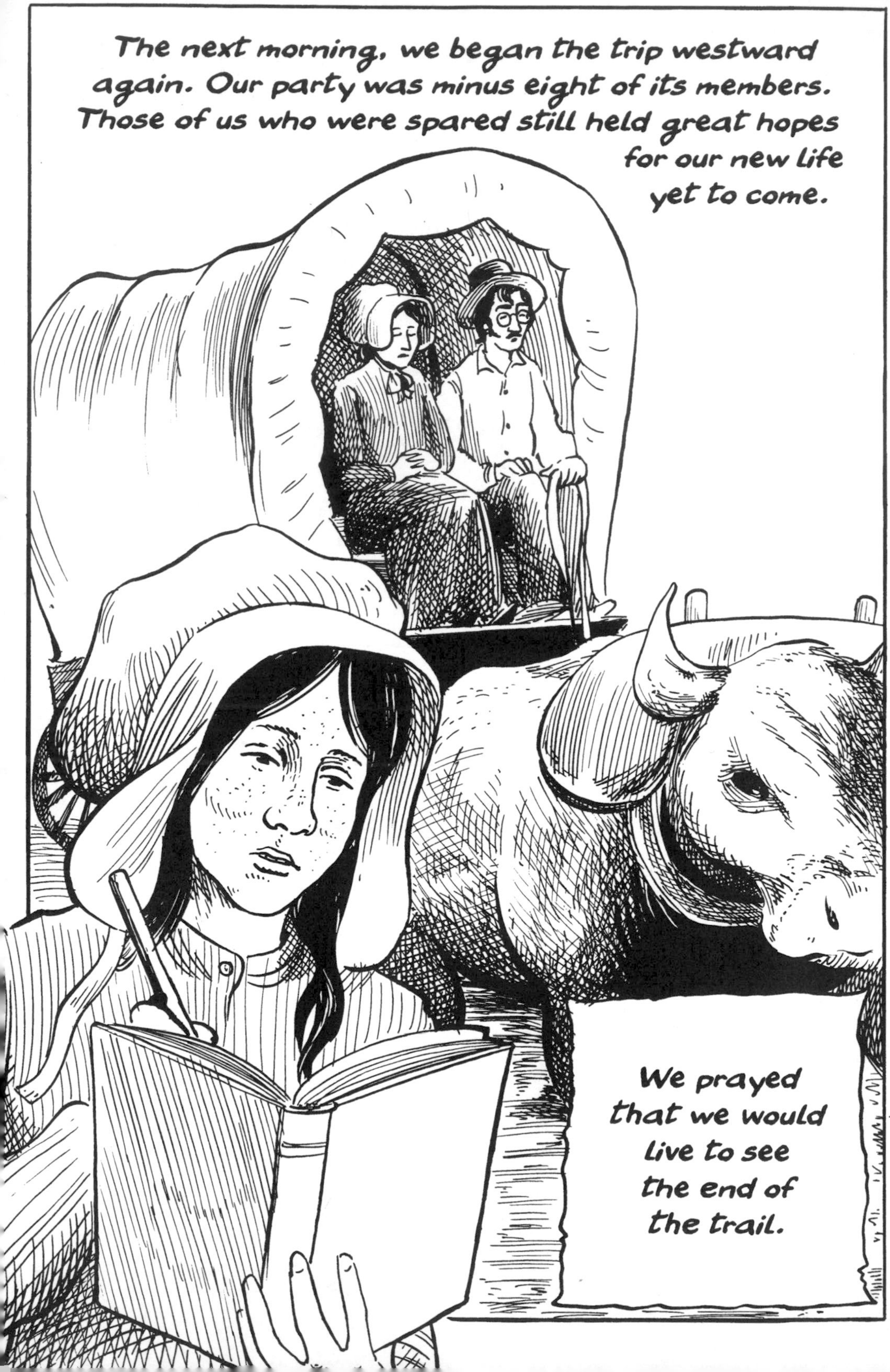

The next morning, we began the trip westward again. Our party was minus eight of its members. Those of us who were spared still held great hopes for our new life yet to come.
We prayed that we would live to see the end of the trail.

Chapter SEVEN
AMONG the Pawnee

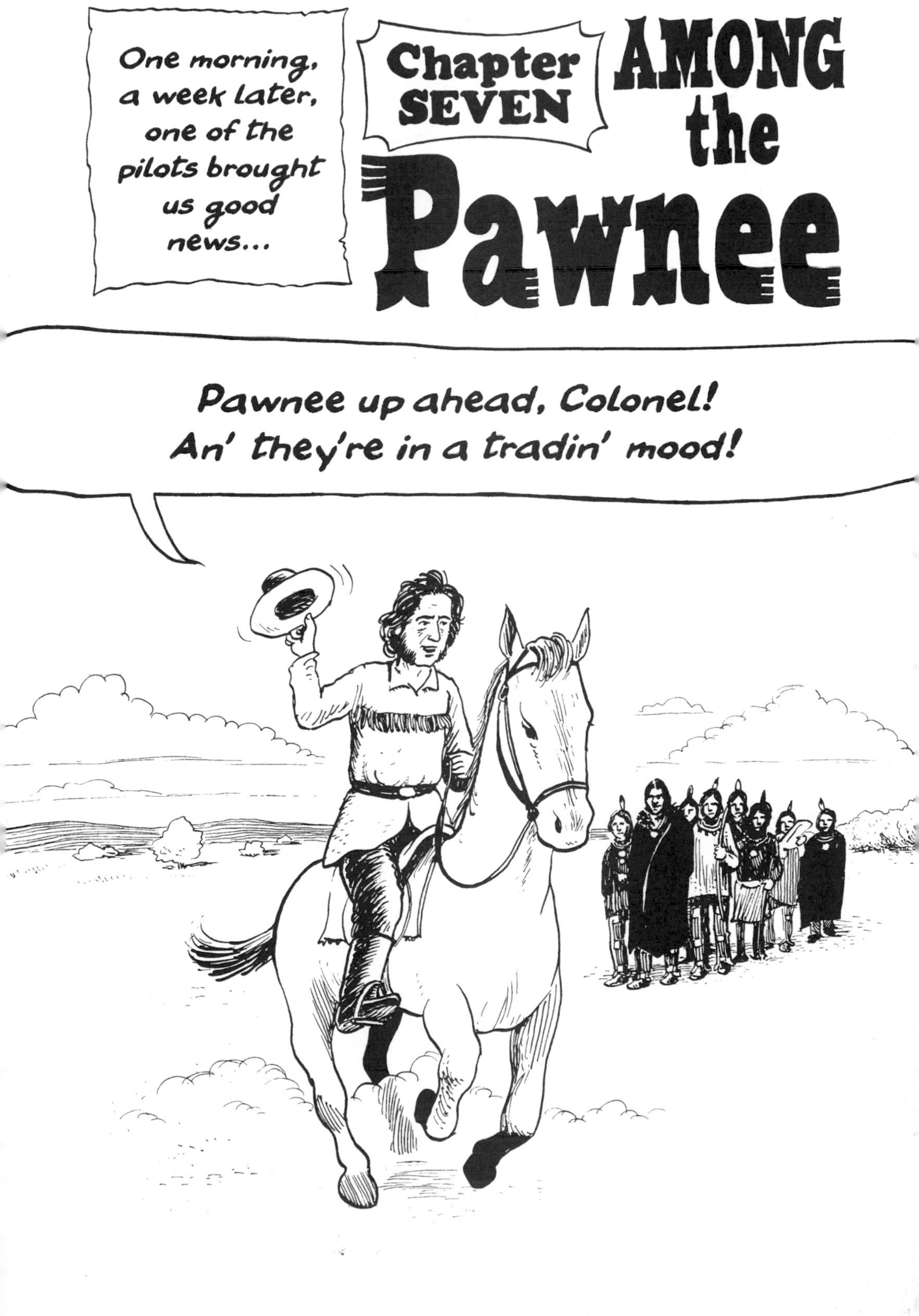

One morning, a week later, one of the pilots brought us good news...
Pawnee up ahead, Colonel! An' they're in a tradin' mood!

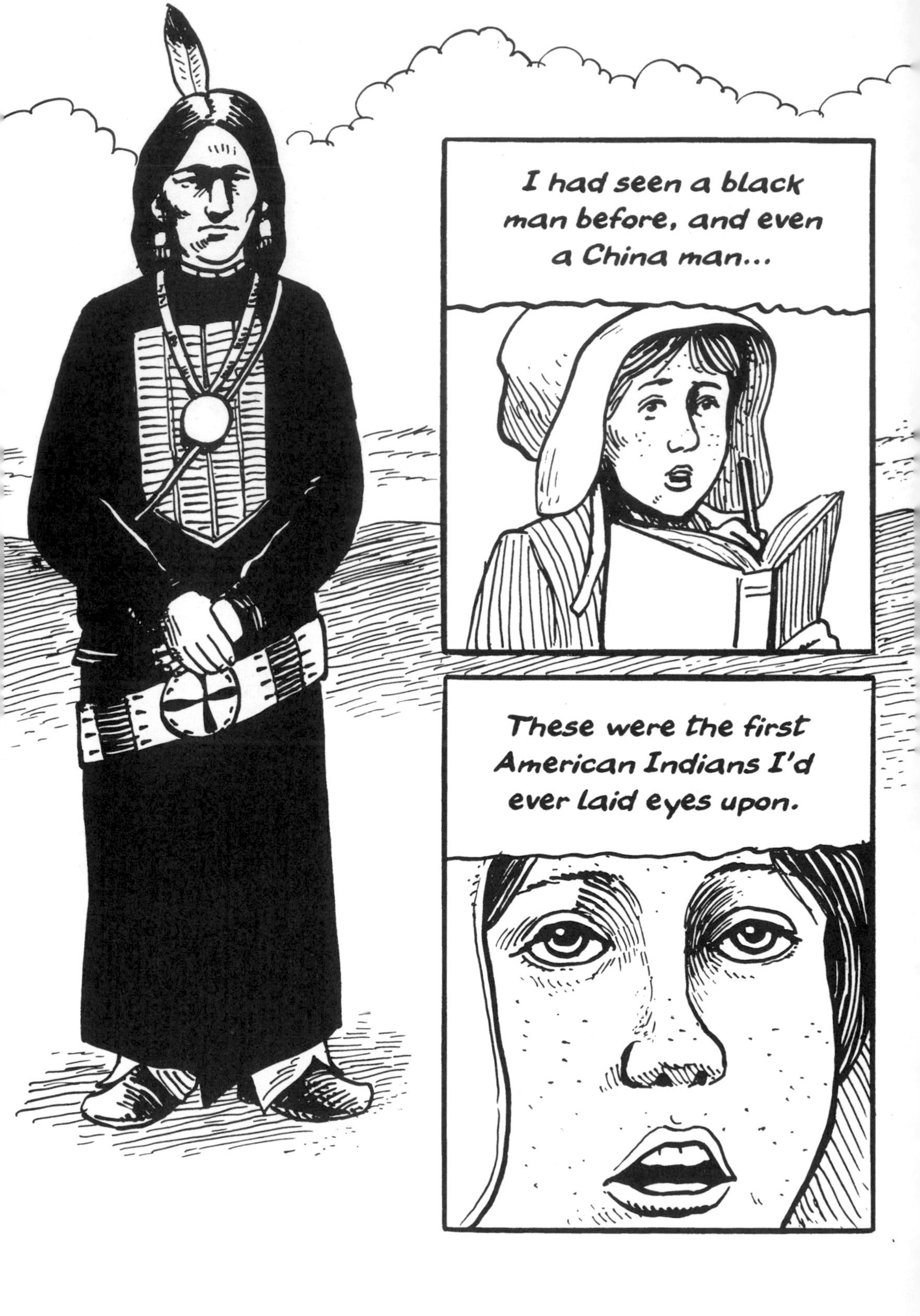
I had seen a black man before, and even a China man...
These were the first American Indians I'd ever laid eyes upon.

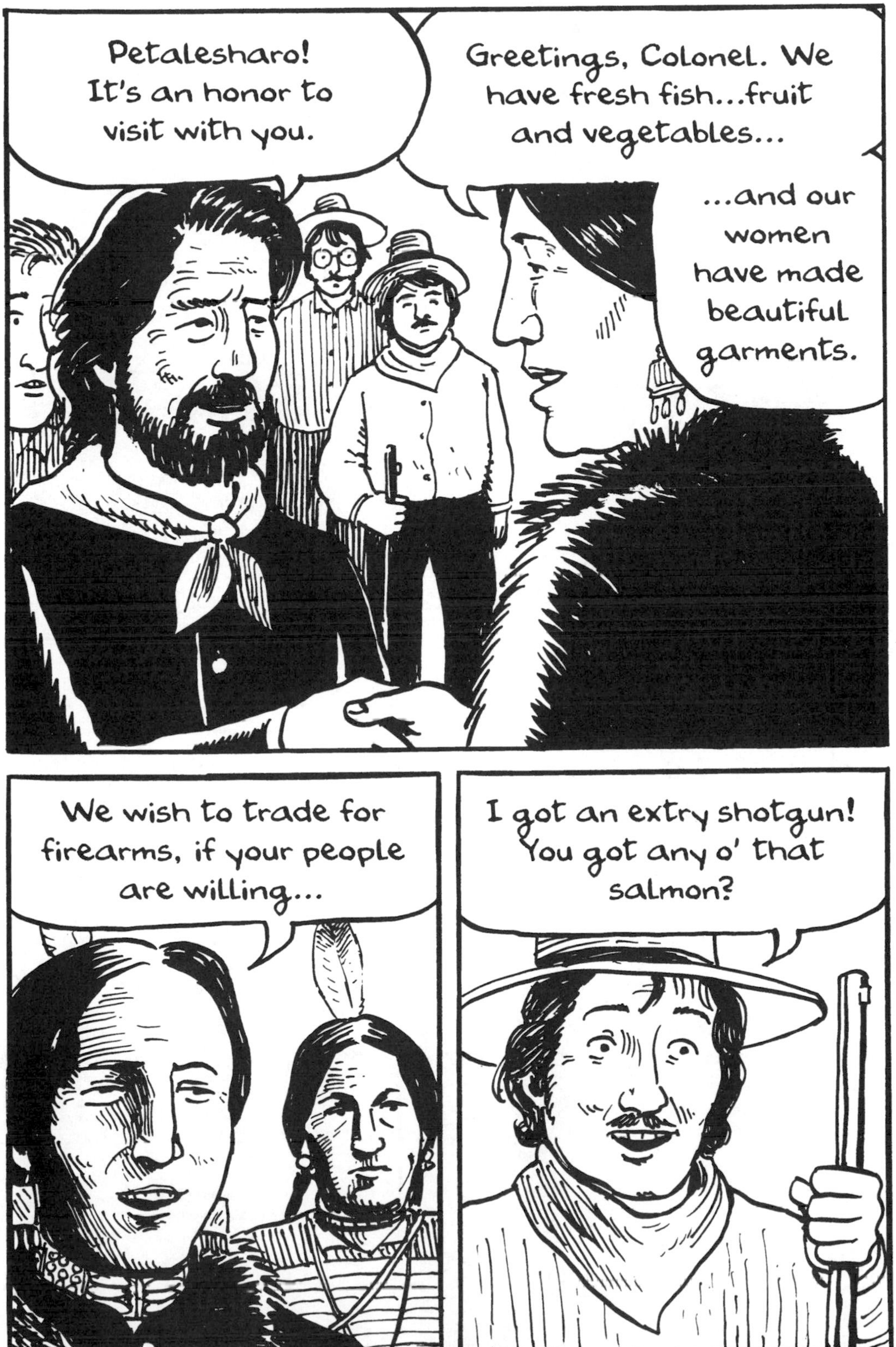
Petalesharo! It's an honor to visit with you.
Greetings, Colonel. We have fresh fish...fruit and vegetables...
...and our women have made beautiful garments.
We wish to trade for firearms, if your people are willing...
I got an extry shotgun! You got any o' that salmon?

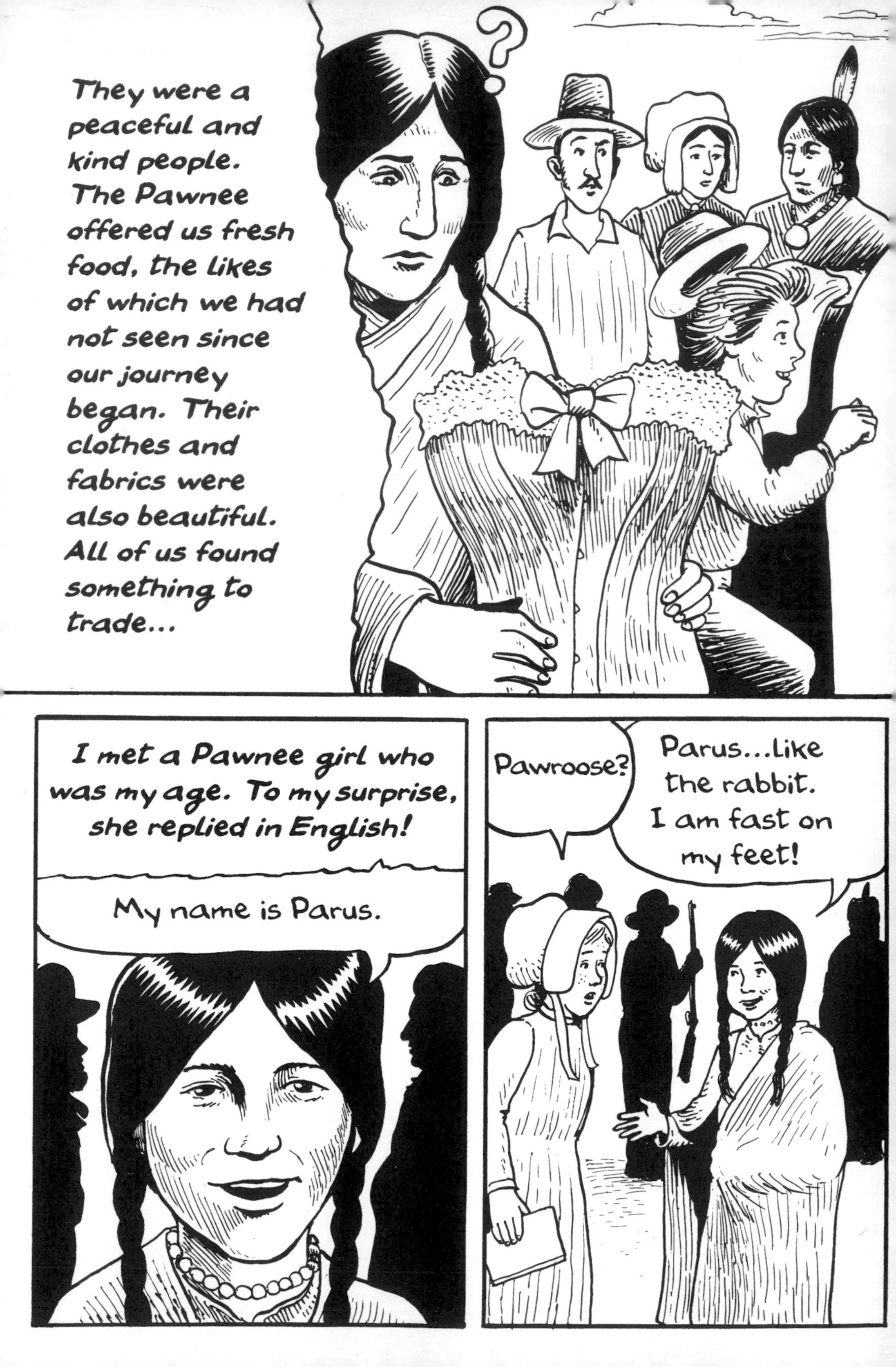

They were a peaceful and kind people. The Pawnee offered us fresh food, the likes of which we had not seen since our journey began. Their clothes and fabrics were also beautiful. All of us found something to trade...
I met a Pawnee girl who was my age. To my surprise, she replied in English!
My name is Parus.
Pawroose?
Parus...like the rabbit. I am fast on my feet!

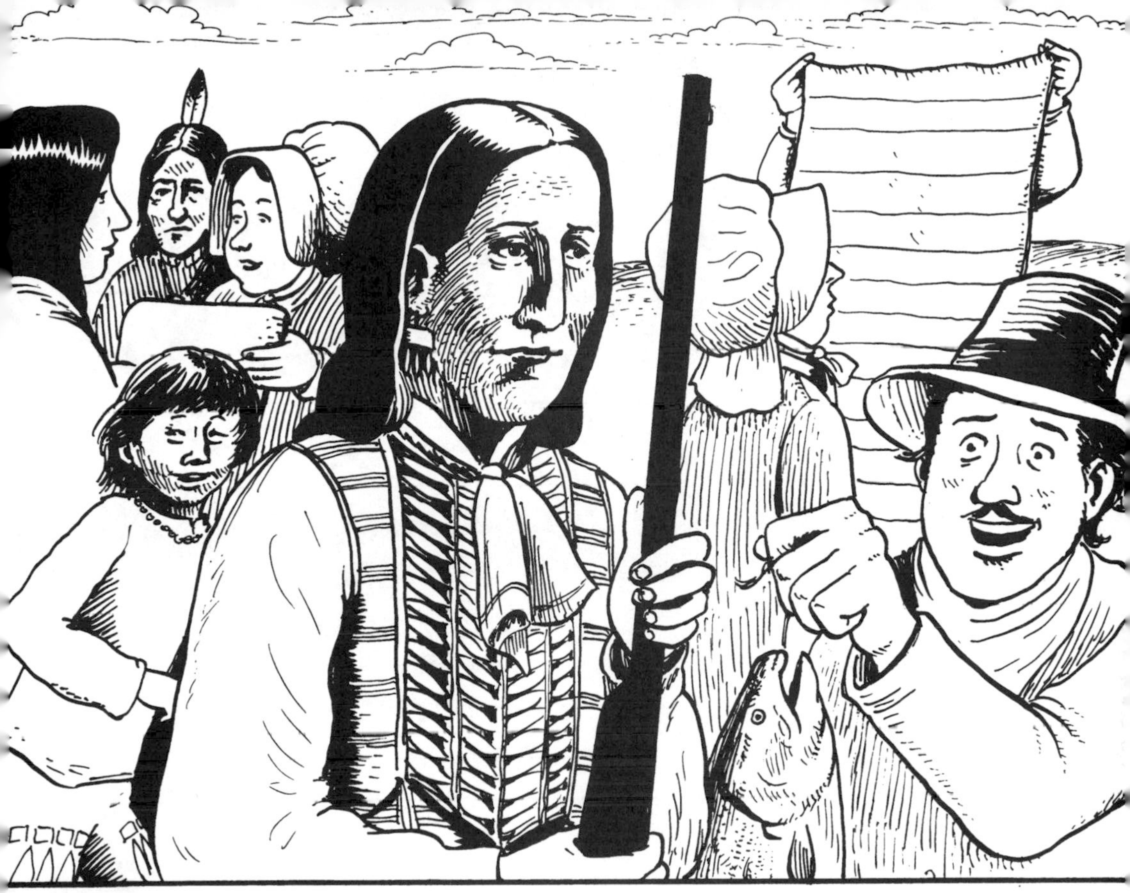

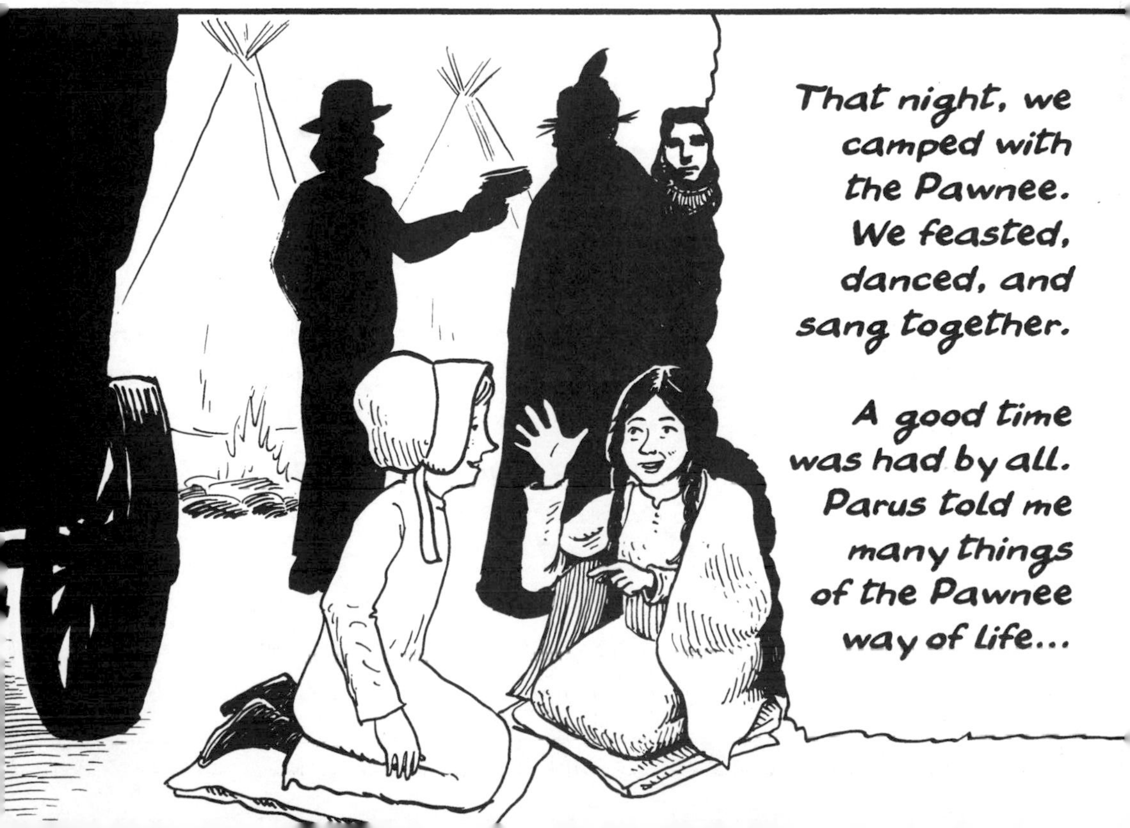
That night, we camped with the Pawnee. We feasted, danced, and sang together.
A good time was had by all. Parus told me many things of the Pawnee way of life...

Pawnee

The Pawnee settled in the Great Plains of America in or around **1200 AD.**

THE PAWNEE's

first name for their tribe was ***Chahiksichahiks.*** *This meant "men of men." "Pawnee" was a word that described their spiky hairstyles,*

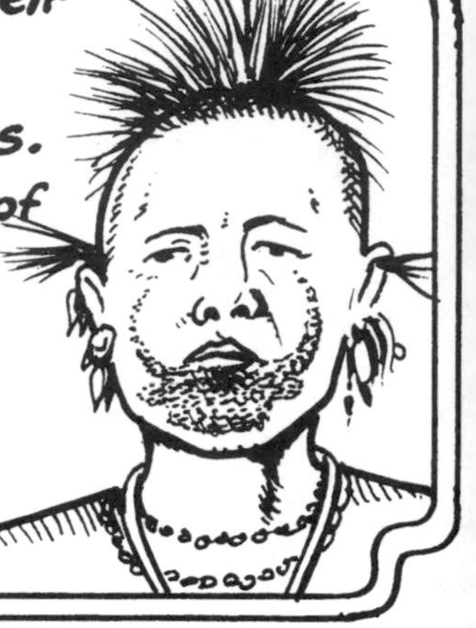

ONE TRIBE, FOUR NAMES

The Pawnee eventually formed four groups:

CHAUI
(Grand)

—

TAPPAGE

—

KITKEHAHAKI
(Republican)

&

SKIDI
(Wolf)

TWO LIVES,

The Pawnee were a semi-sedentary tribe. They lived in two different places every year. Their permanent homes were called ***EARTH LODGES.*** *These were dome-shaped buildings of wood and grass. Up to eight families lived in each lodge. When the Pawnee hunted buffalo in winter months, they used portable homes made of buffalo hide, called* ***TEPEES.***

Life

History & Culture of the Great Plains Tribe

Pawnee artists made comic strip-like paintings and drawings that told the stories of big events, such as their buffalo hunts.

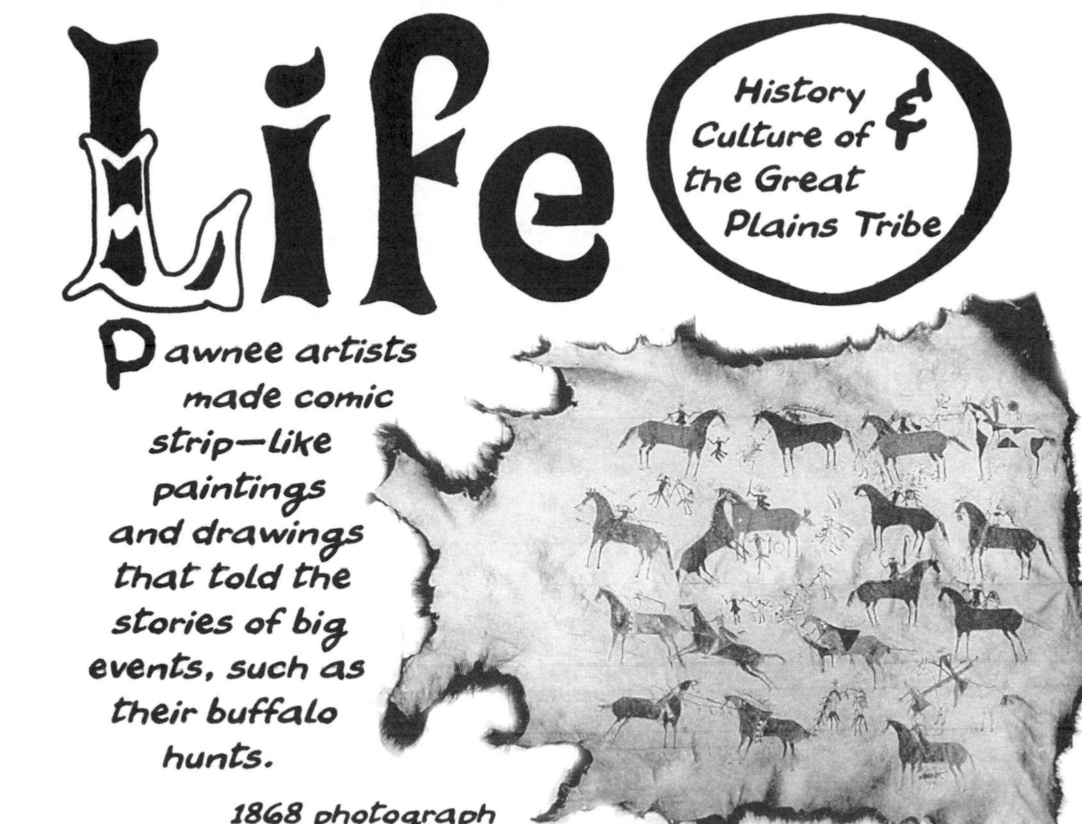

1868 photograph by William Henry Jackson

TWO HOMES

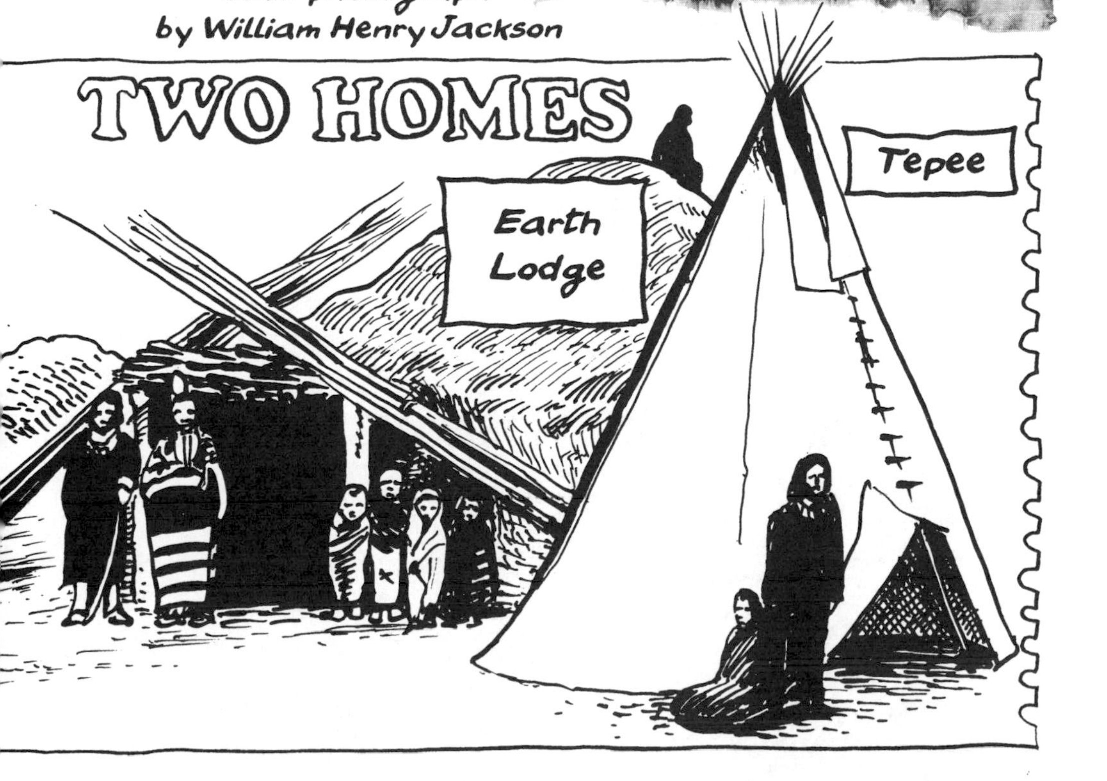
Earth Lodge
Tepee

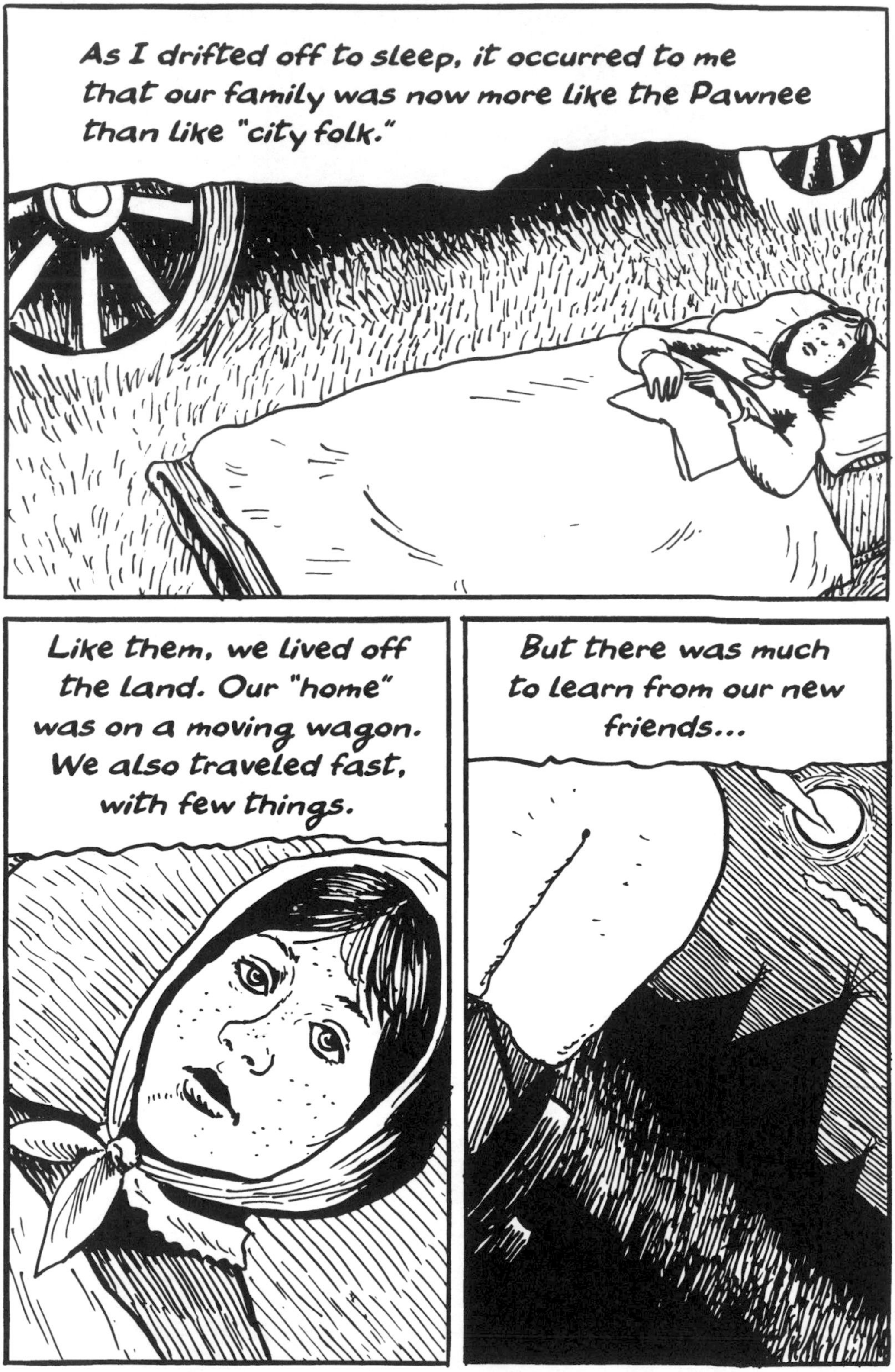
As I drifted off to sleep, it occurred to me that our family was now more like the Pawnee than like "city folk."
Like them, we lived off the land. Our "home" was on a moving wagon. We also traveled fast, with few things.
But there was much to learn from our new friends...

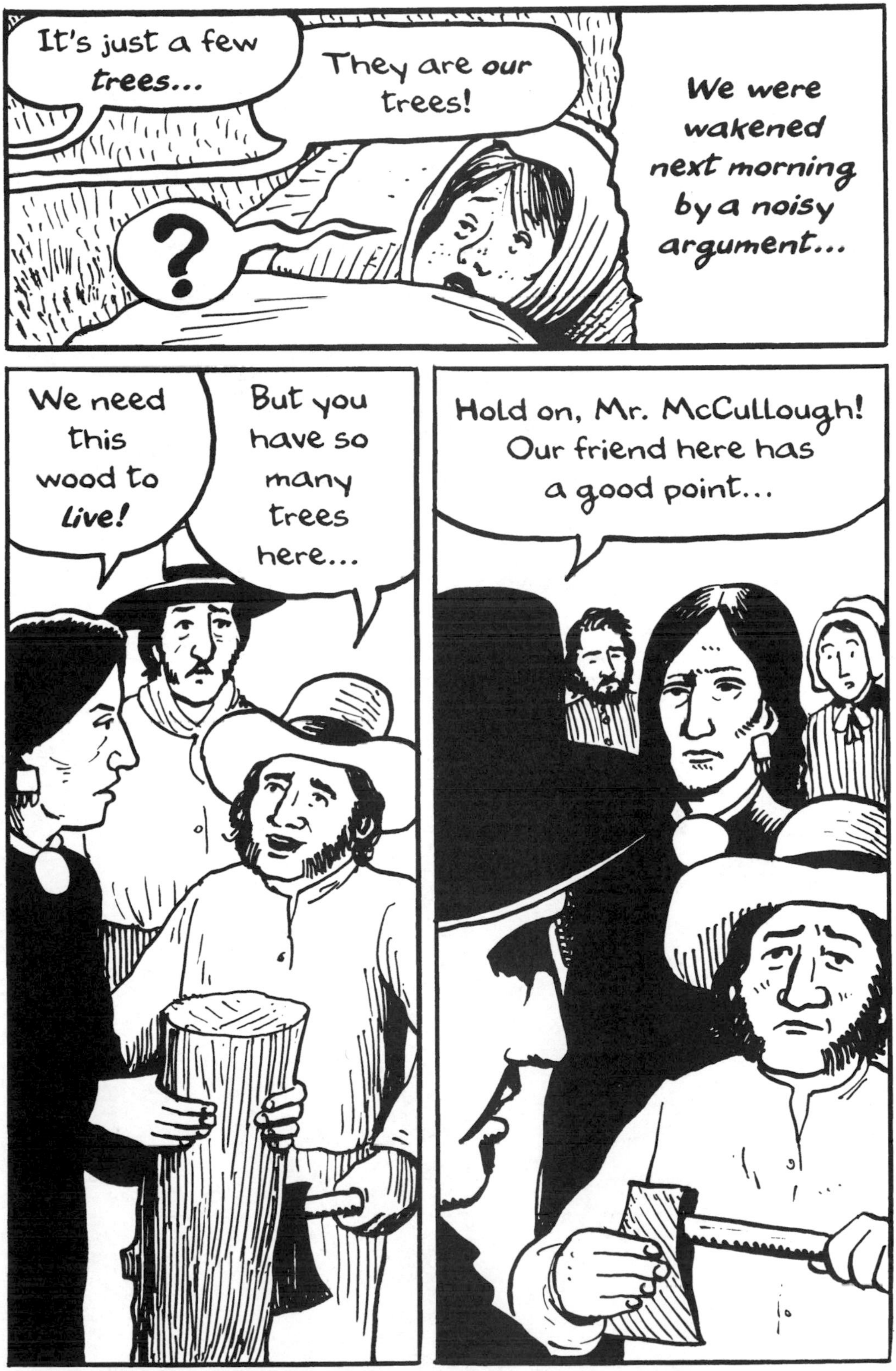
It's just a few *trees*...
They are *our* trees!
?
We were wakened next morning by a noisy argument...
We need this wood to *live!*
But you have so many trees here...
Hold on, Mr. McCullough! Our friend here has a good point...

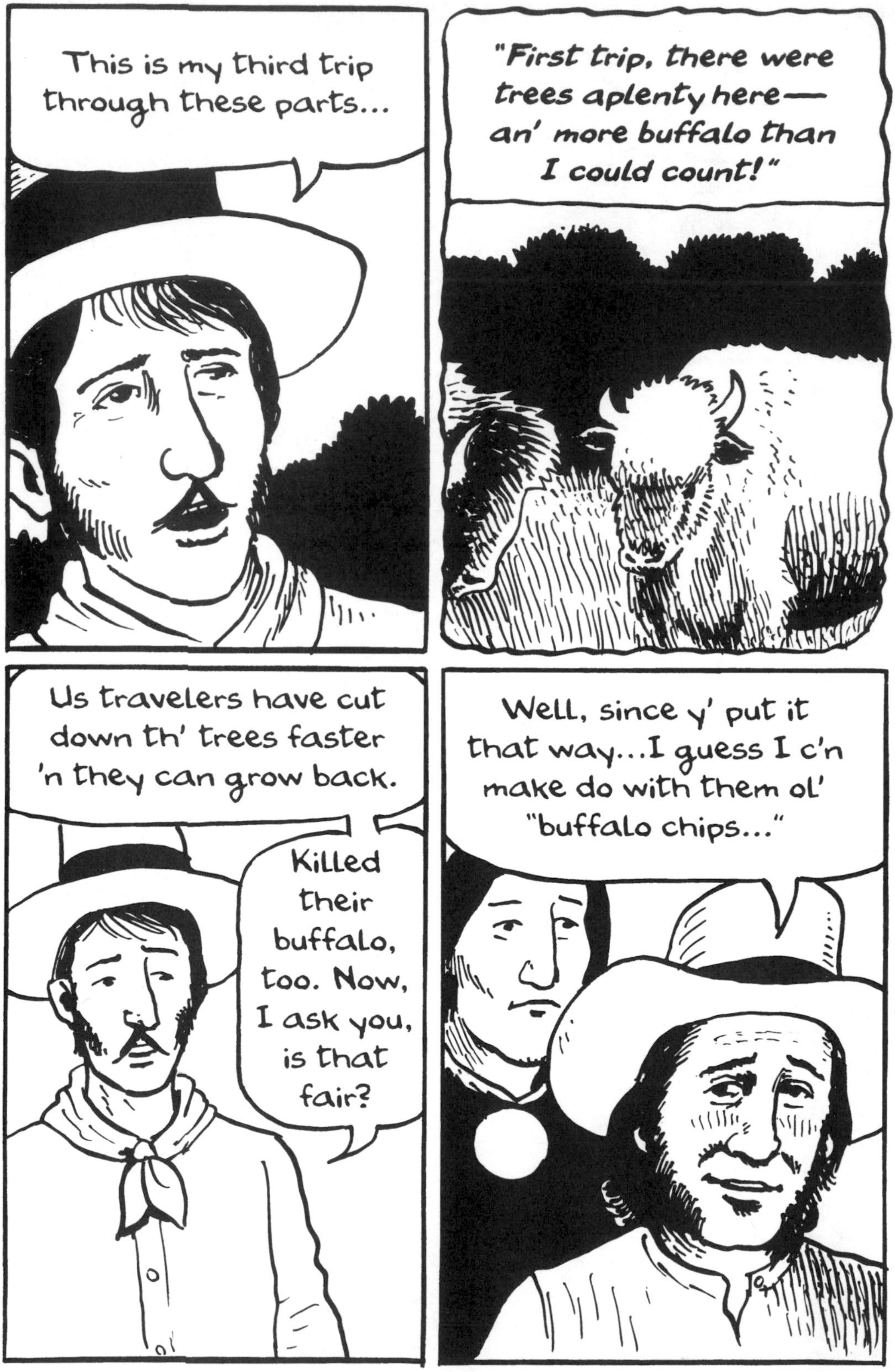
This is my third trip through these parts...
"First trip, there were trees aplenty here— an' more buffalo than I could count!"
Us travelers have cut down th' trees faster 'n they can grow back.
Killed their buffalo, too. Now, I ask you, is that fair?
Well, since y' put it that way...I guess I c'n make do with them ol' "buffalo chips..."

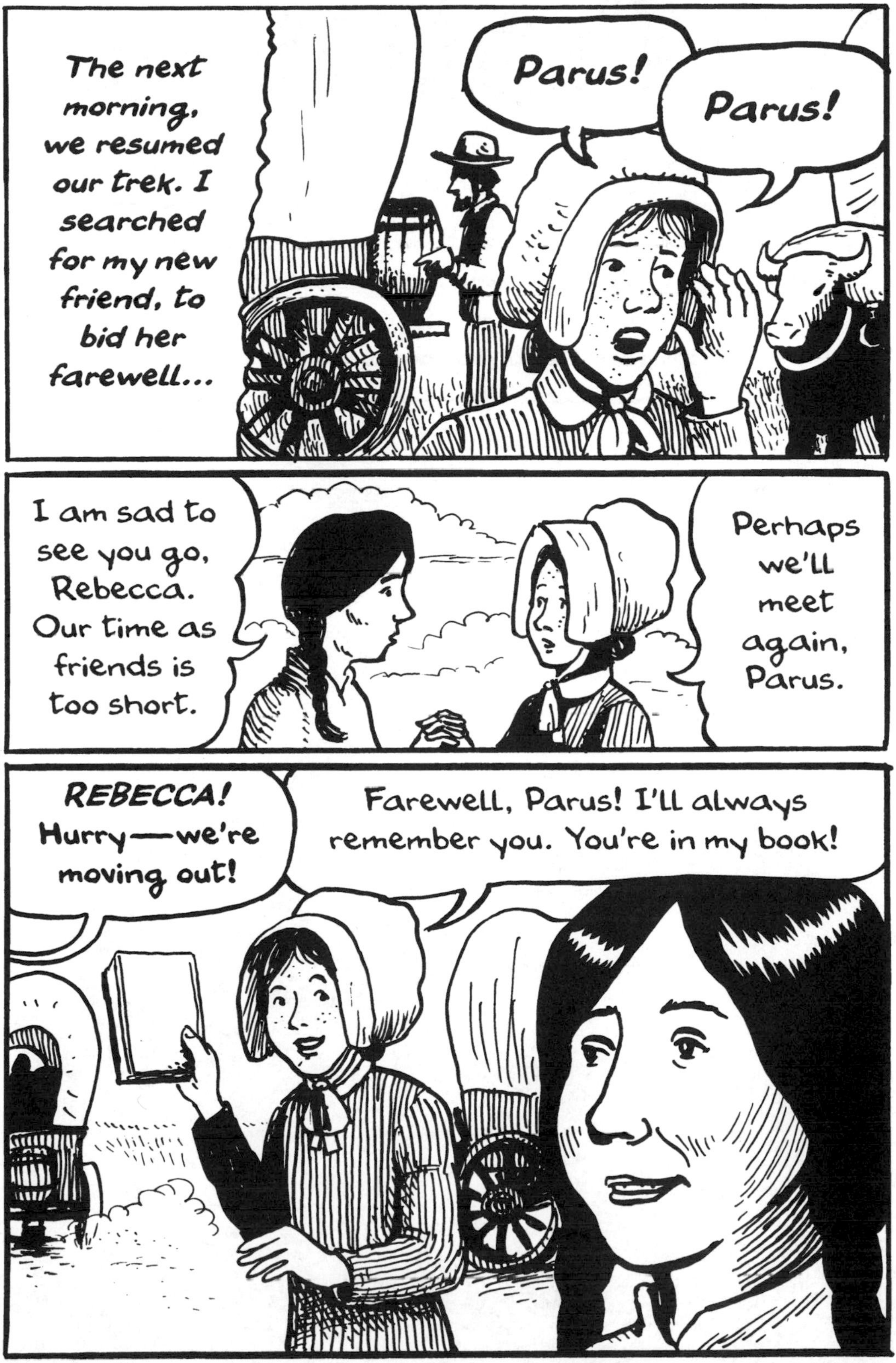
The next morning, we resumed our trek. I searched for my new friend, to bid her farewell...
Parus!
Parus!
I am sad to see you go, Rebecca. Our time as friends is too short.
Perhaps we'll meet again, Parus.
REBECCA! Hurry—we're moving out!
Farewell, Parus! I'll always remember you. You're in my book!

Chapter 8 Fantastic and

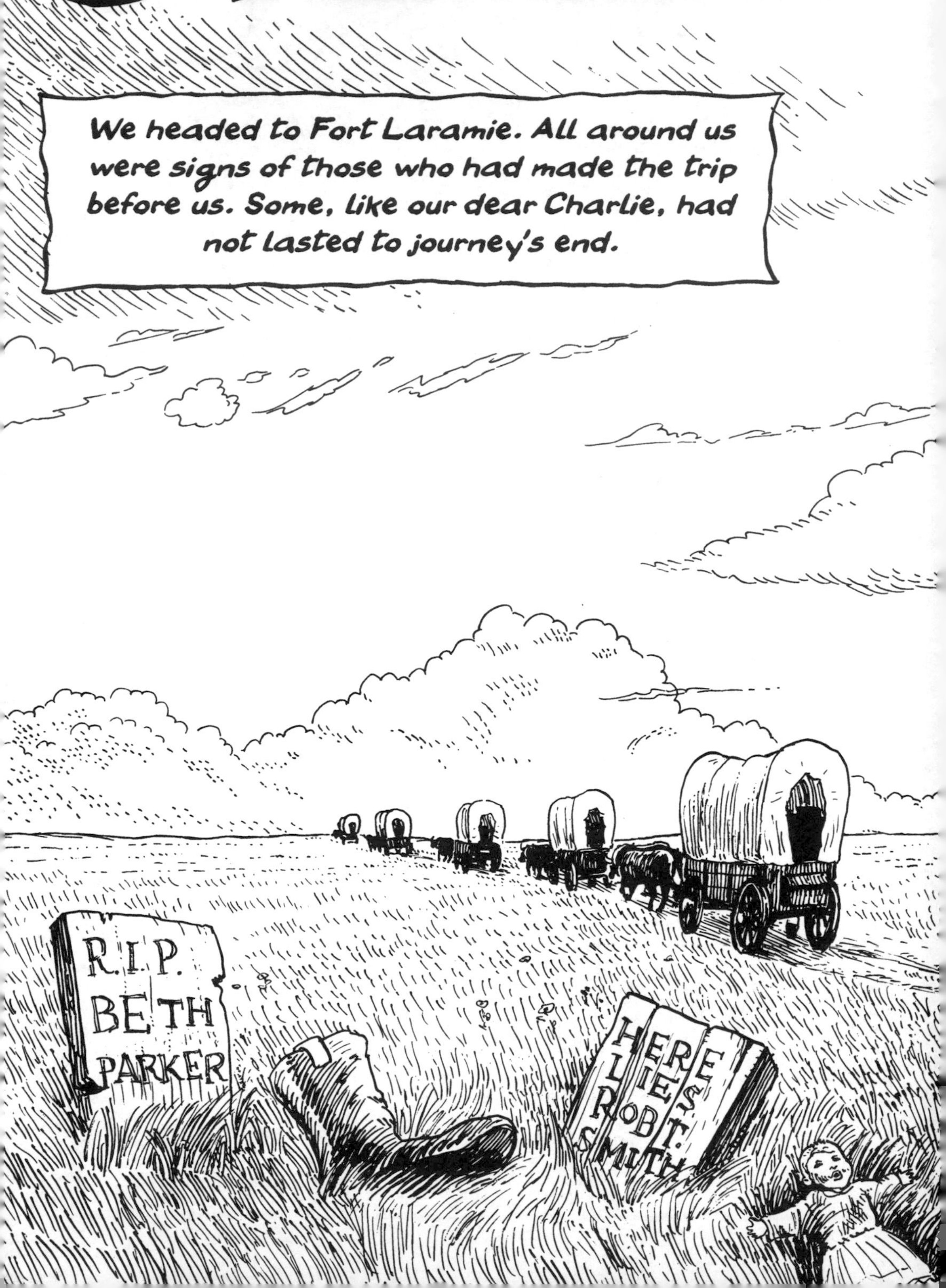

We headed to Fort Laramie. All around us were signs of those who had made the trip before us. Some, like our dear Charlie, had not lasted to journey's end.
R.I.P. BETH PARKER
HERE LIES ROBT. SMITH

Familiar Sights

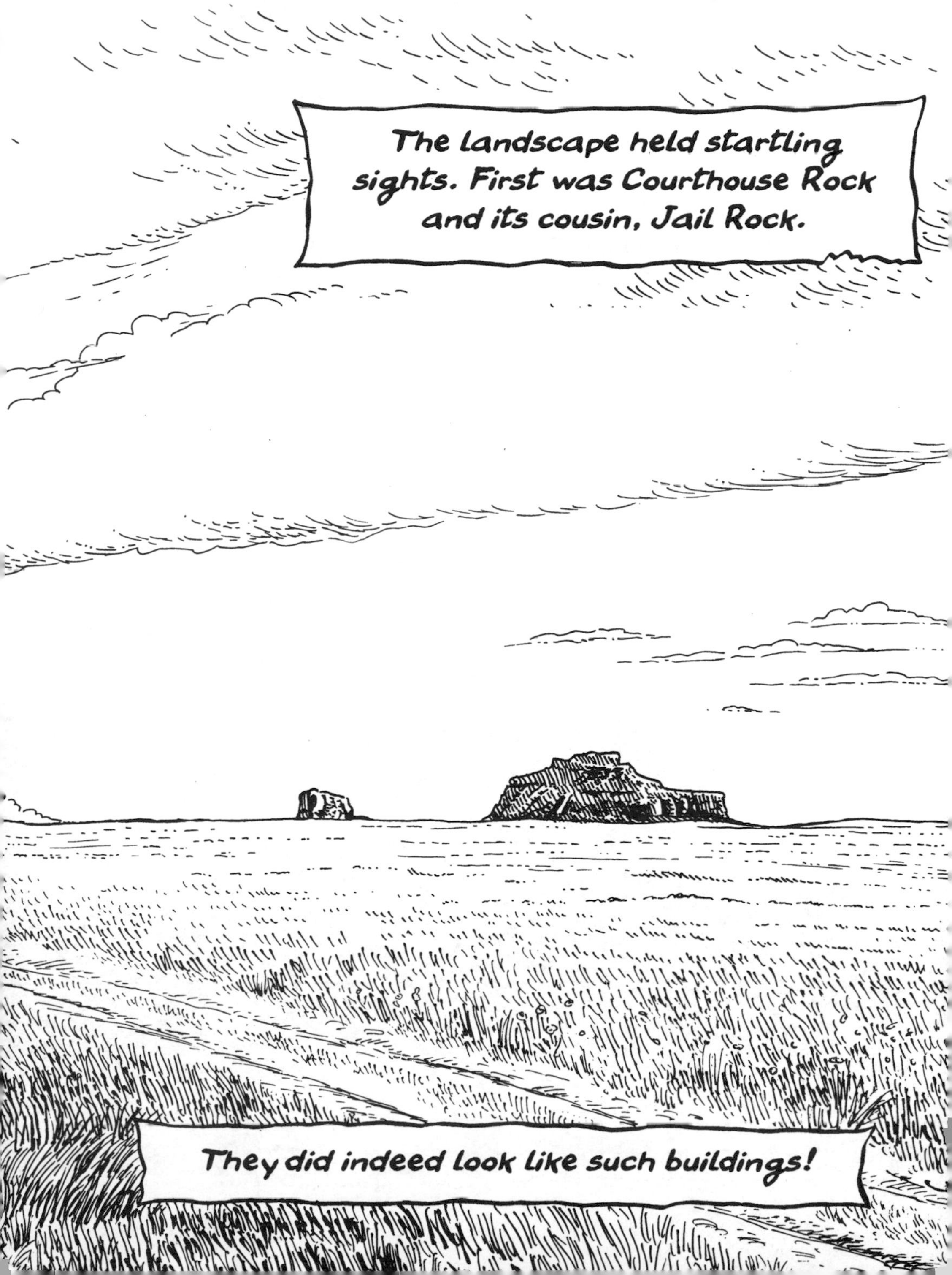
The landscape held startling sights. First was Courthouse Rock and its cousin, Jail Rock.
They did indeed look like such buildings!

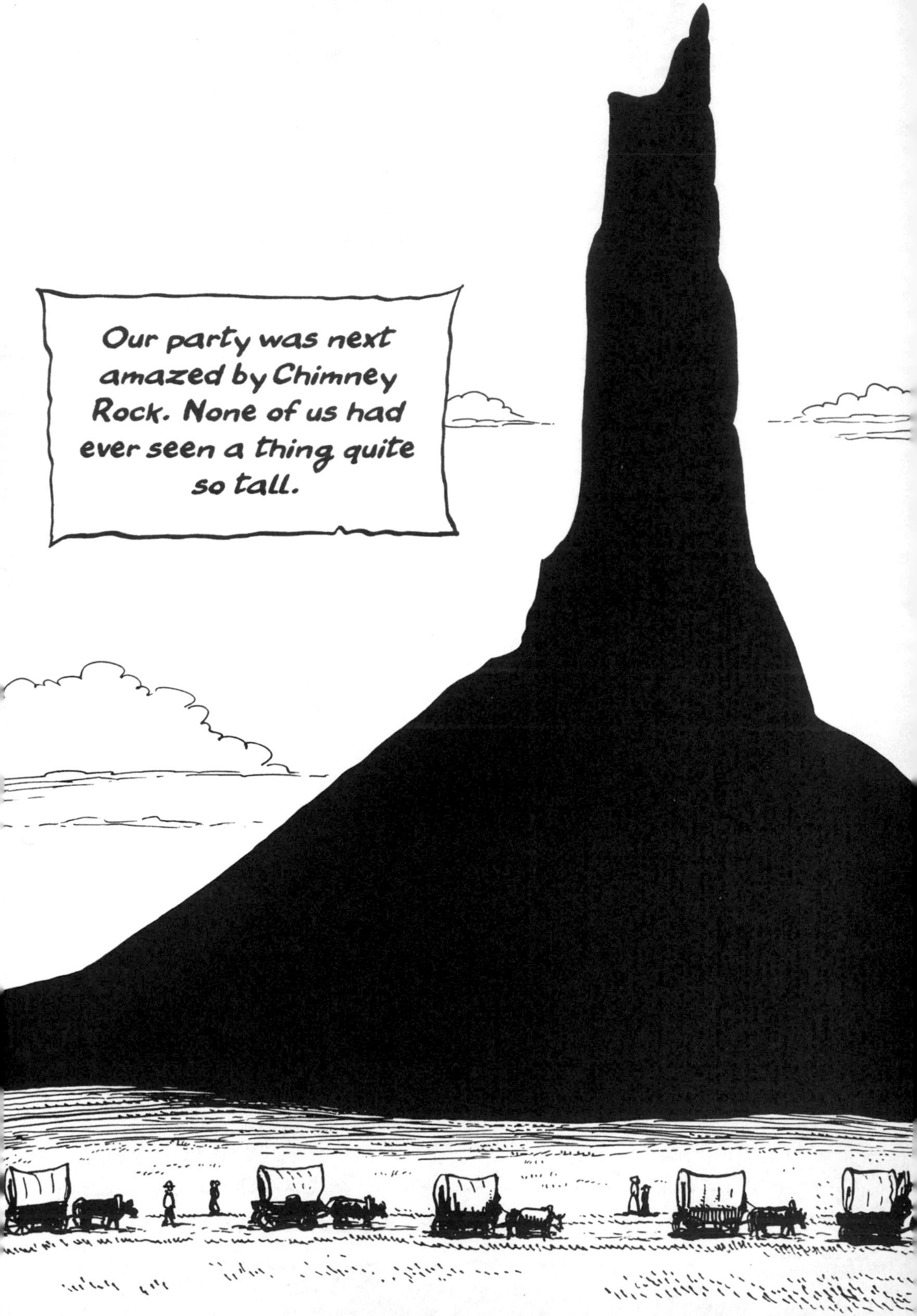
Our party was next amazed by Chimney Rock. None of us had ever seen a thing quite so tall.

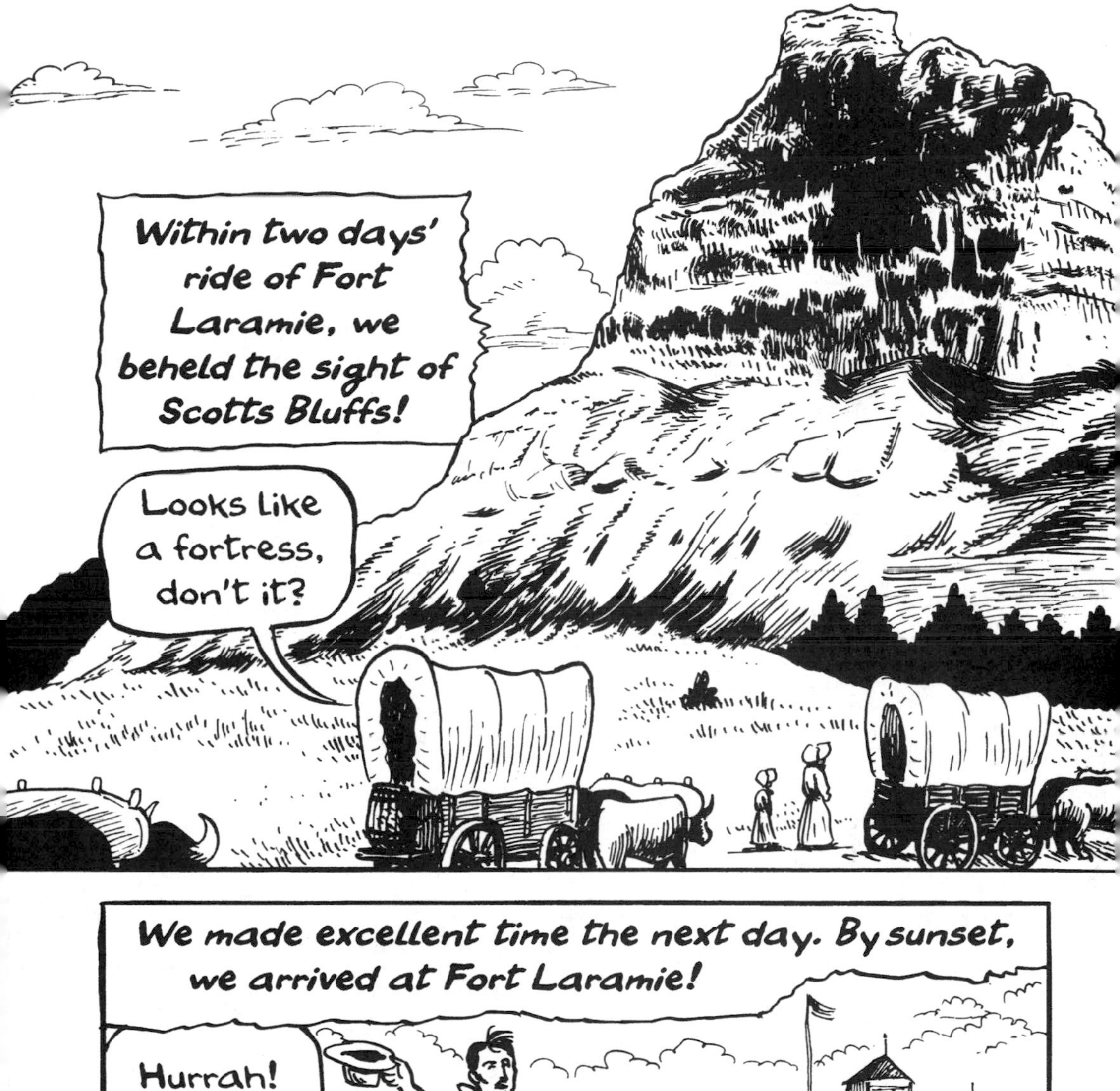
Within two days' ride of Fort Laramie, we beheld the sight of Scotts Bluffs!
Looks like a fortress, don't it?

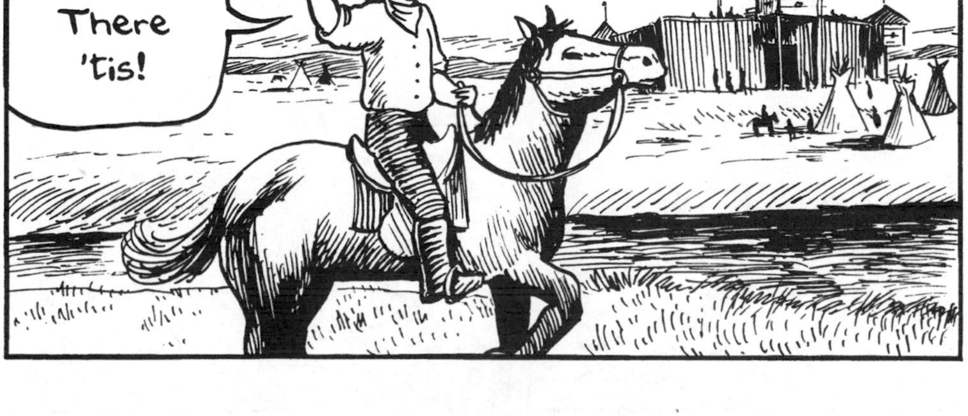
We made excellent time the next day. By sunset, we arrived at Fort Laramie!
Hurrah! There 'tis!

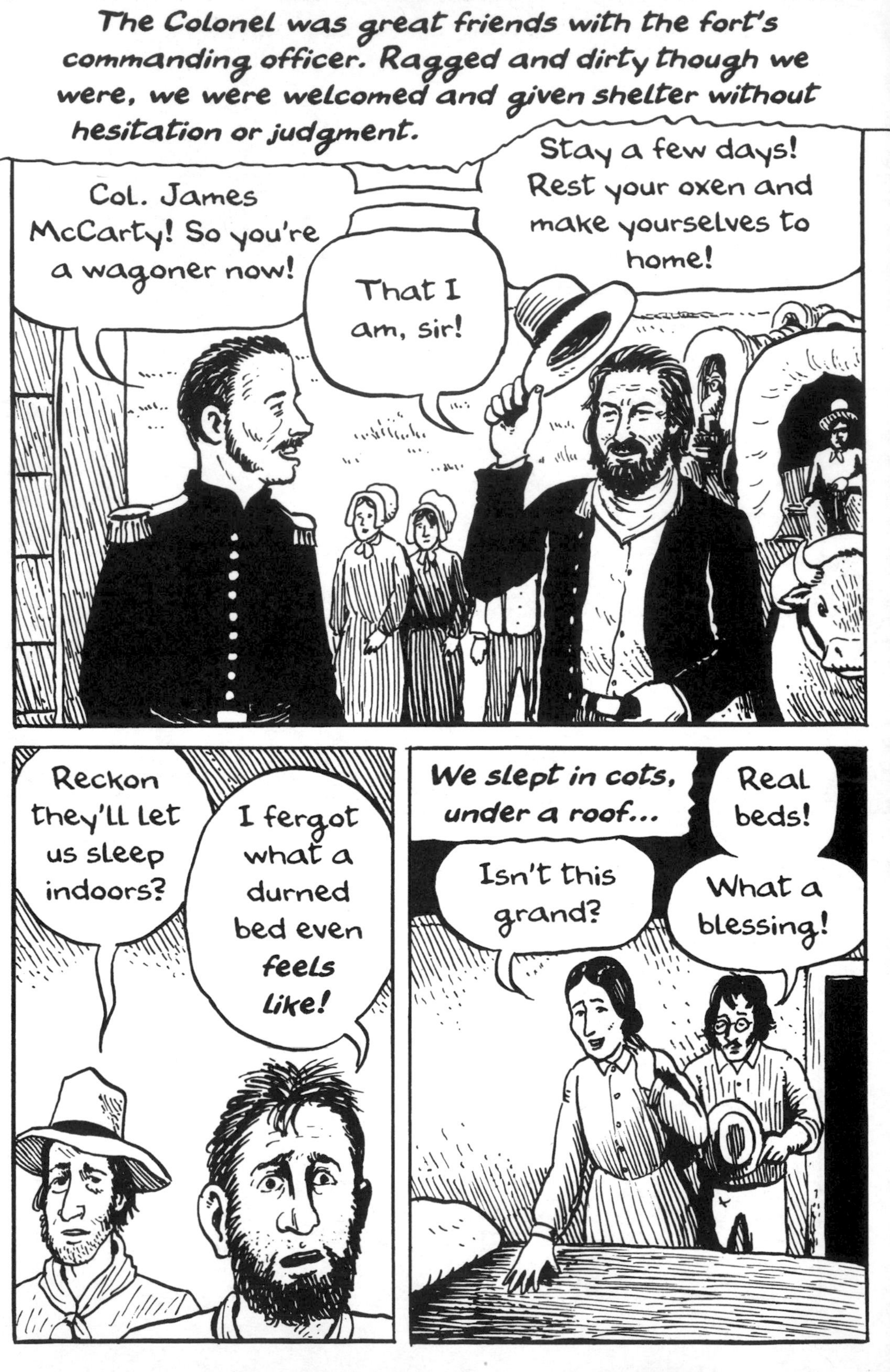

The Colonel was great friends with the fort's commanding officer. Ragged and dirty though we were, we were welcomed and given shelter without hesitation or judgment.
Col. James McCarty! So you're a wagoner now!
That I am, sir!
Stay a few days! Rest your oxen and make yourselves to home!
Reckon they'll let us sleep indoors?
I fergot what a durned bed even feels like!
We slept in cots, under a roof...
Real beds!
Isn't this grand?
What a blessing!

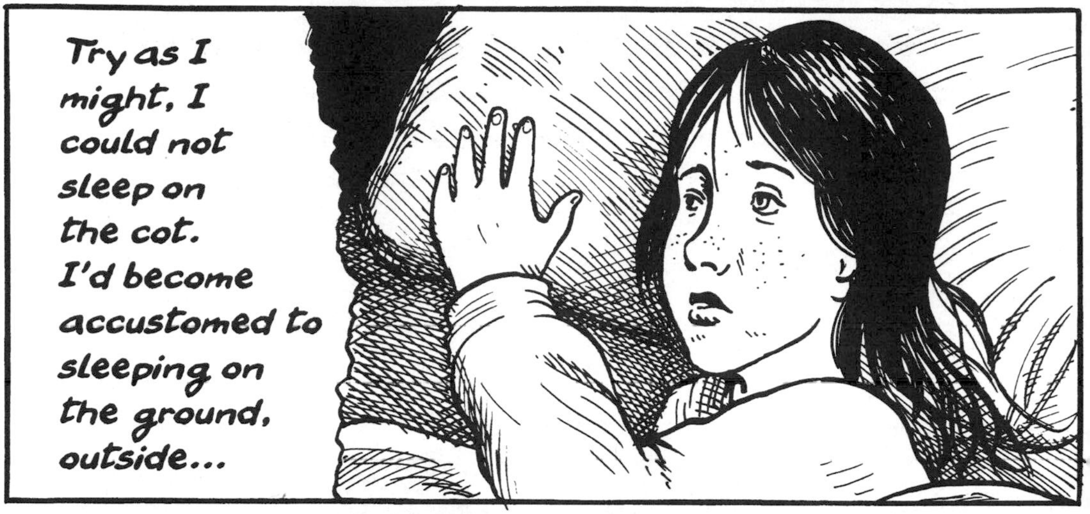
Try as I might, I could not sleep on the cot. I'd become accustomed to sleeping on the ground, outside...

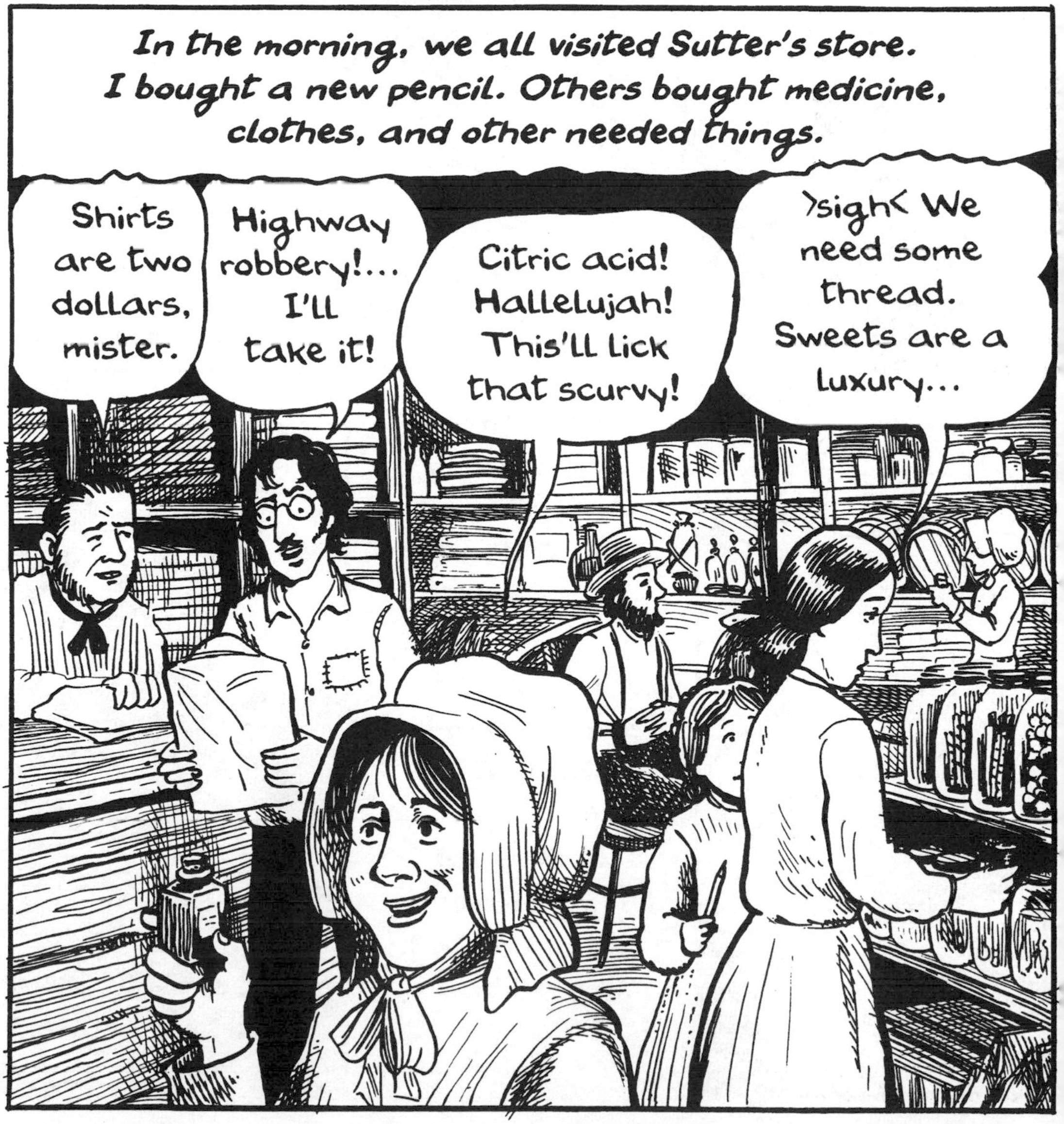
In the morning, we all visited Sutter's store. I bought a new pencil. Others bought medicine, clothes, and other needed things.
Shirts are two dollars, mister.
Highway robbery!... I'll take it!
Citric acid! Hallelujah! This'll lick that scurvy!
>sigh< We need some thread. Sweets are a luxury...

We moved on. Eight days later, we reached Independence Rock. Many who had made the trip before us carved their names onto its surface.

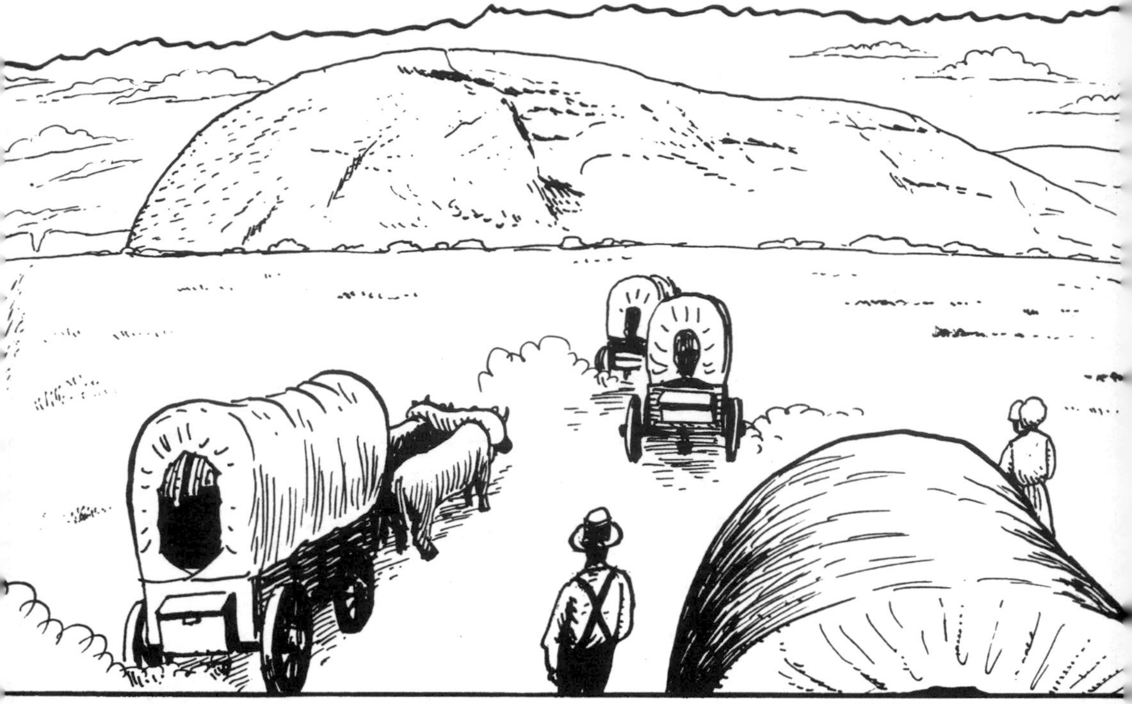

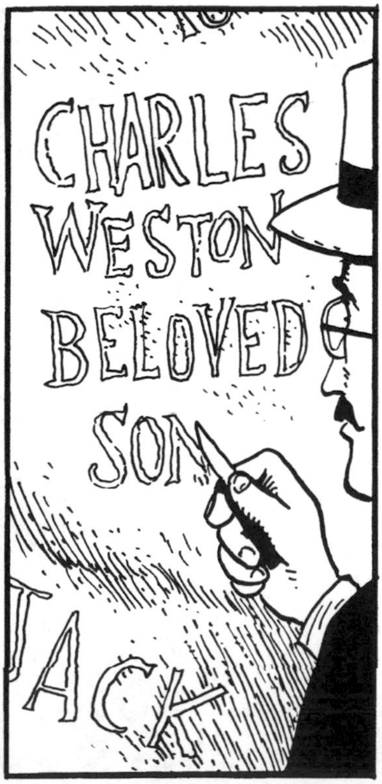
CHARLES
WESTON
BELOVED
SON

Father carved a tribute to dear Charlie upon it. Mother and I wept.

I saw a tear trickle down my father's face.

It was as though Charlie did make the trip with us.

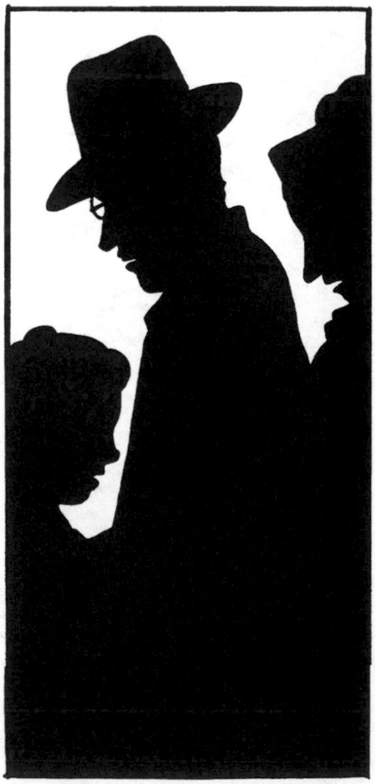

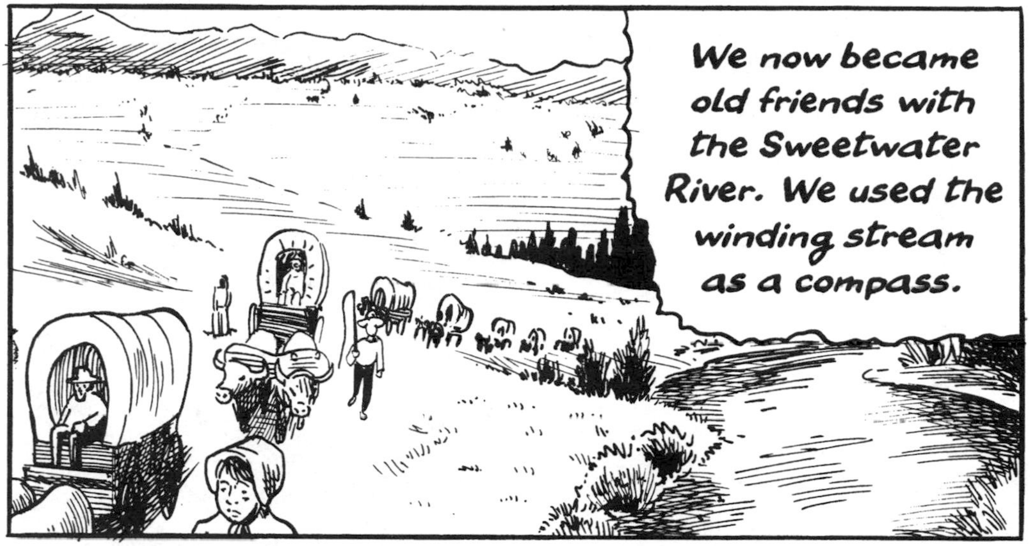
We now became old friends with the Sweetwater River. We used the winding stream as a compass.

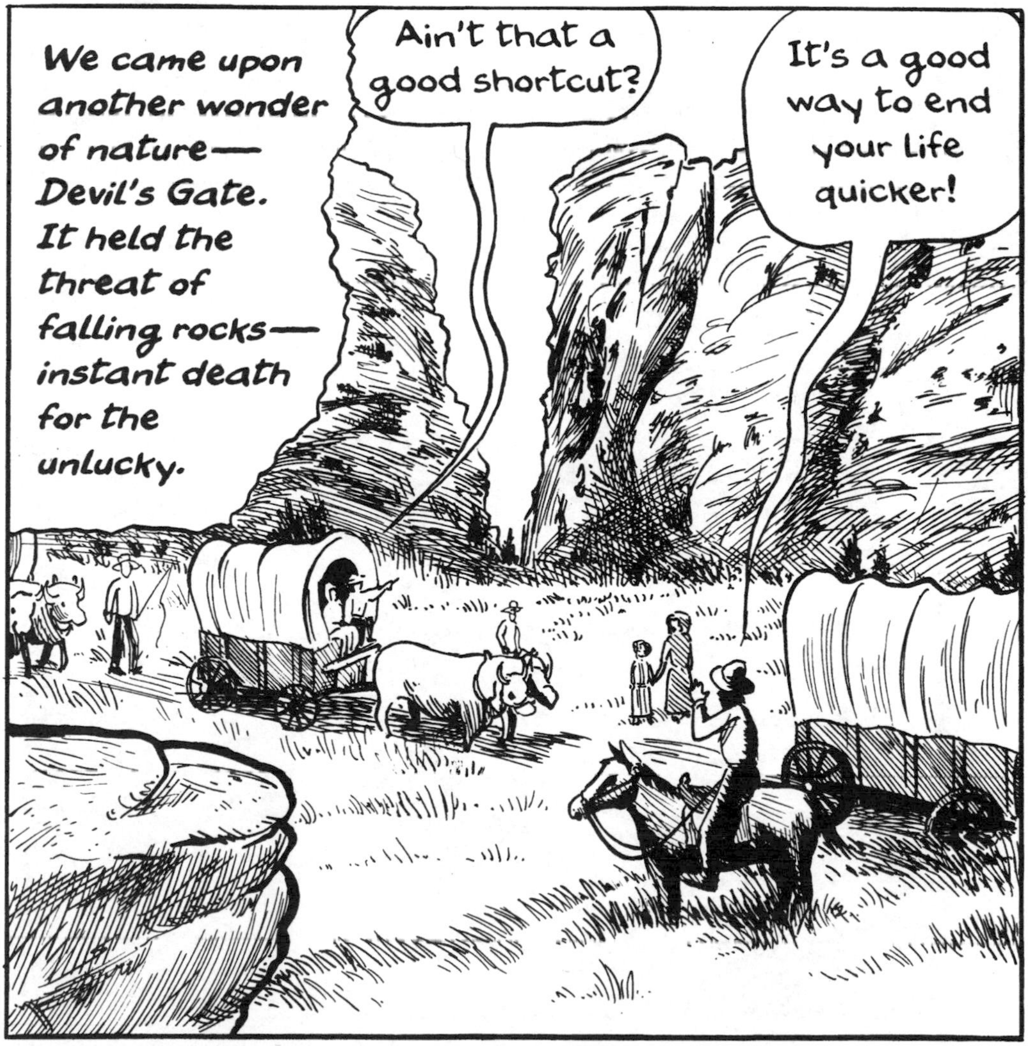
We came upon another wonder of nature—Devil's Gate. It held the threat of falling rocks—instant death for the unlucky.
Ain't that a good shortcut?
It's a good way to end your life quicker!

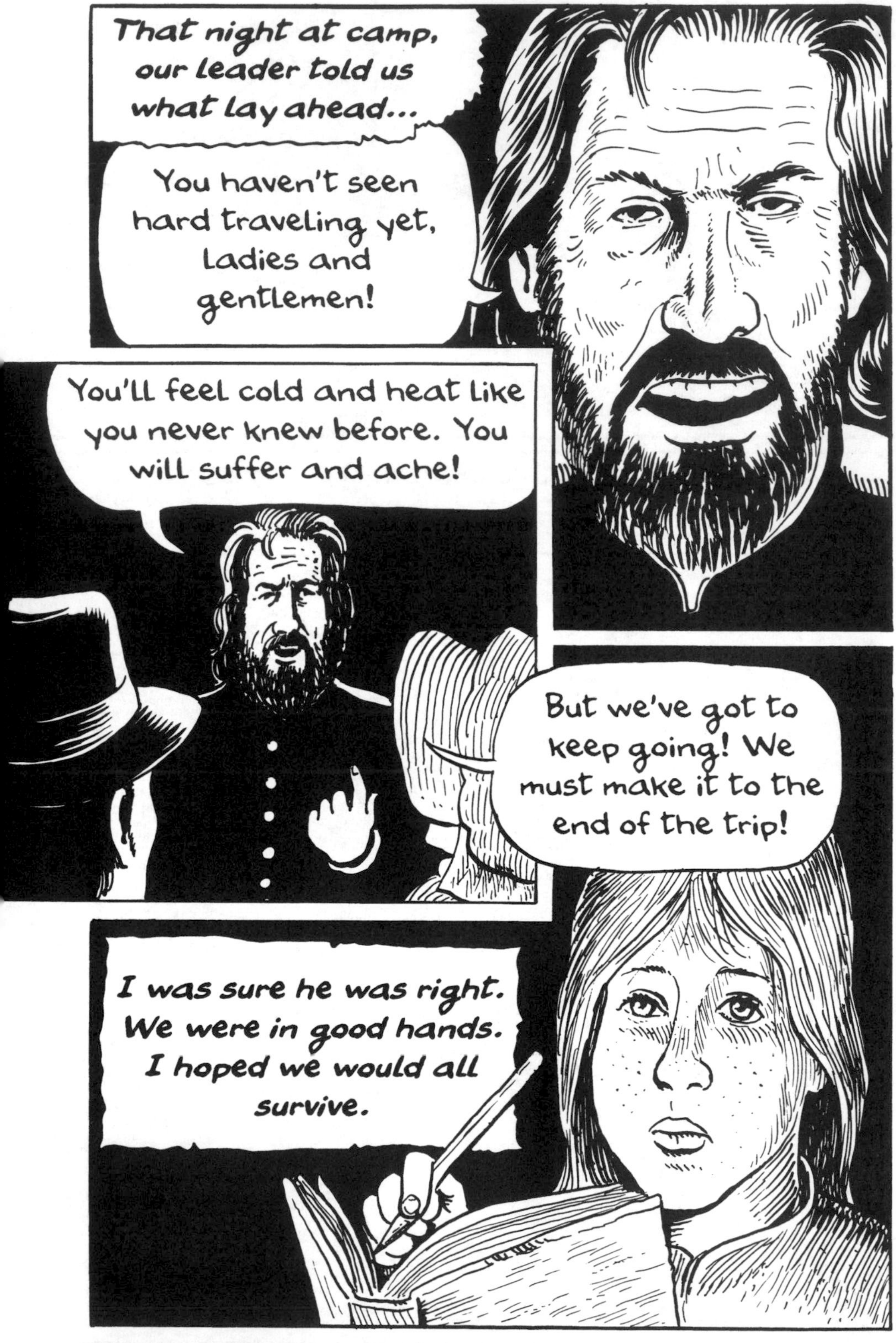
That night at camp, our leader told us what lay ahead...
You haven't seen hard traveling yet, ladies and gentlemen!
You'll feel cold and heat like you never knew before. You will suffer and ache!
But we've got to keep going! We must make it to the end of the trip!
I was sure he was right. We were in good hands. I hoped we would all survive.

CHAPTER NINE

Through the Continental Divide!

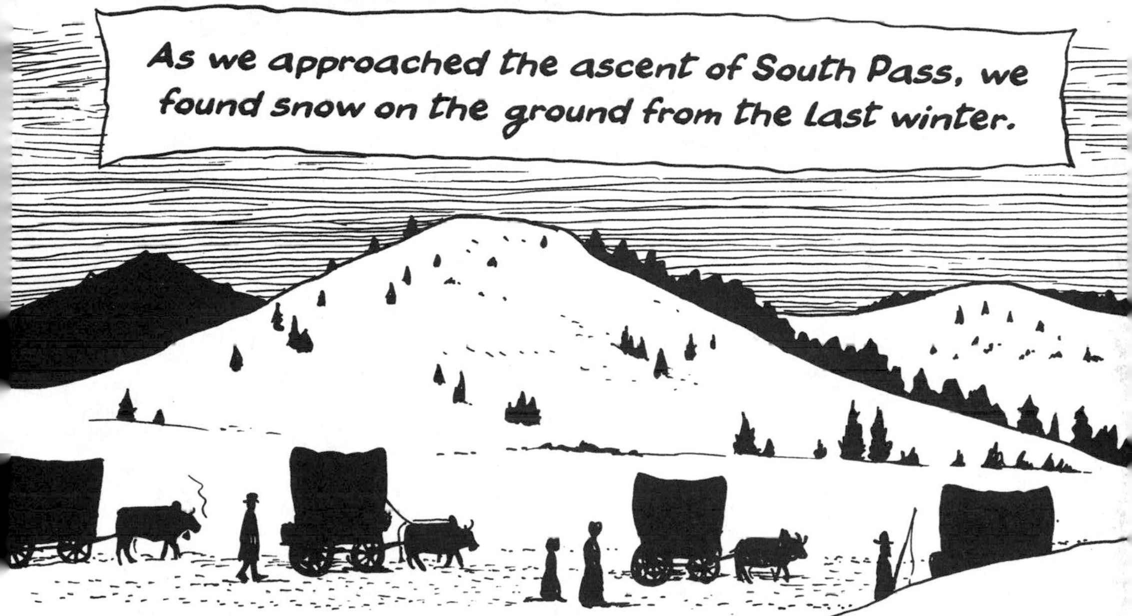
As we approached the ascent of South Pass, we found snow on the ground from the last winter.

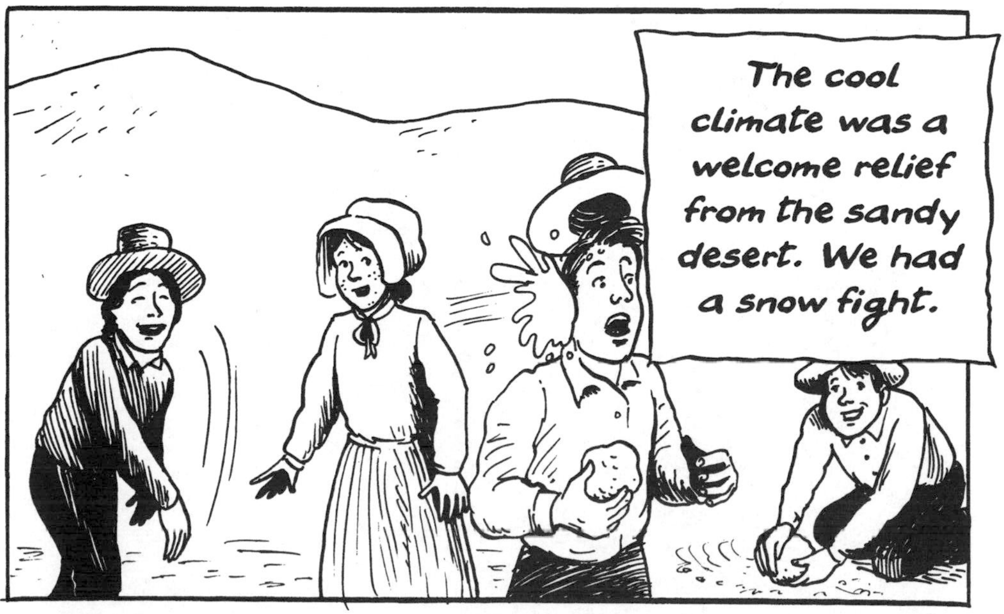
The cool climate was a welcome relief from the sandy desert. We had a snow fight.

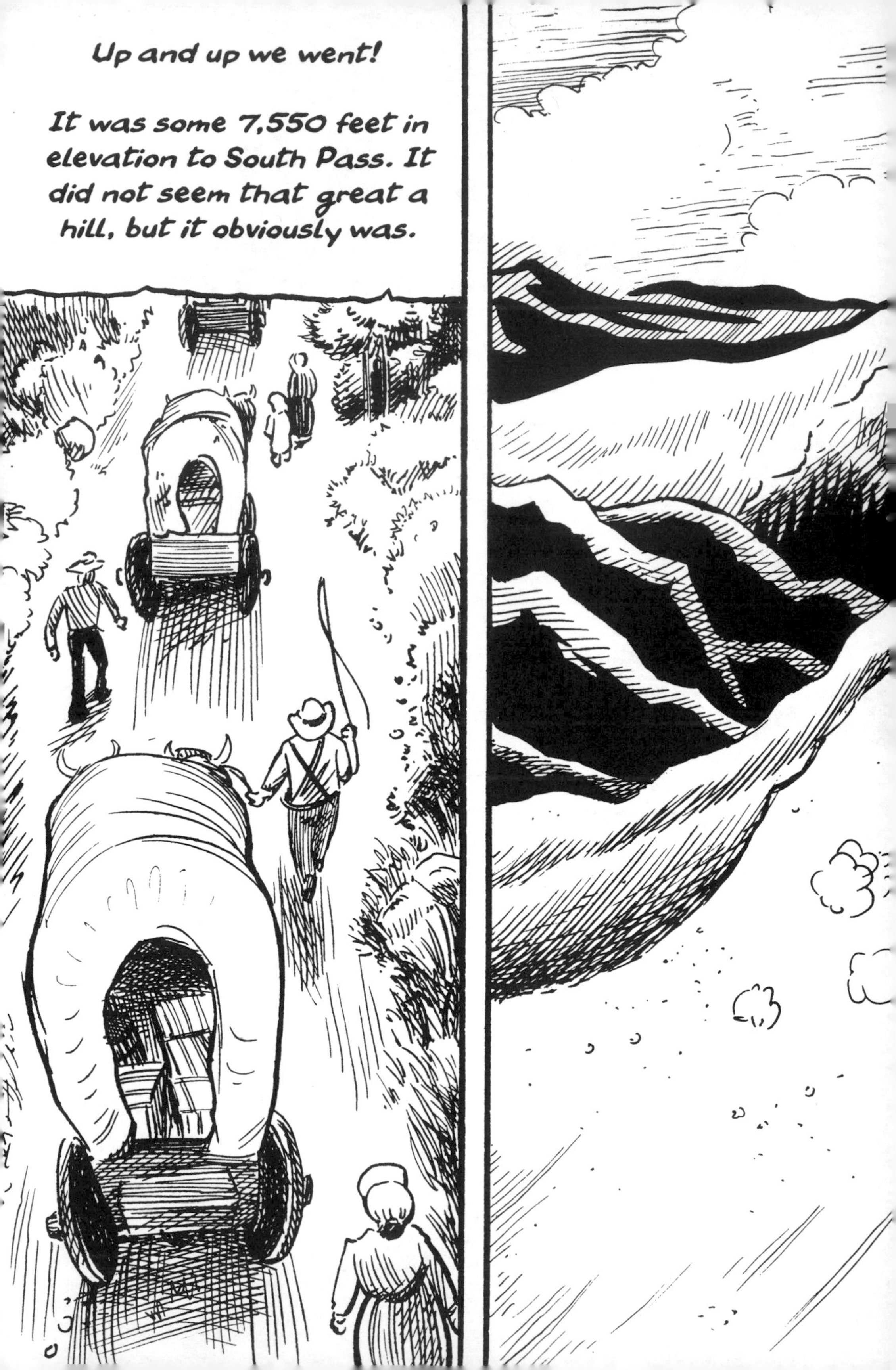
Up and up we went!
It was some 7,550 feet in elevation to South Pass. It did not seem that great a hill, but it obviously was.

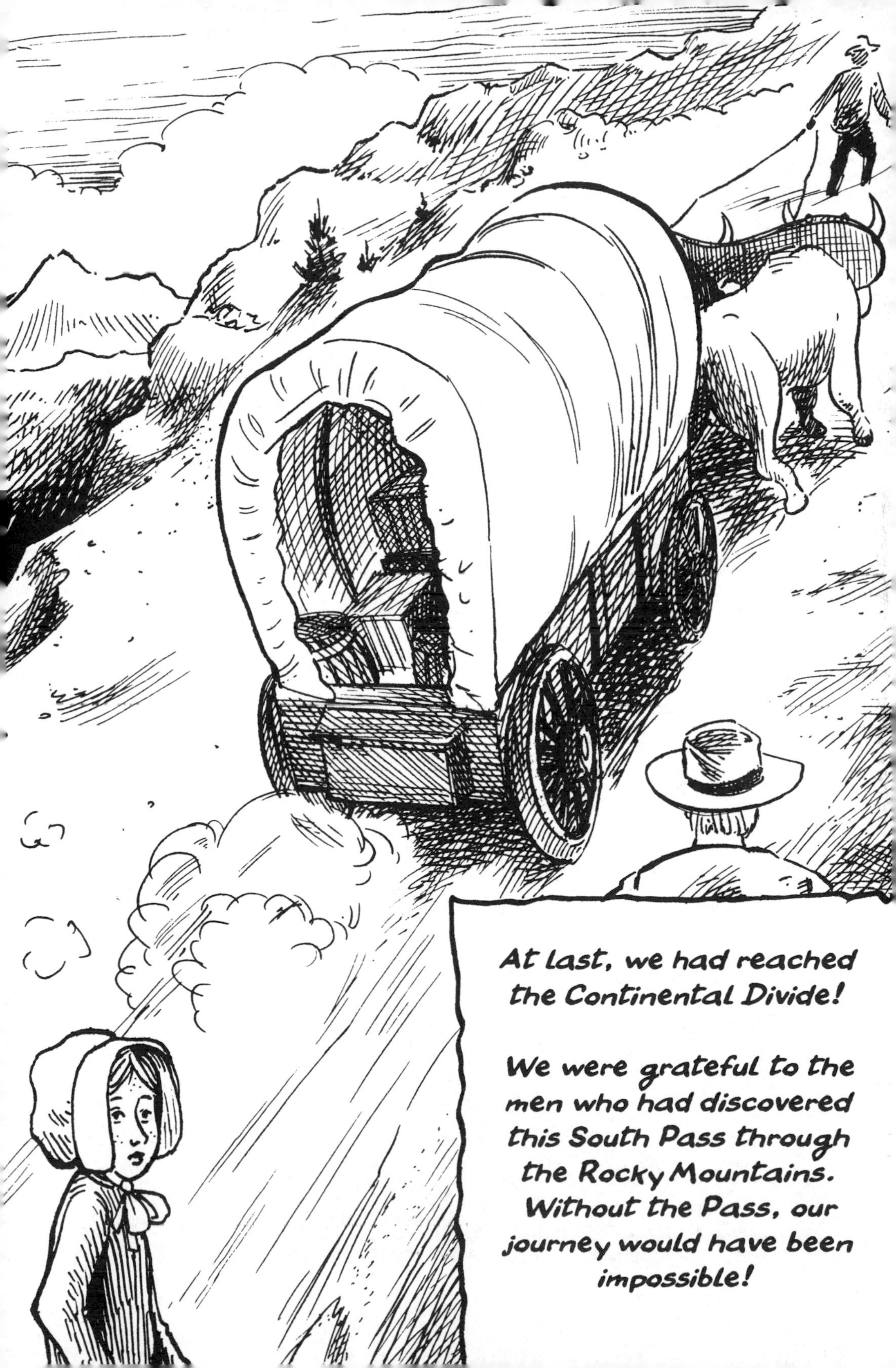
At last, we had reached the Continental Divide!
We were grateful to the men who had discovered this South Pass through the Rocky Mountains. Without the Pass, our journey would have been impossible!

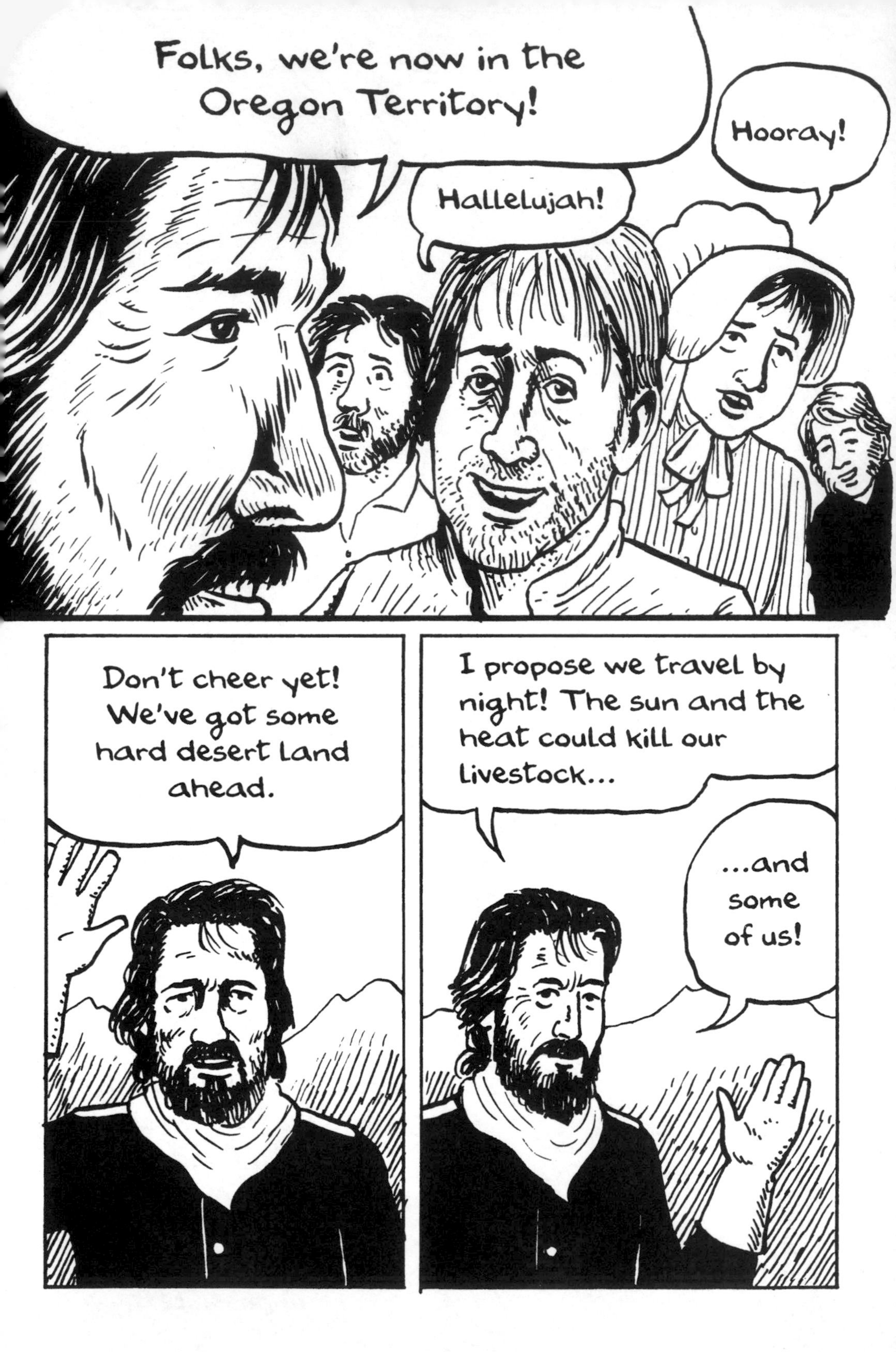
Folks, we're now in the Oregon Territory!
Hallelujah!
Hooray!
Don't cheer yet! We've got some hard desert land ahead.
I propose we travel by night! The sun and the heat could kill our livestock...
...and some of us!

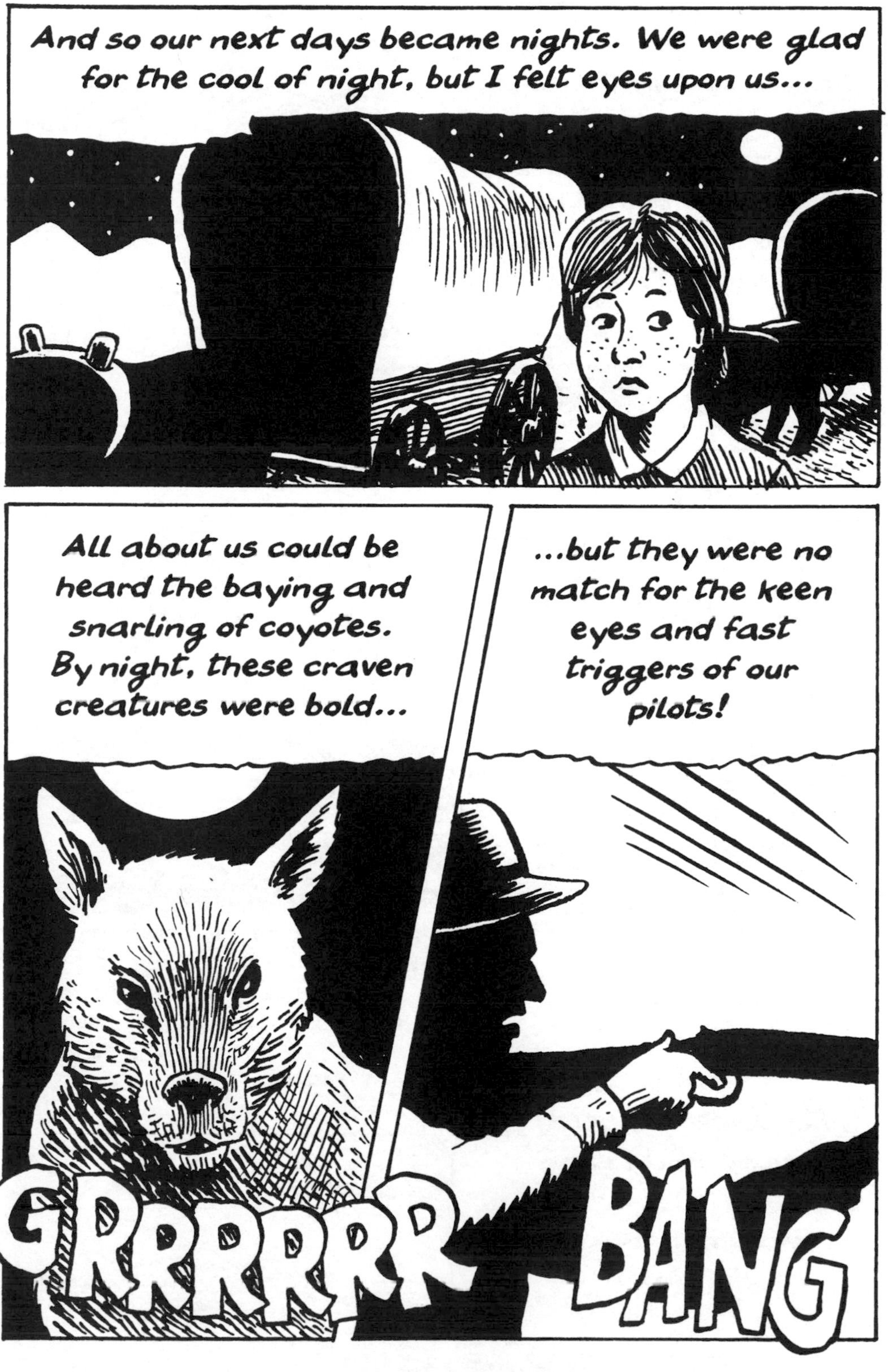
And so our next days became nights. We were glad for the cool of night, but I felt eyes upon us...
All about us could be heard the baying and snarling of coyotes. By night, these craven creatures were bold...
GRRRRRR
...but they were no match for the keen eyes and fast triggers of our pilots!
BANG

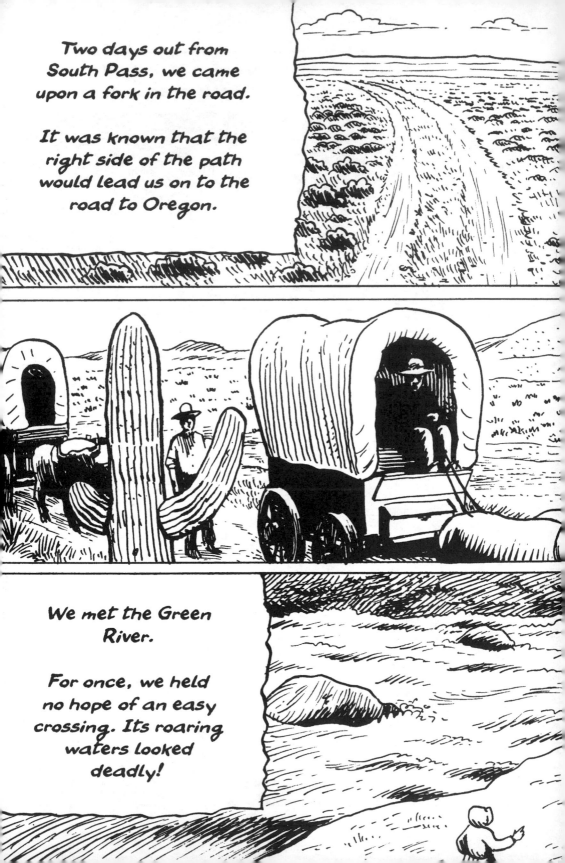

Two days out from South Pass, we came upon a fork in the road.

It was known that the right side of the path would lead us on to the road to Oregon.

We met the Green River.

For once, we held no hope of an easy crossing. Its roaring waters looked deadly!

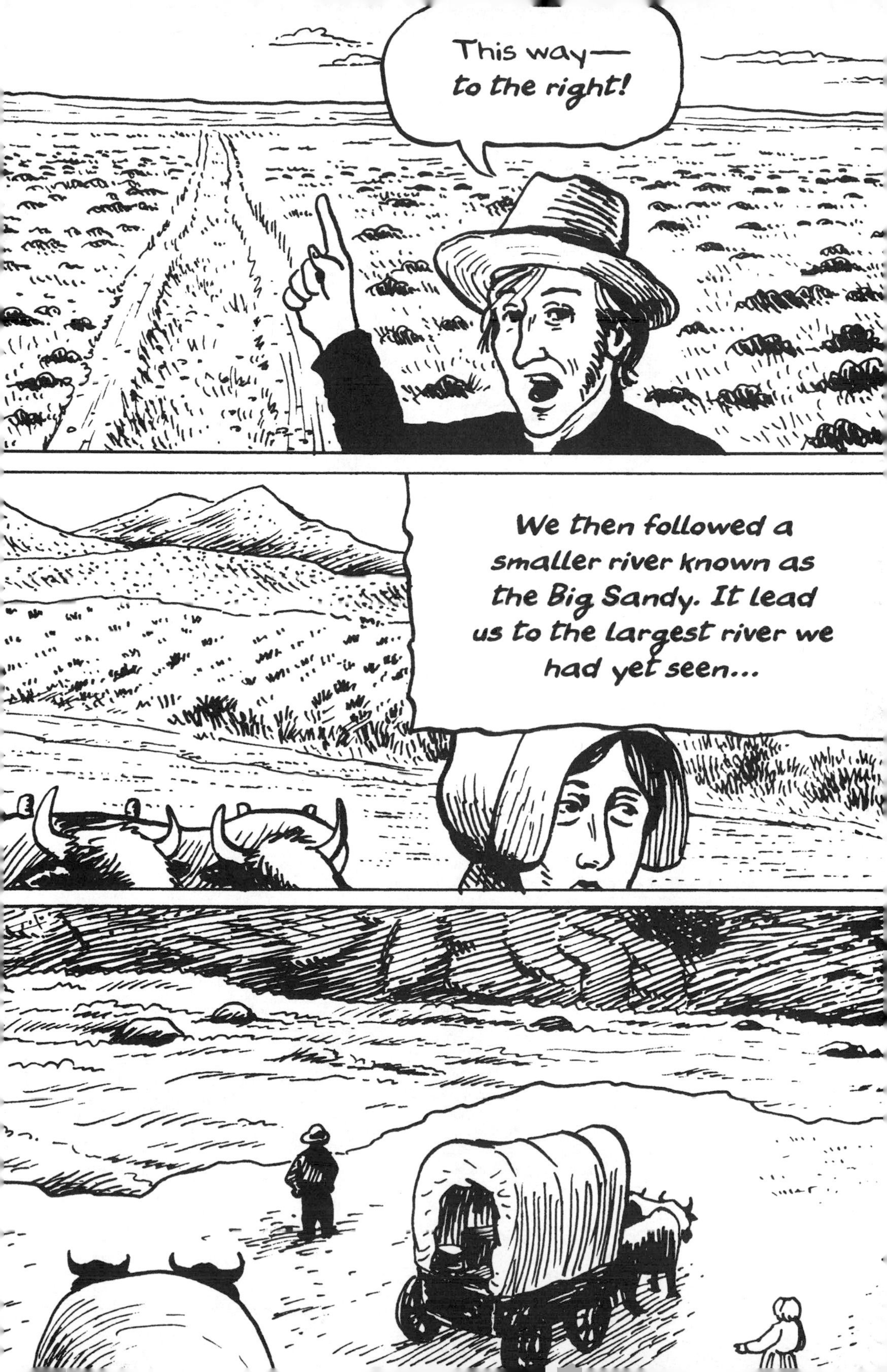
This way—
to the right!
We then followed a smaller river known as the Big Sandy. It lead us to the largest river we had yet seen...

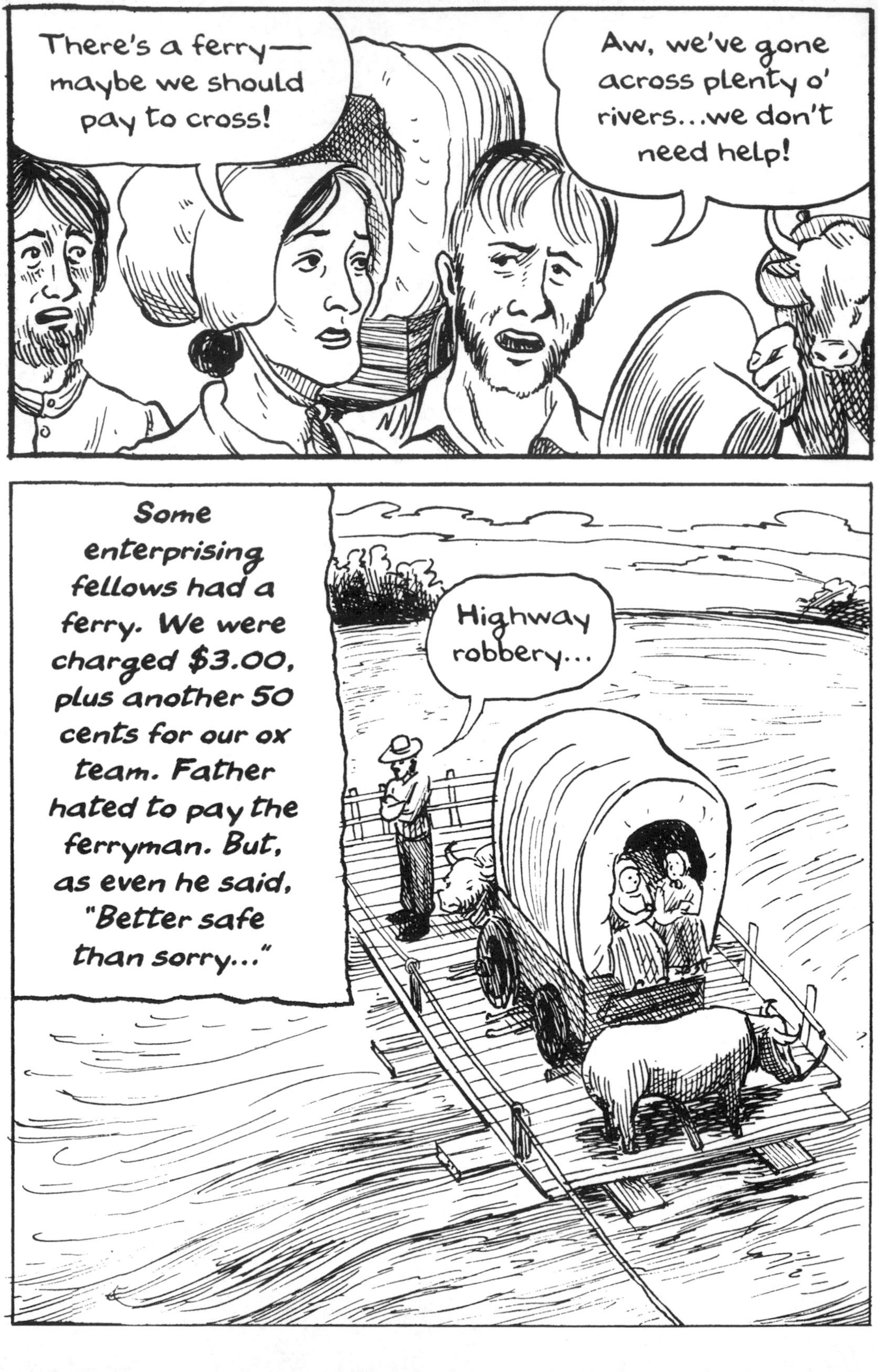
There's a ferry—maybe we should pay to cross!
Aw, we've gone across plenty o' rivers...we don't need help!
Some enterprising fellows had a ferry. We were charged $3.00, plus another 50 cents for our ox team. Father hated to pay the ferryman. But, as even he said, "Better safe than sorry..."
Highway robbery...

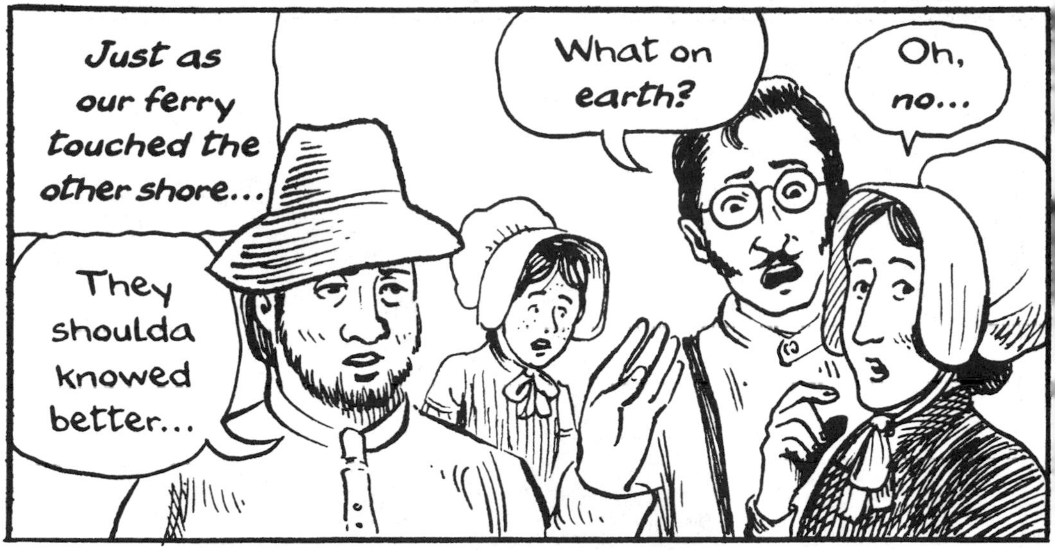
Just as our ferry touched the other shore...
They shoulda knowed better...
What on earth?
Oh, no...

One wagon tried to cross the river on its own...

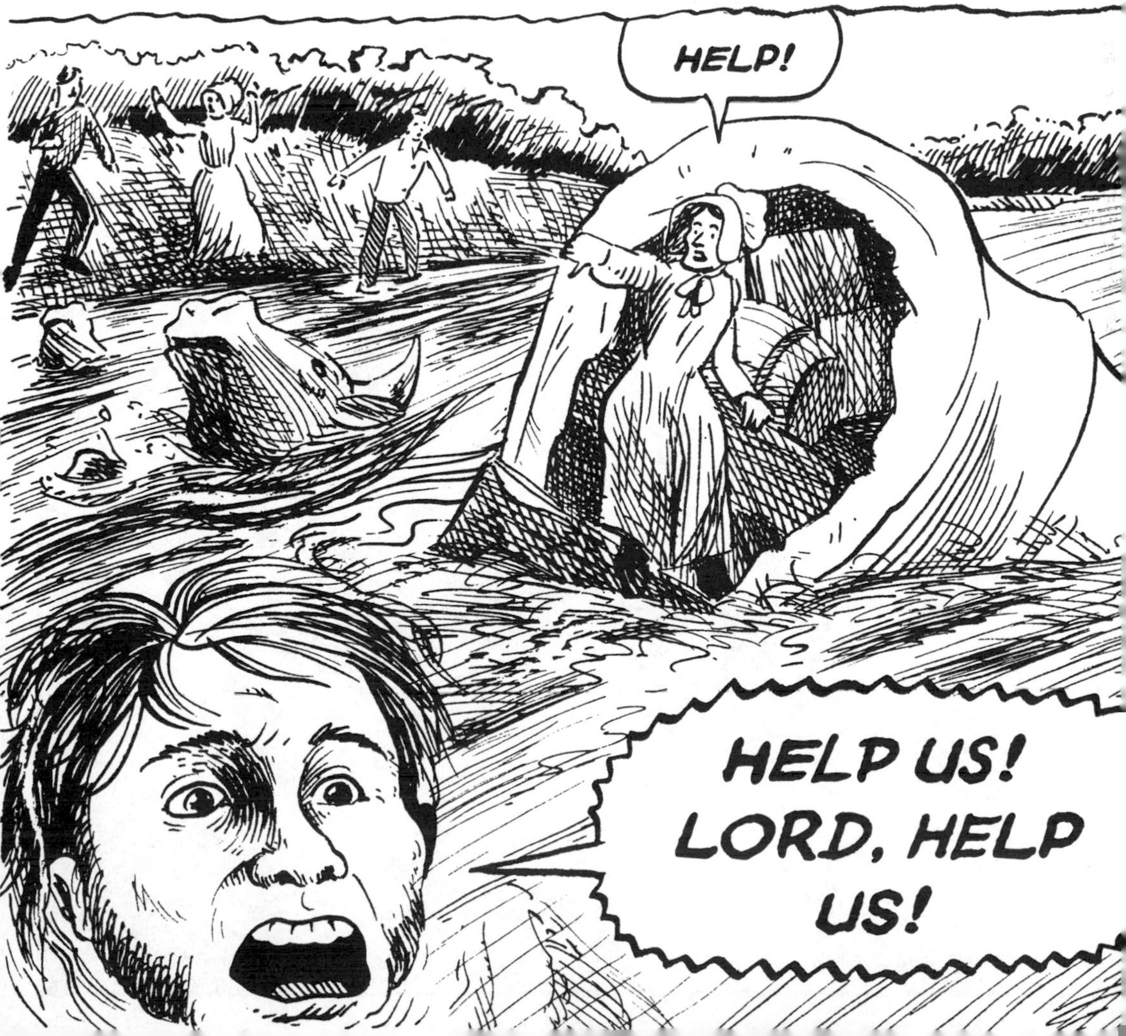
HELP!
HELP US! LORD, HELP US!

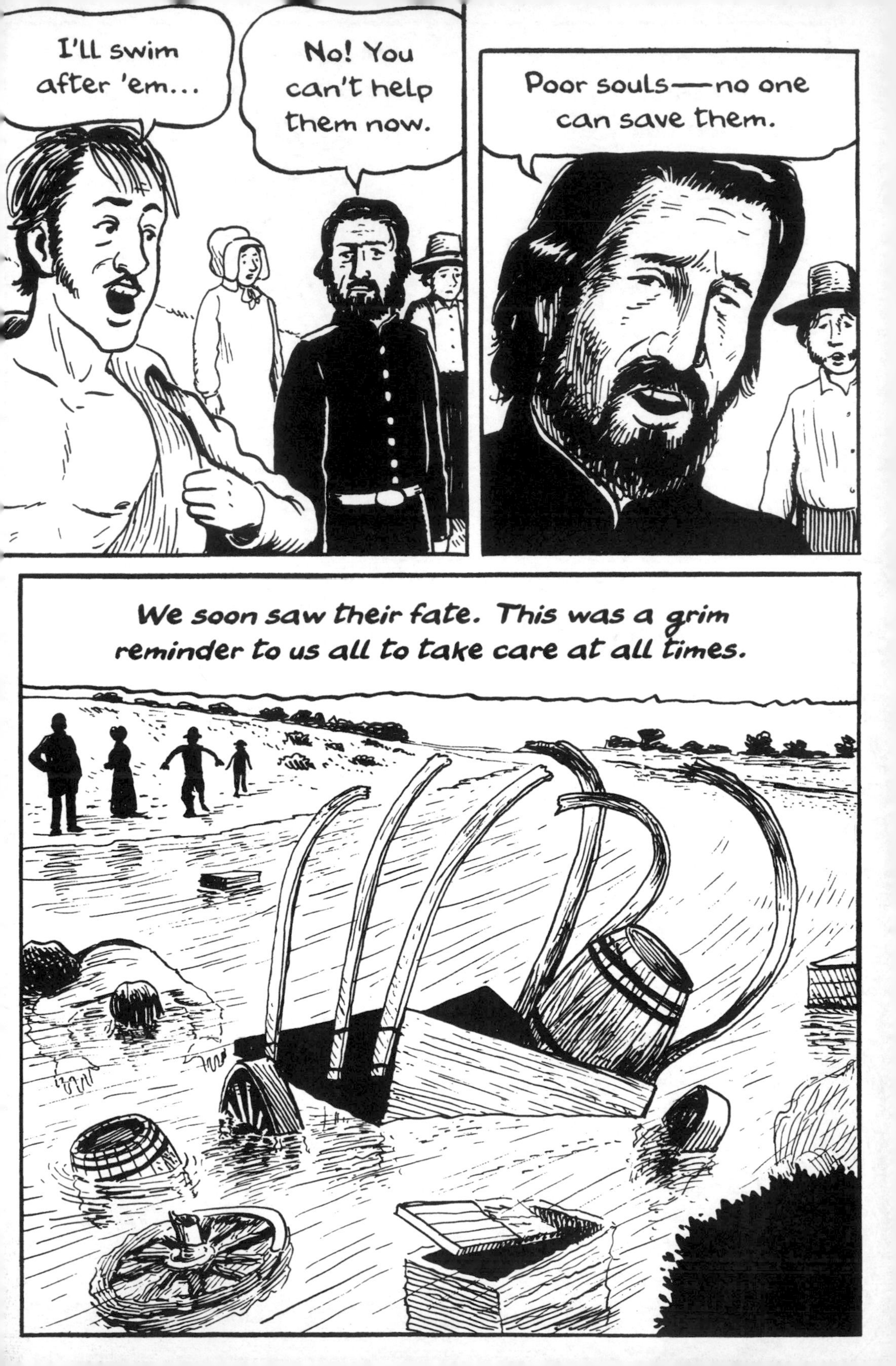
I'LL swim after 'em...
No! You can't help them now.
Poor souls—no one can save them.
We soon saw their fate. This was a grim reminder to us all to take care at all times.

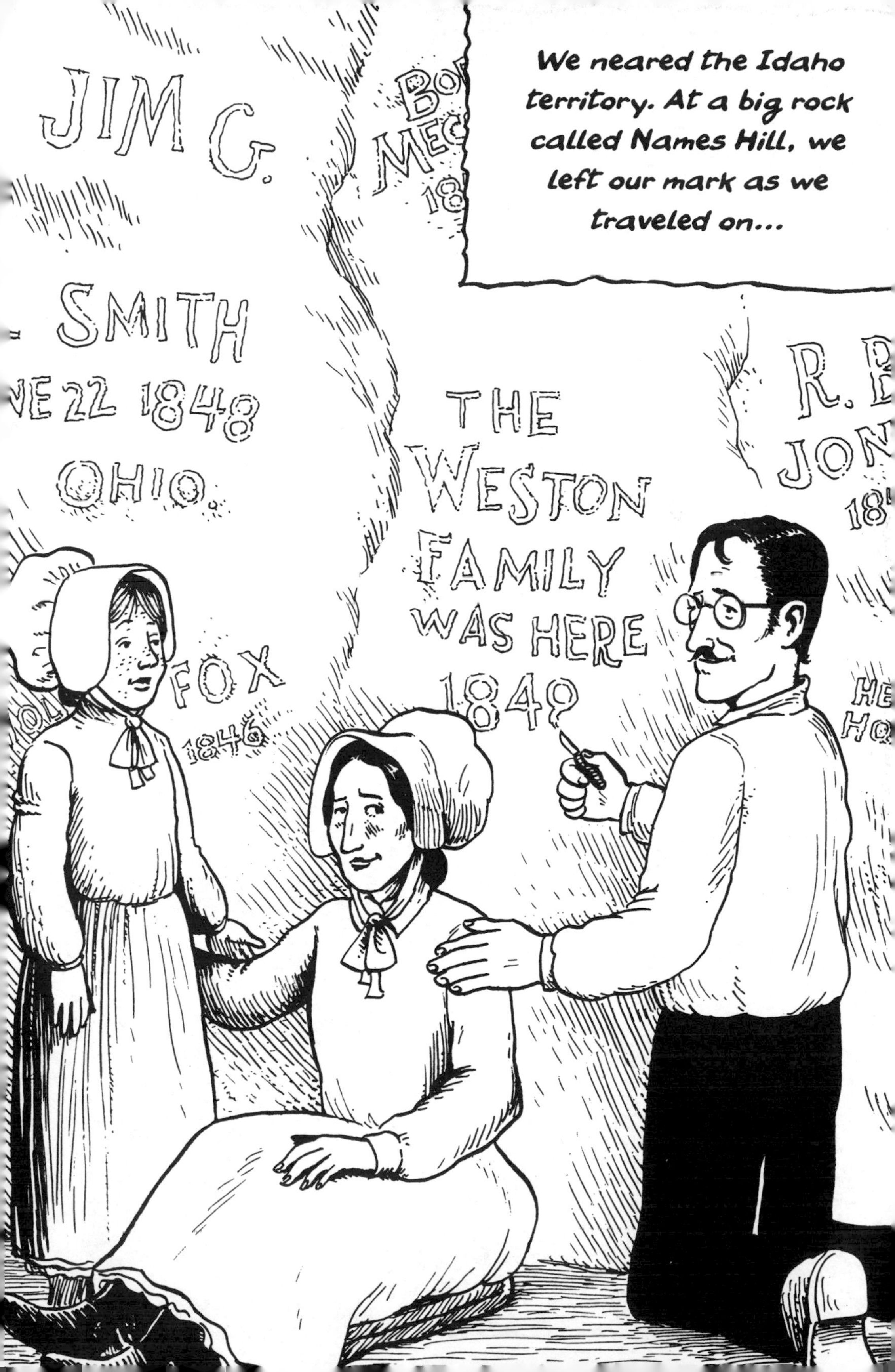

We neared the Idaho territory. At a big rock called Names Hill, we left our mark as we traveled on...
JIM G.
SMITH
1848
OHIO.
THE WESTON FAMILY WAS HERE 1849
FOX
1846

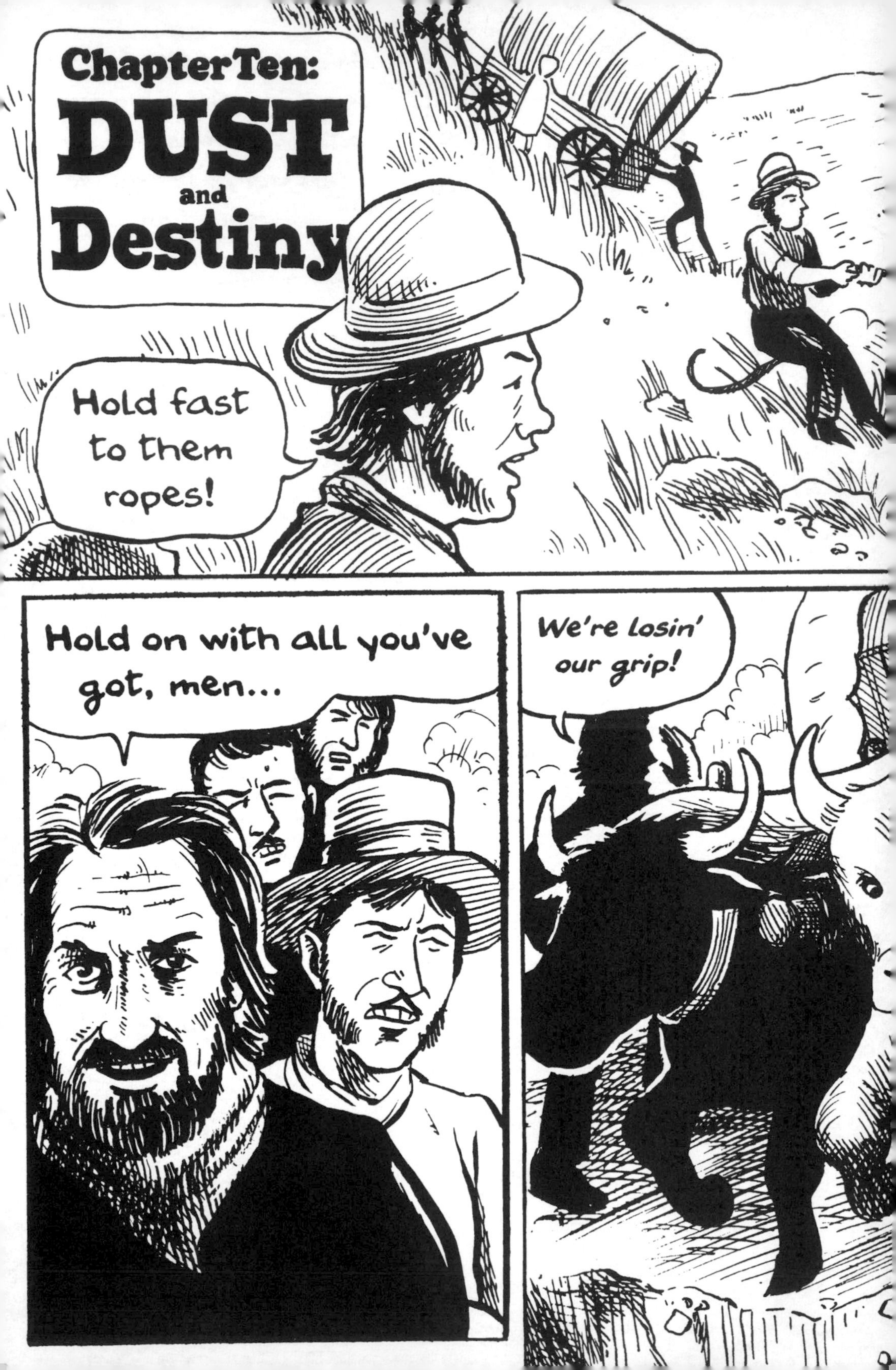
Chapter Ten:
DUST
and
Destiny
Hold fast to them ropes!
Hold on with all you've got, men...
We're losin' our grip!

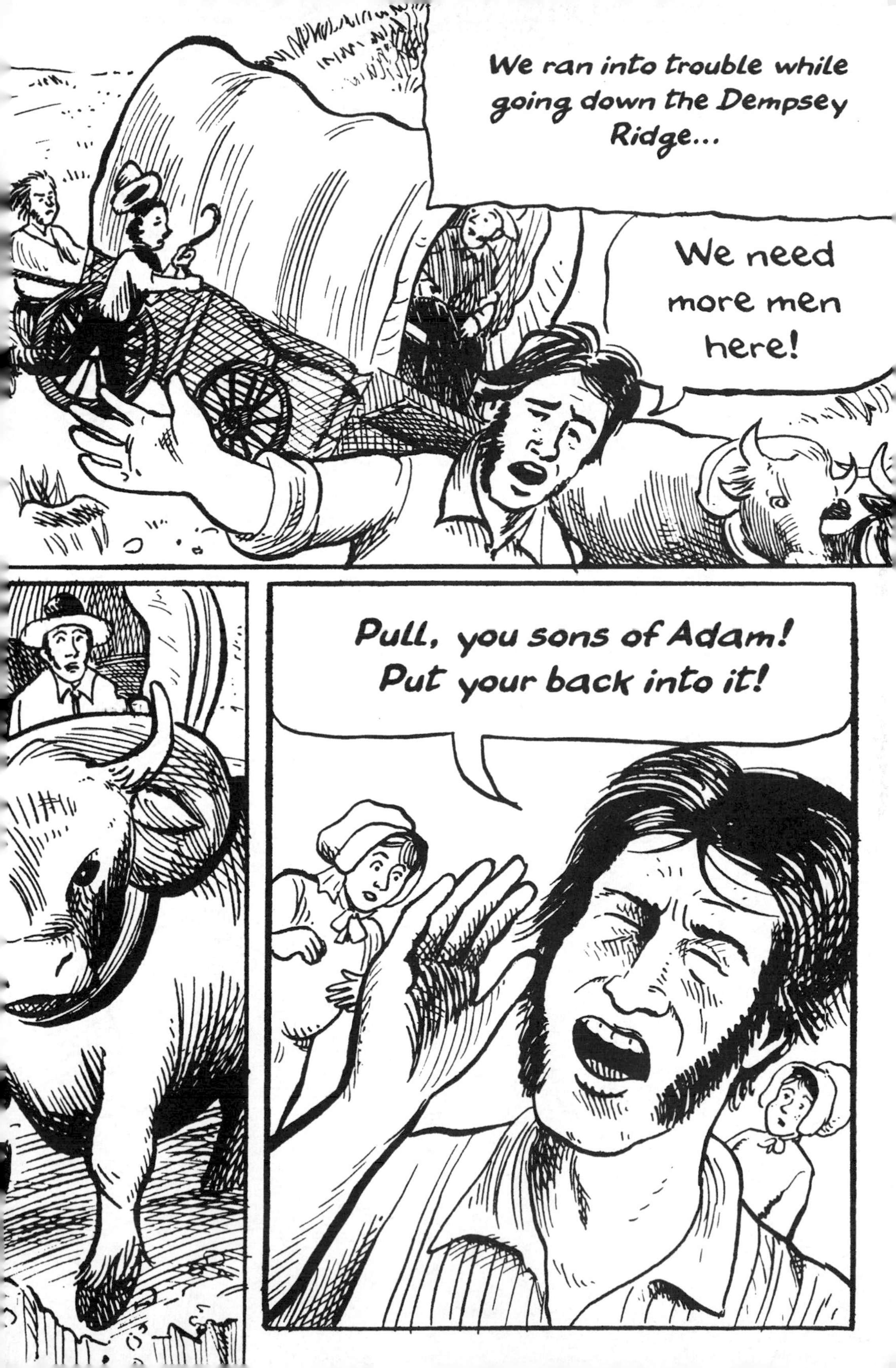
We ran into trouble while going down the Dempsey Ridge...
We need more men here!
Pull, you sons of Adam! Put your back into it!

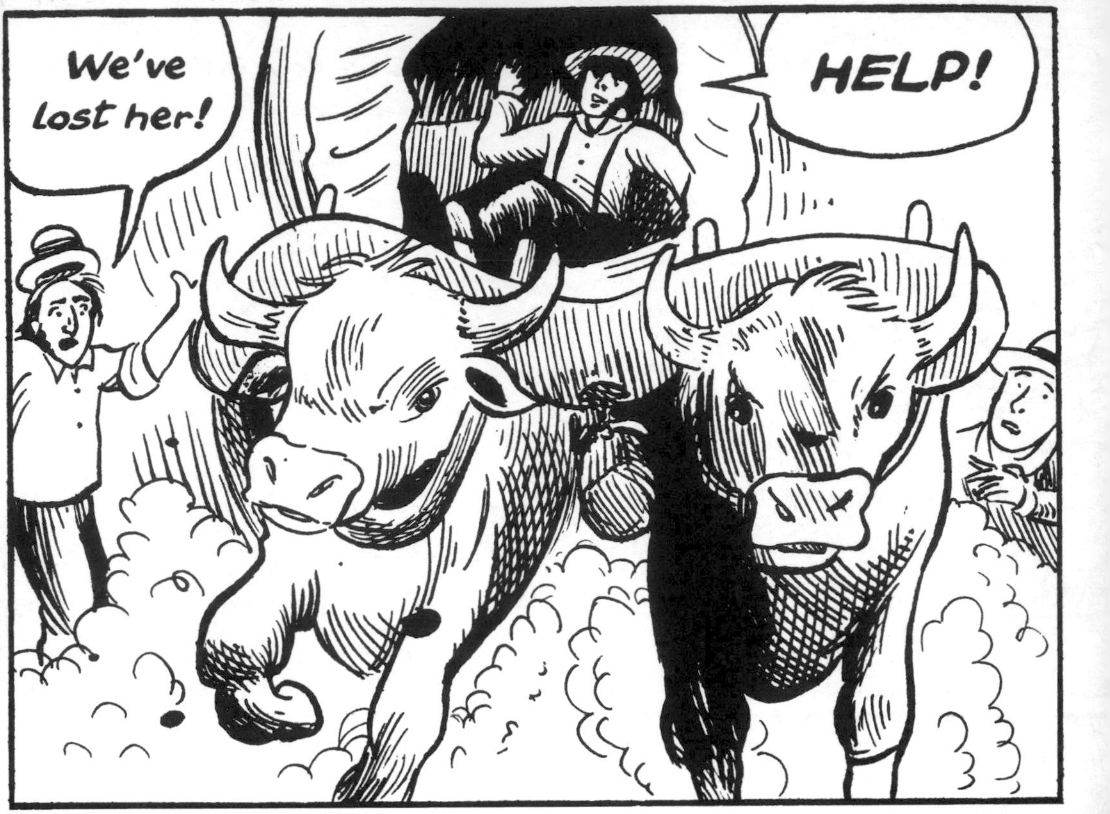
We've lost her!
HELP!
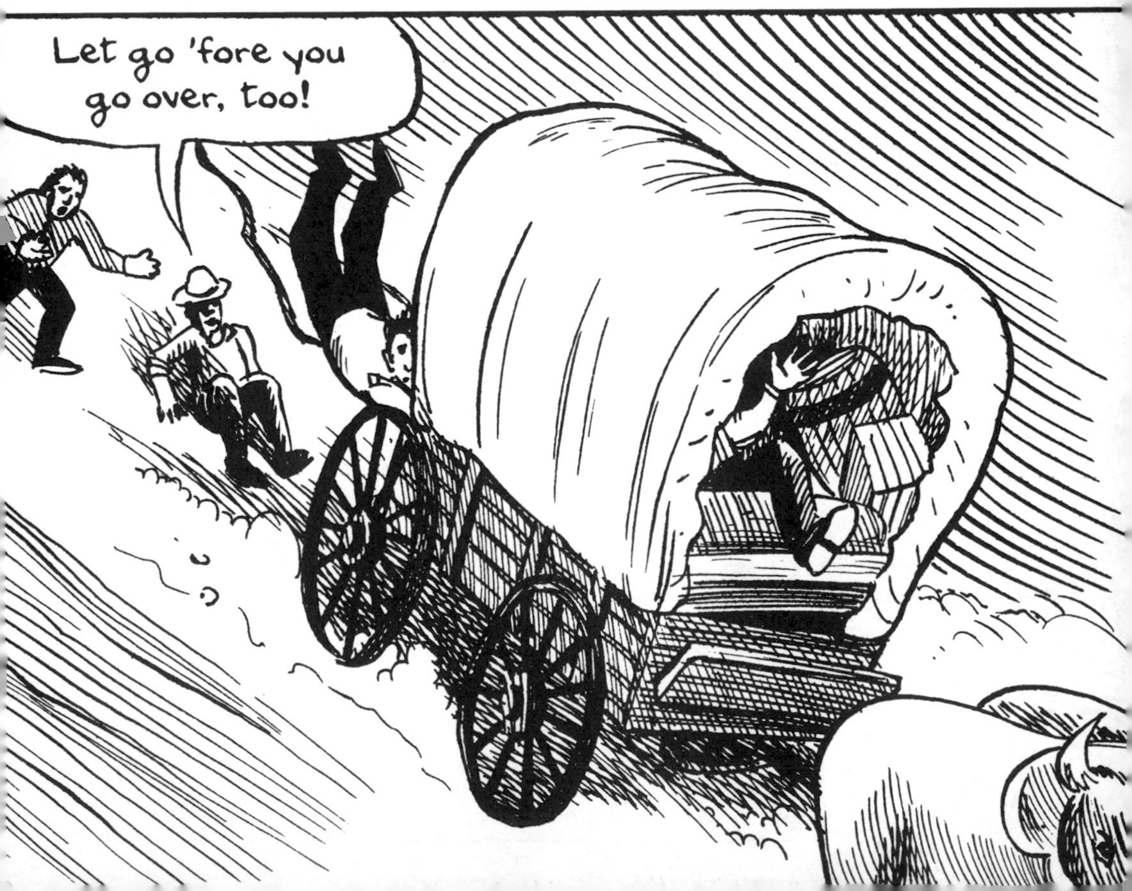
Let go 'fore you go over, too!

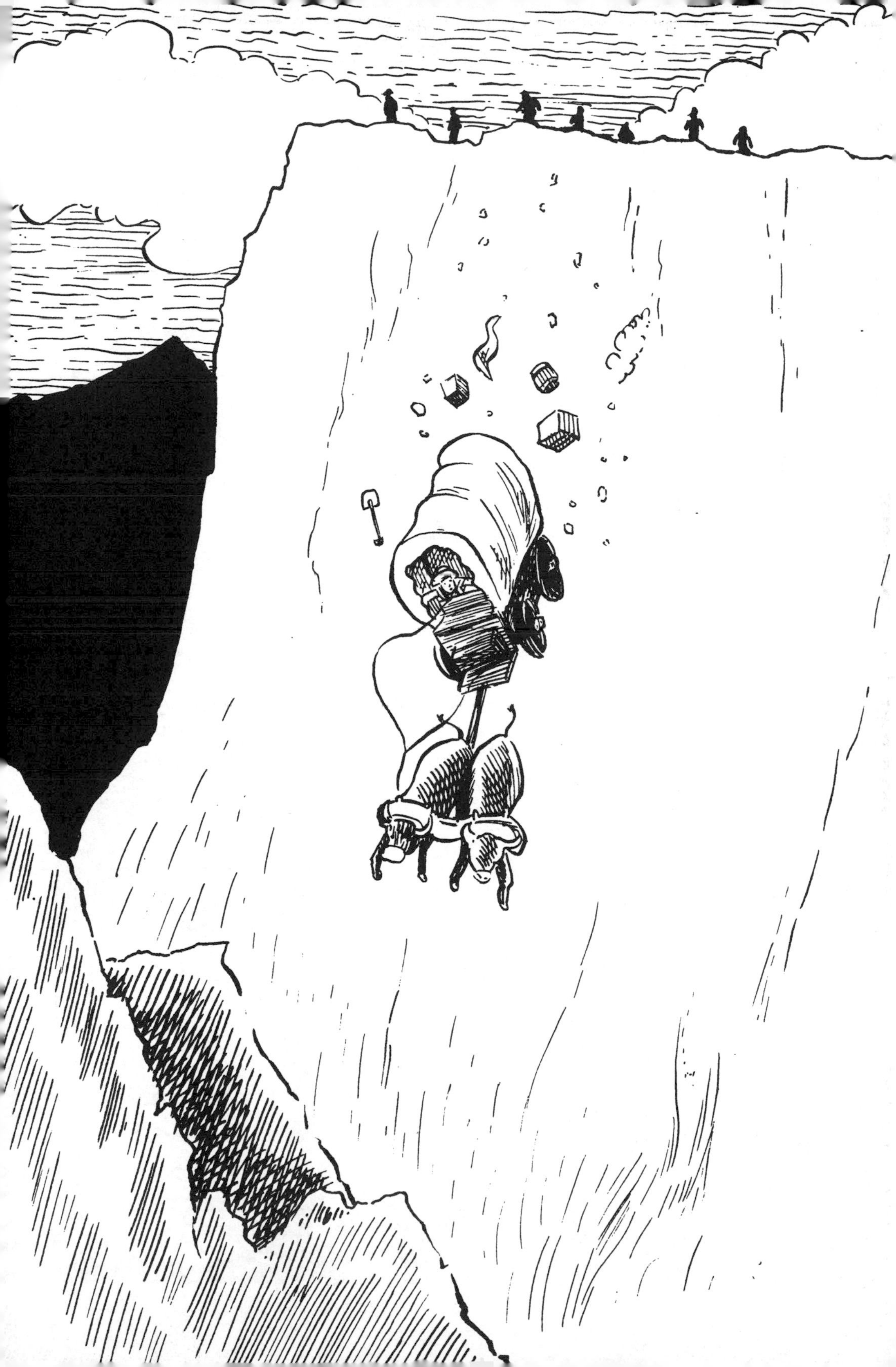

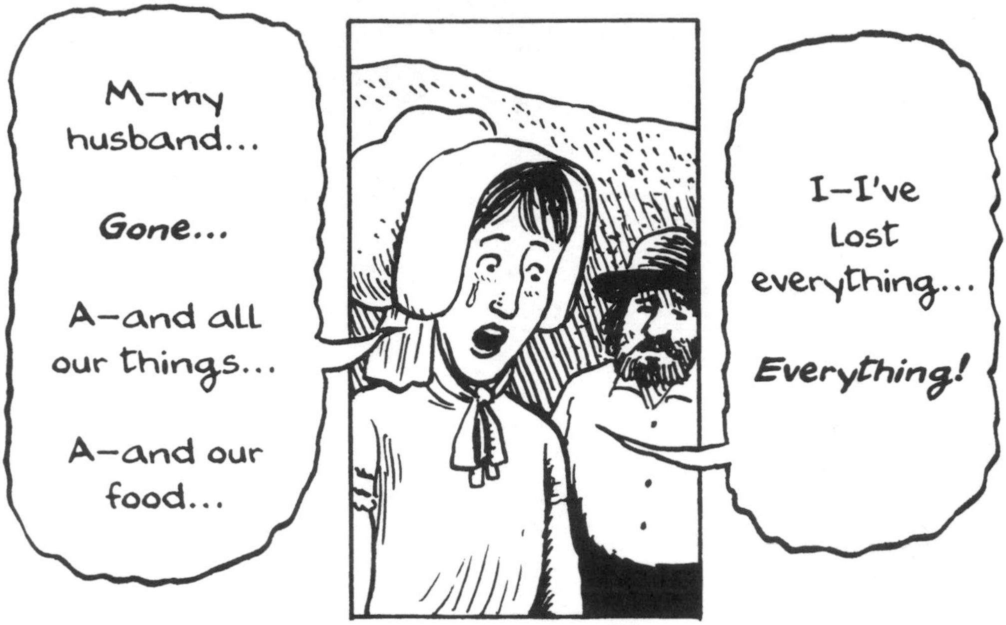
M–my husband...
Gone...
A–and all our things...
A–and our food...
I–I've lost everything...
Everything!

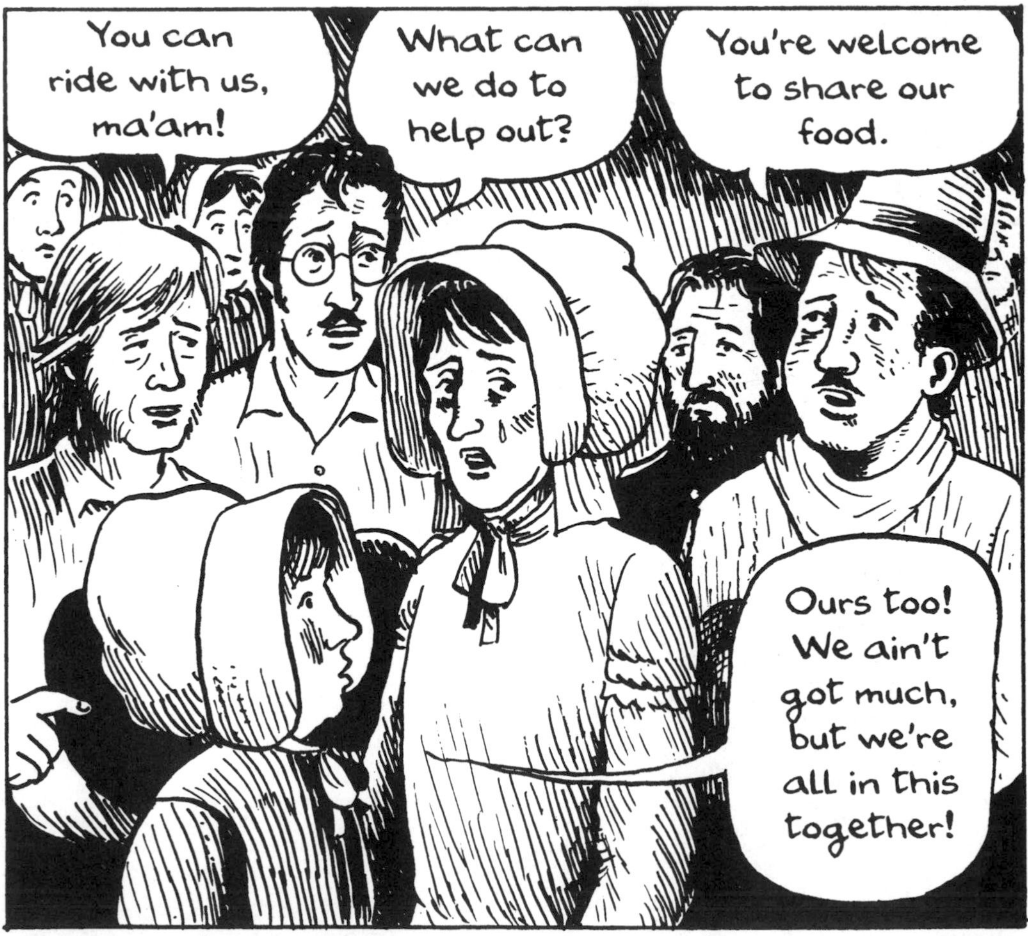
You can ride with us, ma'am!
What can we do to help out?
You're welcome to share our food.
Ours too! We ain't got much, but we're all in this together!

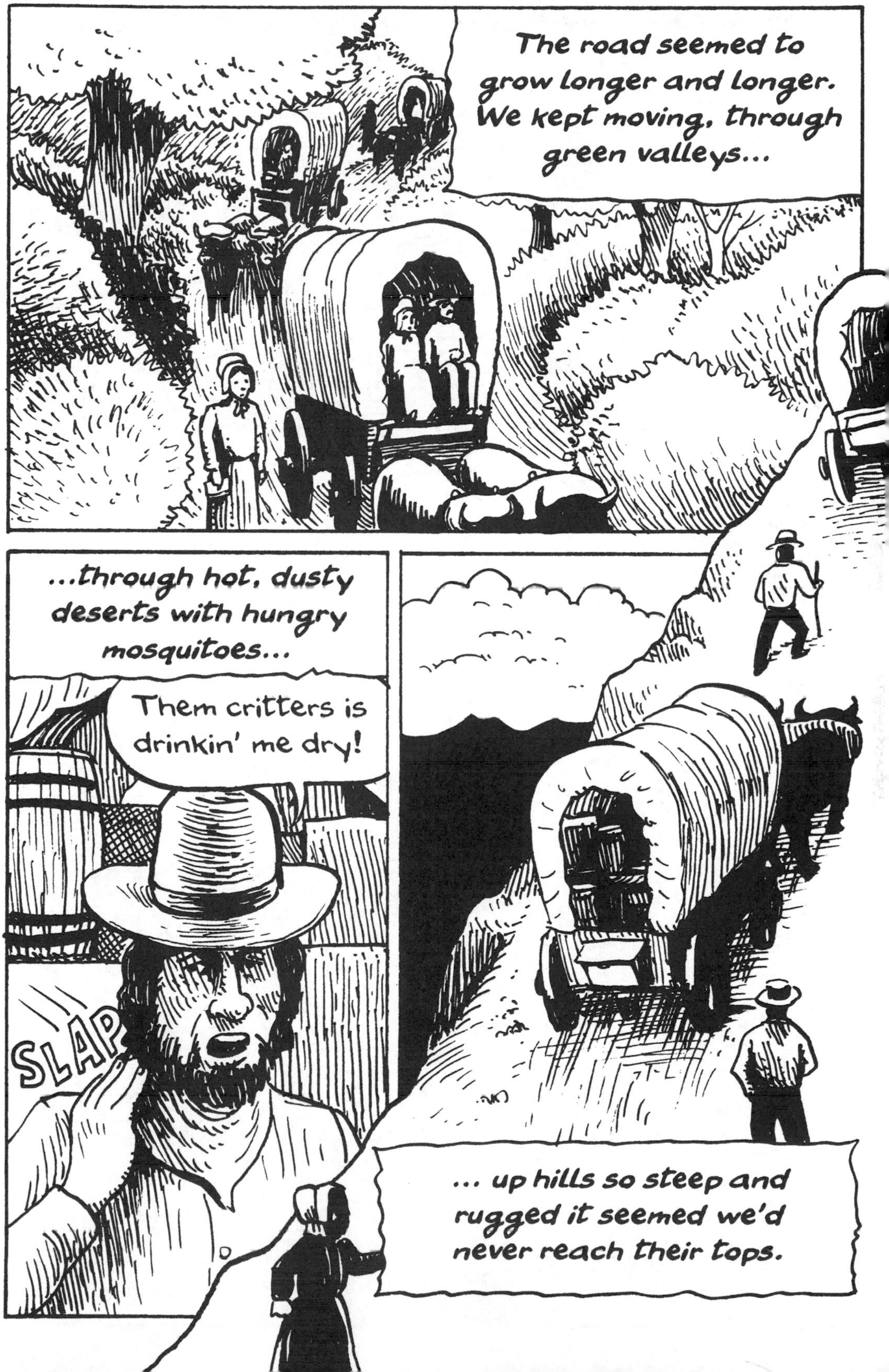
The road seemed to grow longer and longer. We kept moving, through green valleys...
...through hot, dusty deserts with hungry mosquitoes...
Them critters is drinkin' me dry!
SLAP
... up hills so steep and rugged it seemed we'd never reach their tops.

At Fort Hall, we thought our journey nearly over. But that was only a pipe dream...

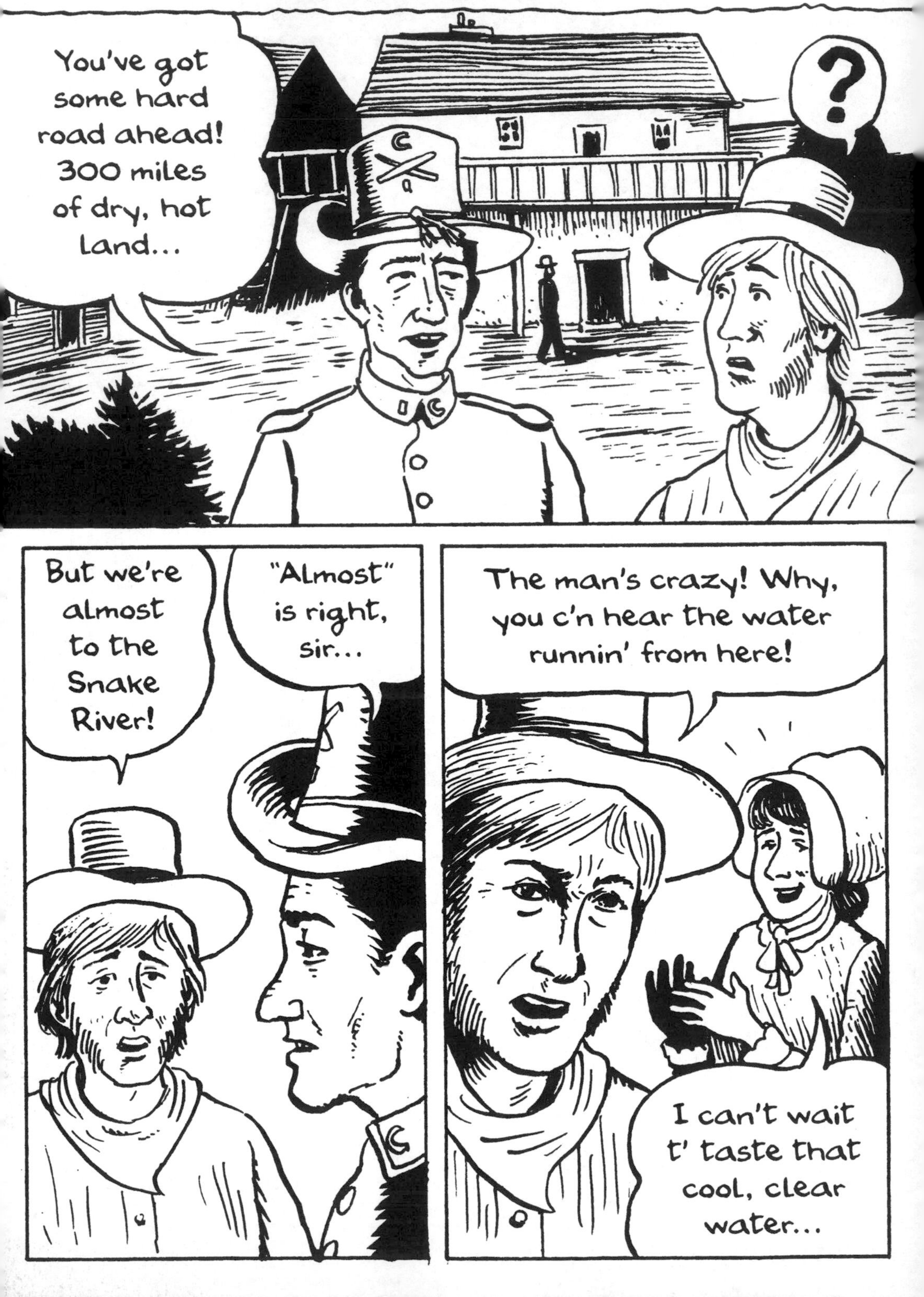
You've got some hard road ahead! 300 miles of dry, hot land...
?
But we're almost to the Snake River!
"Almost" is right, sir...
The man's crazy! Why, you c'n hear the water runnin' from here!
I can't wait t' taste that cool, clear water...

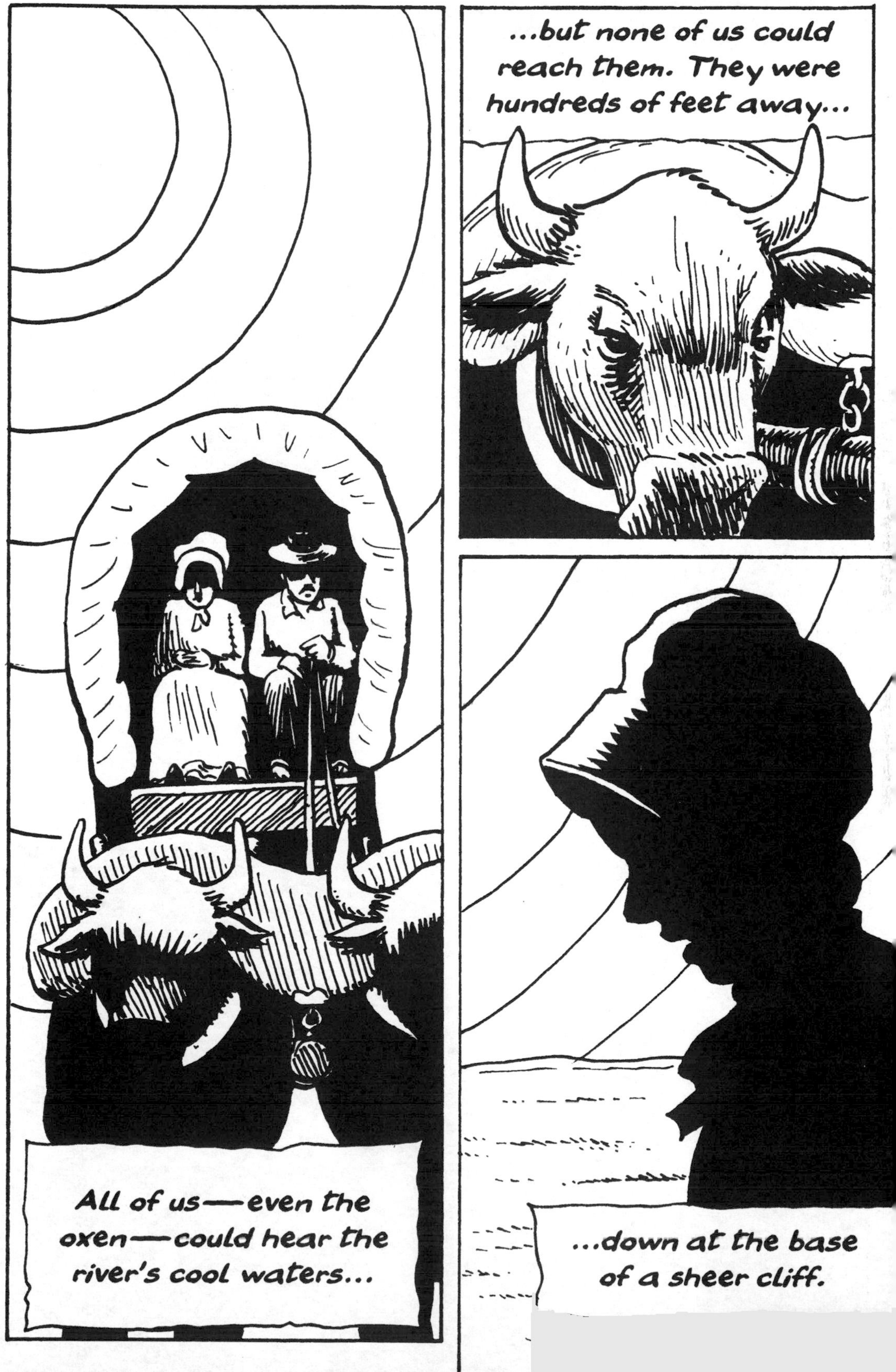
All of us—even the oxen—could hear the river's cool waters...
...but none of us could reach them. They were hundreds of feet away...
...down at the base of a sheer cliff.

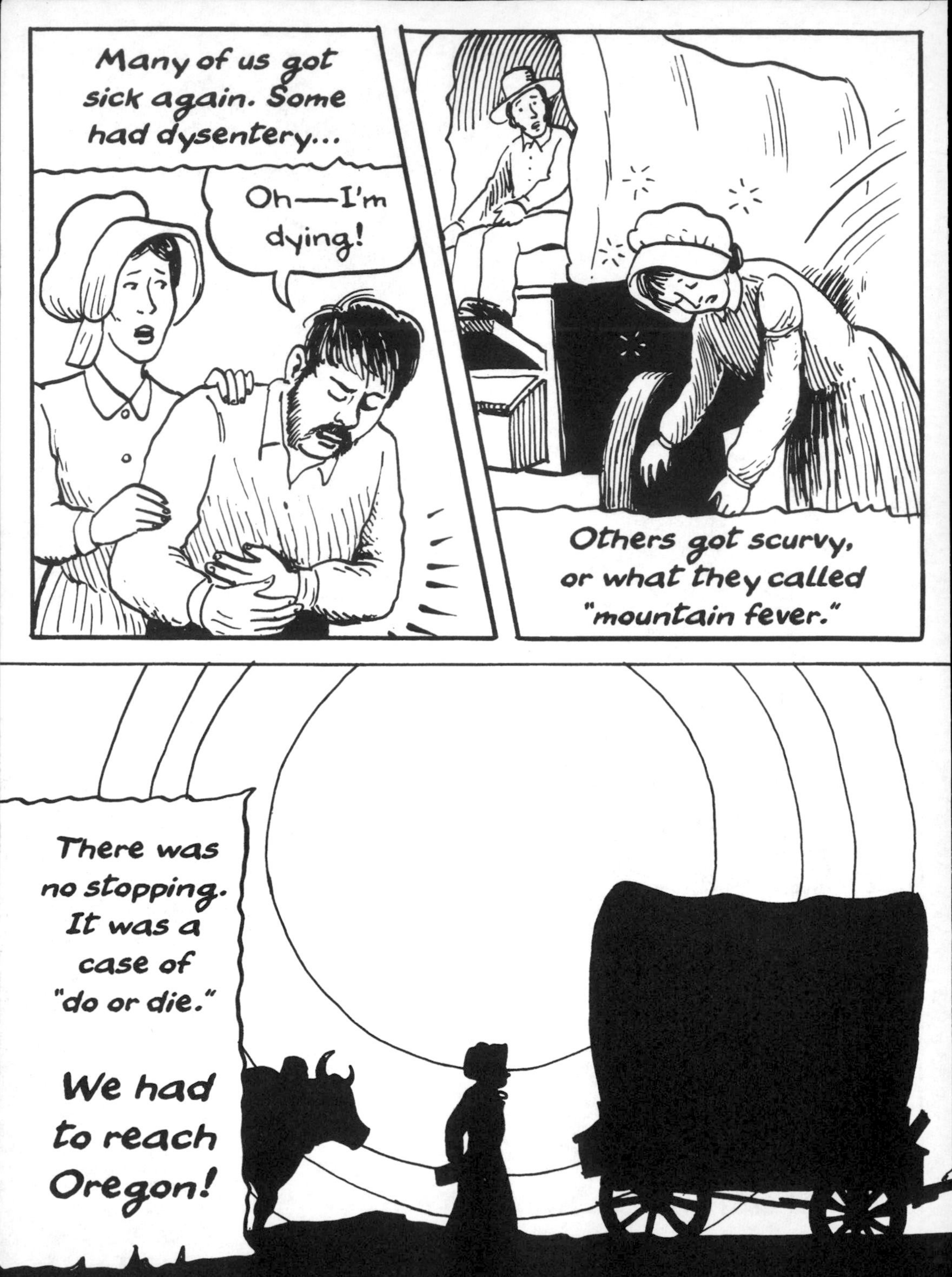
Many of us got sick again. Some had dysentery...
Oh—I'm dying!
Others got scurvy, or what they called "mountain fever."
There was no stopping. It was a case of "do or die."
We had to reach Oregon!

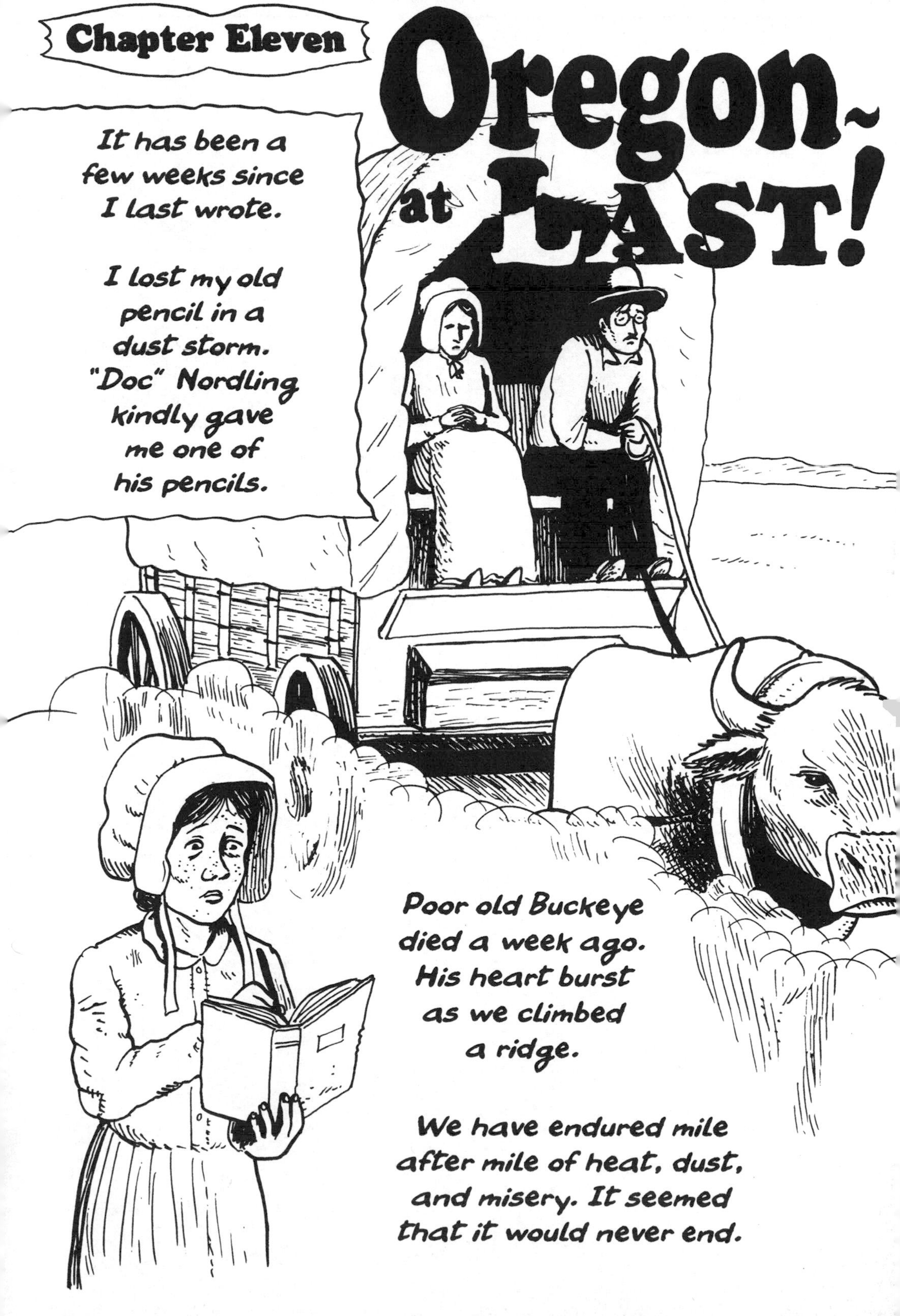
Chapter Eleven
Oregon at LAST!
It has been a few weeks since I last wrote.
I lost my old pencil in a dust storm. "Doc" Nordling kindly gave me one of his pencils.
Poor old Buckeye died a week ago. His heart burst as we climbed a ridge.
We have endured mile after mile of heat, dust, and misery. It seemed that it would never end.

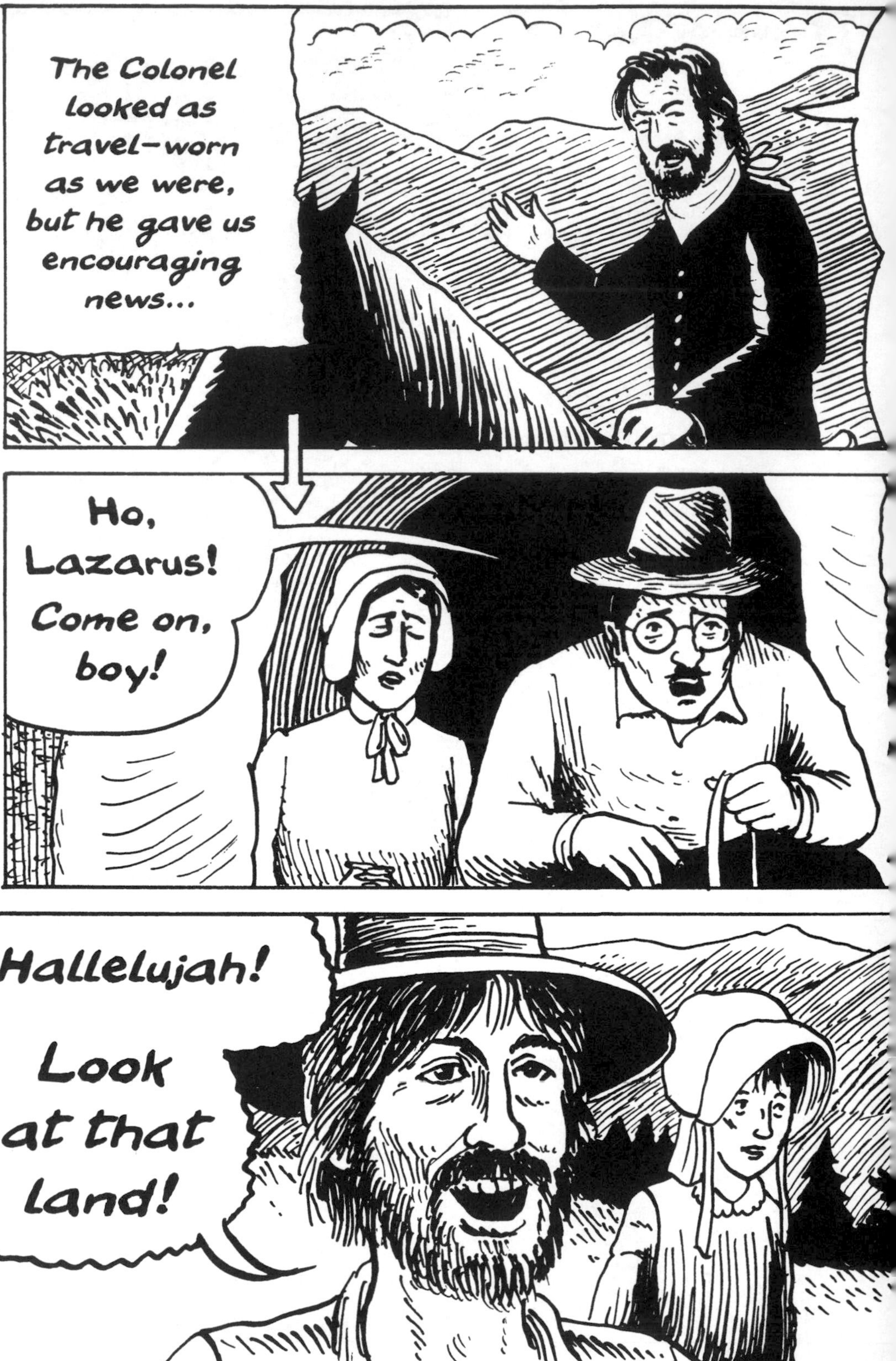
The Colonel looked as travel-worn as we were, but he gave us encouraging news...
Ho, Lazarus! Come on, boy!
Hallelujah!
Look at that land!

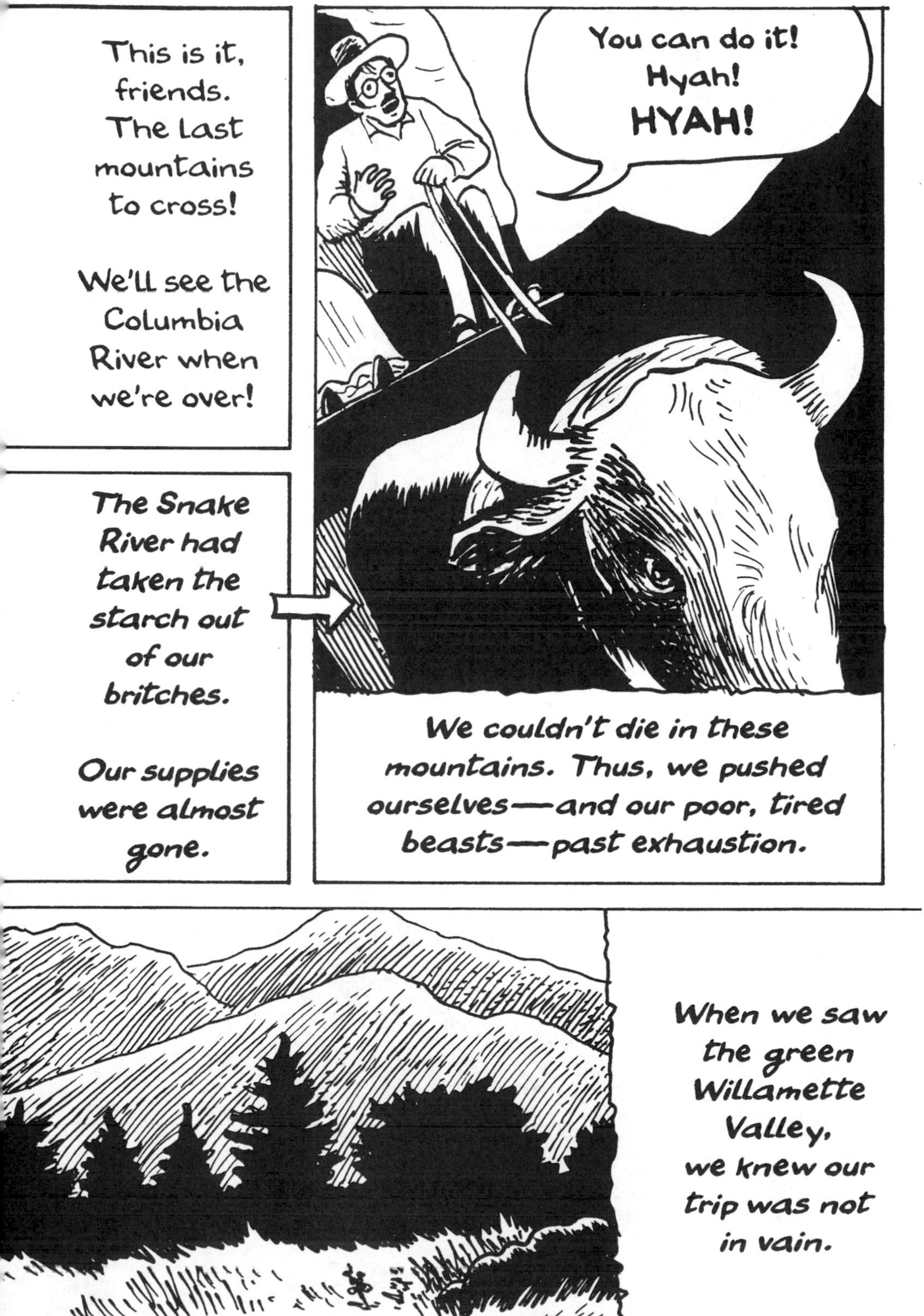
This is it, friends. The last mountains to cross!
We'll see the Columbia River when we're over!
You can do it! Hyah! HYAH!
The Snake River had taken the starch out of our britches.
Our supplies were almost gone.
We couldn't die in these mountains. Thus, we pushed ourselves—and our poor, tired beasts—past exhaustion.
When we saw the green Willamette Valley, we knew our trip was not in vain.

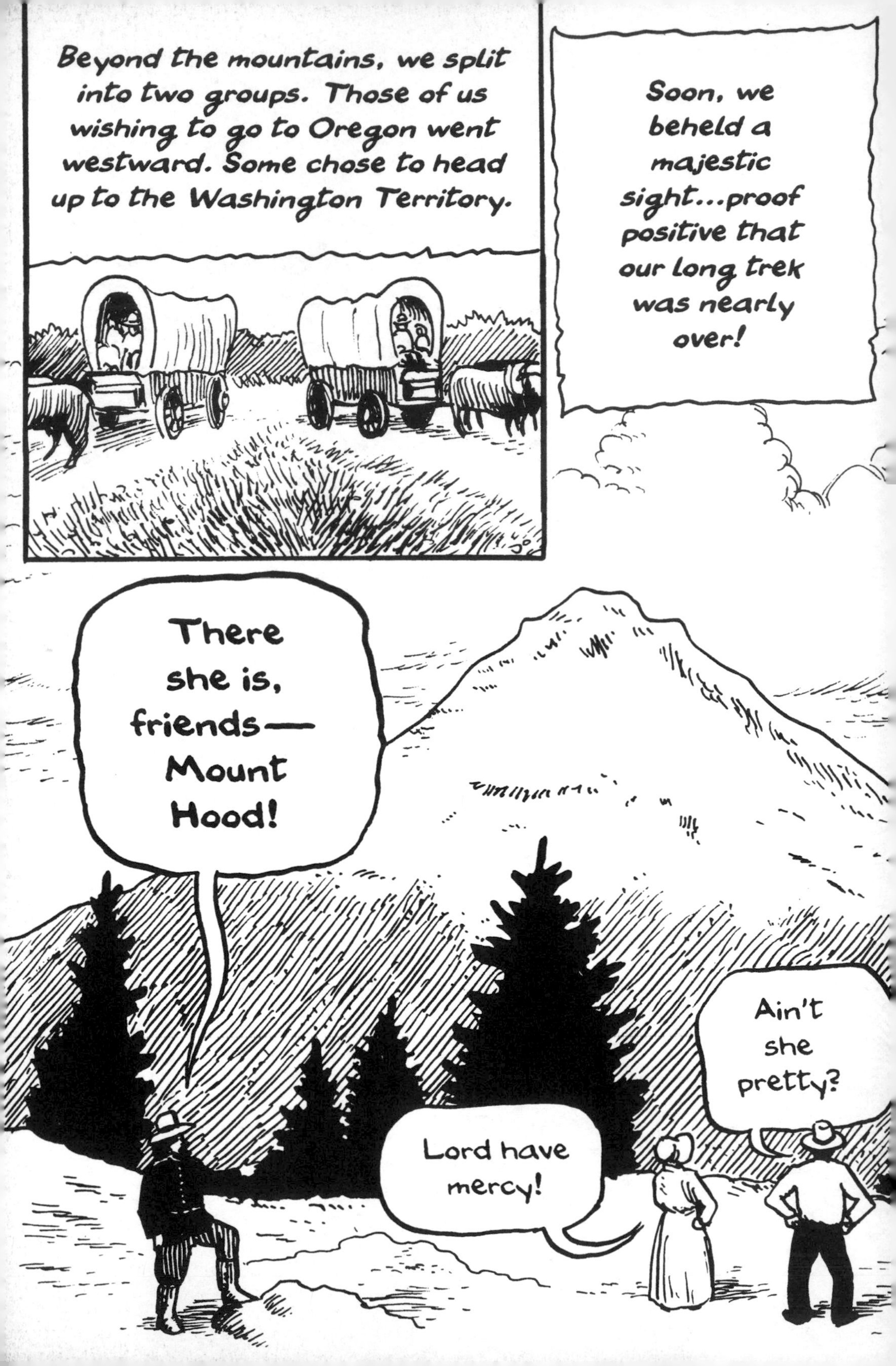
Beyond the mountains, we split into two groups. Those of us wishing to go to Oregon went westward. Some chose to head up to the Washington Territory.
Soon, we beheld a majestic sight...proof positive that our long trek was nearly over!
There she is, friends— Mount Hood!
Ain't she pretty?
Lord have mercy!

This,
Col. McCarty
told us, was
the end of
the Trail.

You've got
three ways to
finish this trip,
friends...

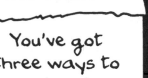

"Number one: you can buy
passage down the Columbia
River..."

"Number two: you can go 'round
Mt. Hood on the Lolo Pass..."

I think
we're lost.
again...

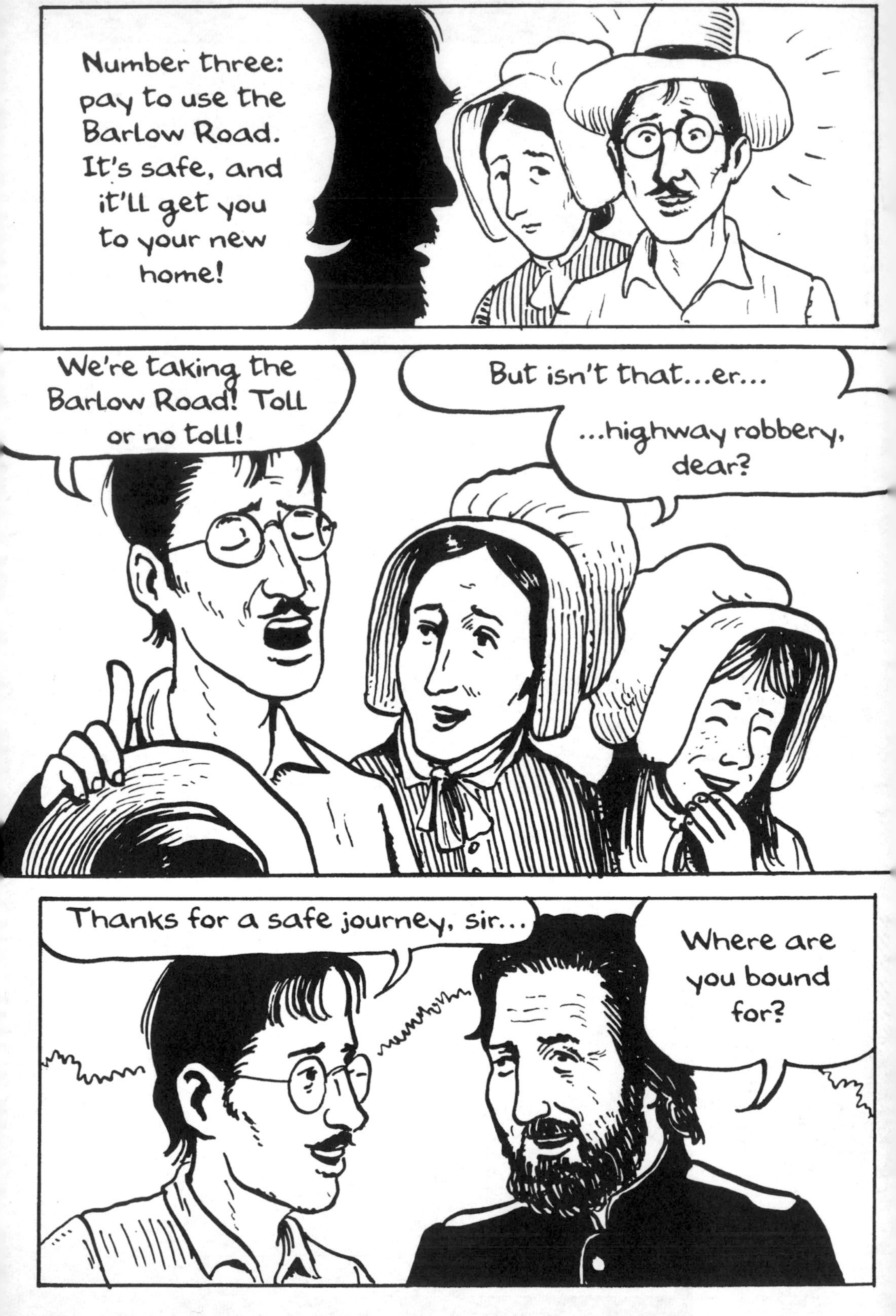
Number three: pay to use the Barlow Road. It's safe, and it'll get you to your new home!
We're taking the Barlow Road! Toll or no toll!
But isn't that...er...
...highway robbery, dear?
Thanks for a safe journey, sir...
Where are you bound for?

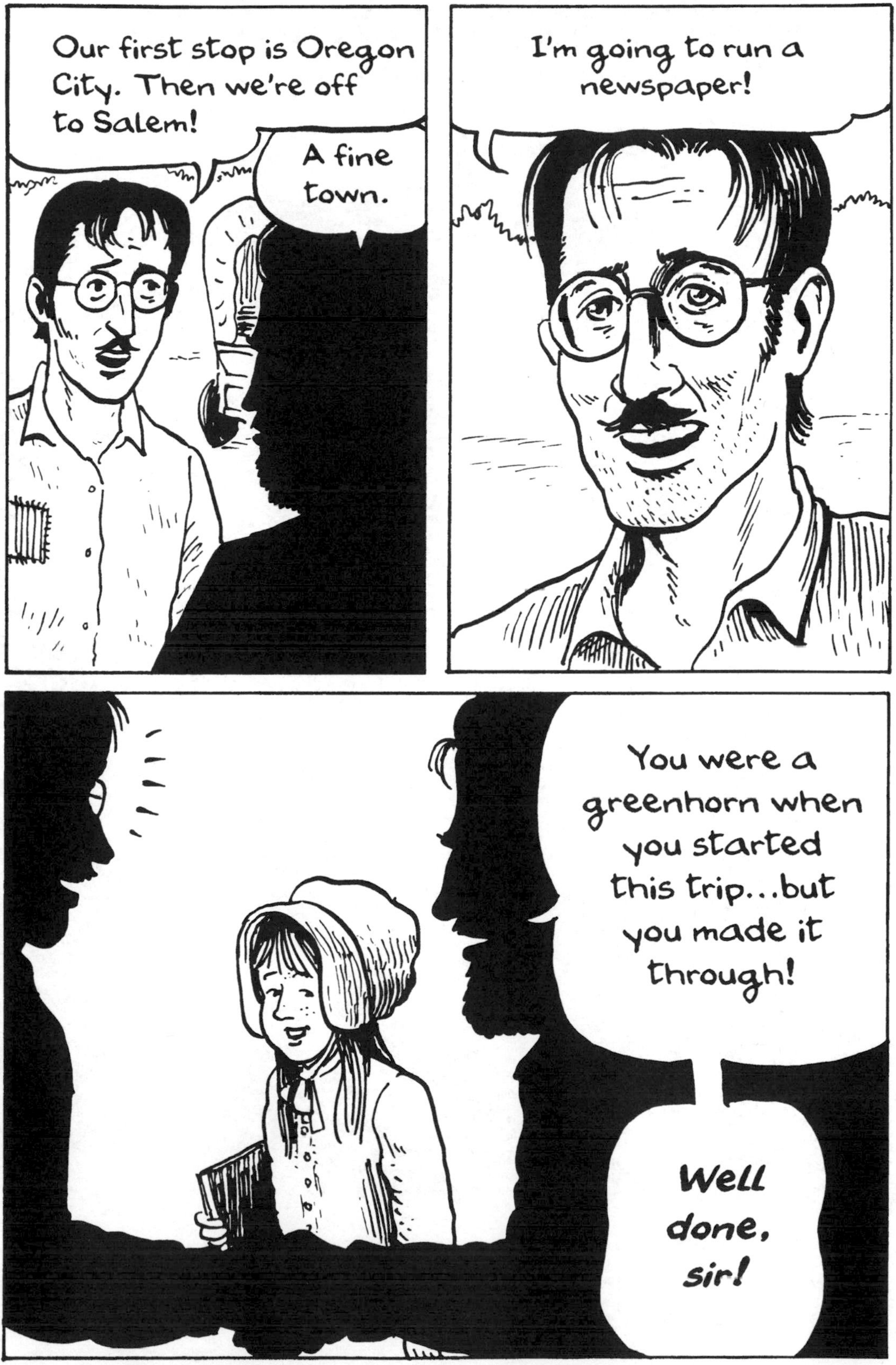
Our first stop is Oregon City. Then we're off to Salem!
A fine town.
I'm going to run a newspaper!
You were a greenhorn when you started this trip...but you made it through!
Well done, sir!

We traveled for six days on the Barlow Road. Our food and water were almost gone...

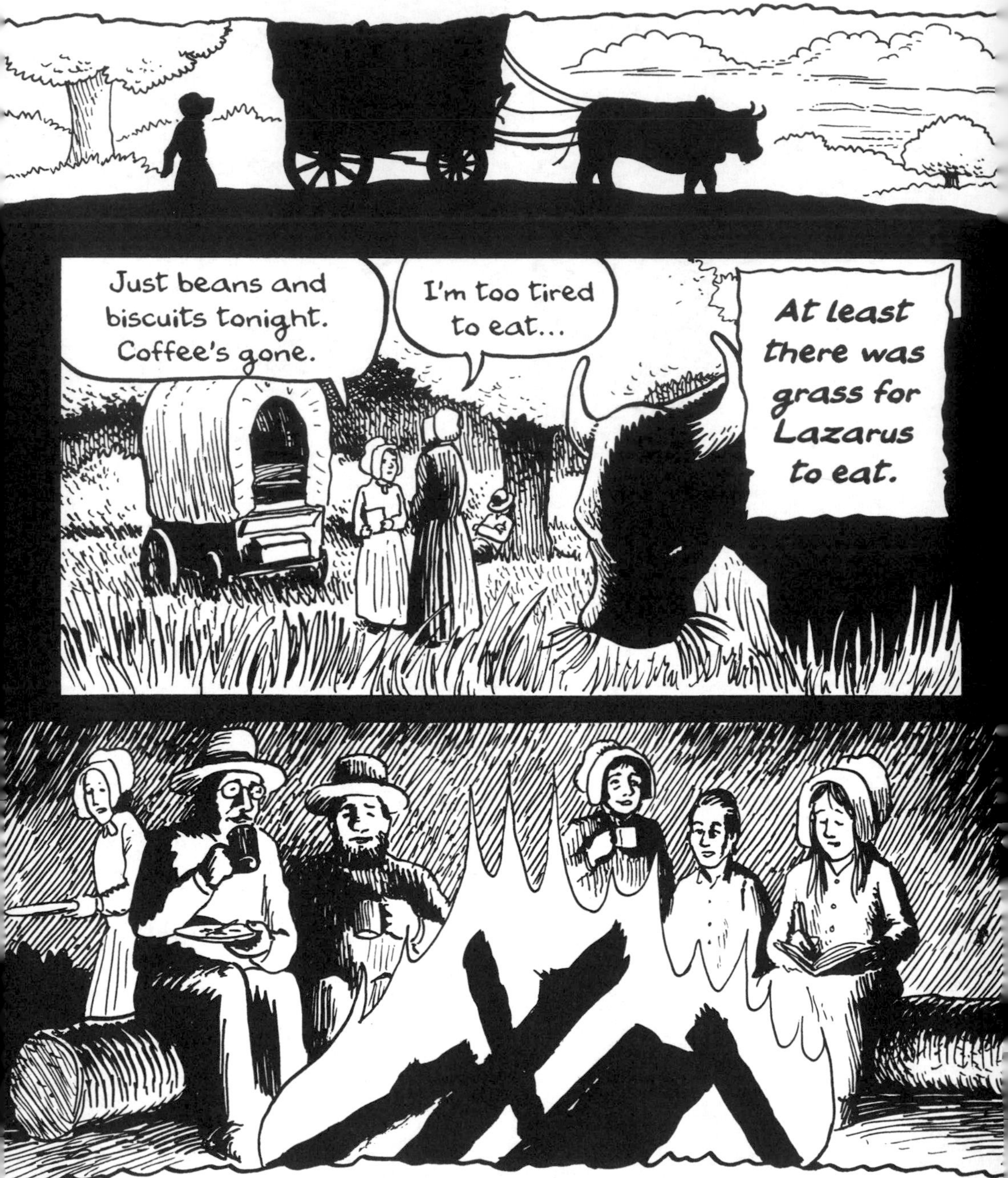
Just beans and biscuits tonight. Coffee's gone.
I'm too tired to eat...
At least there was grass for Lazarus to eat.

We stumbled upon a place simply called Campground. Some fellow travelers shared their beans and bread with us. We were thankful for their kindness.

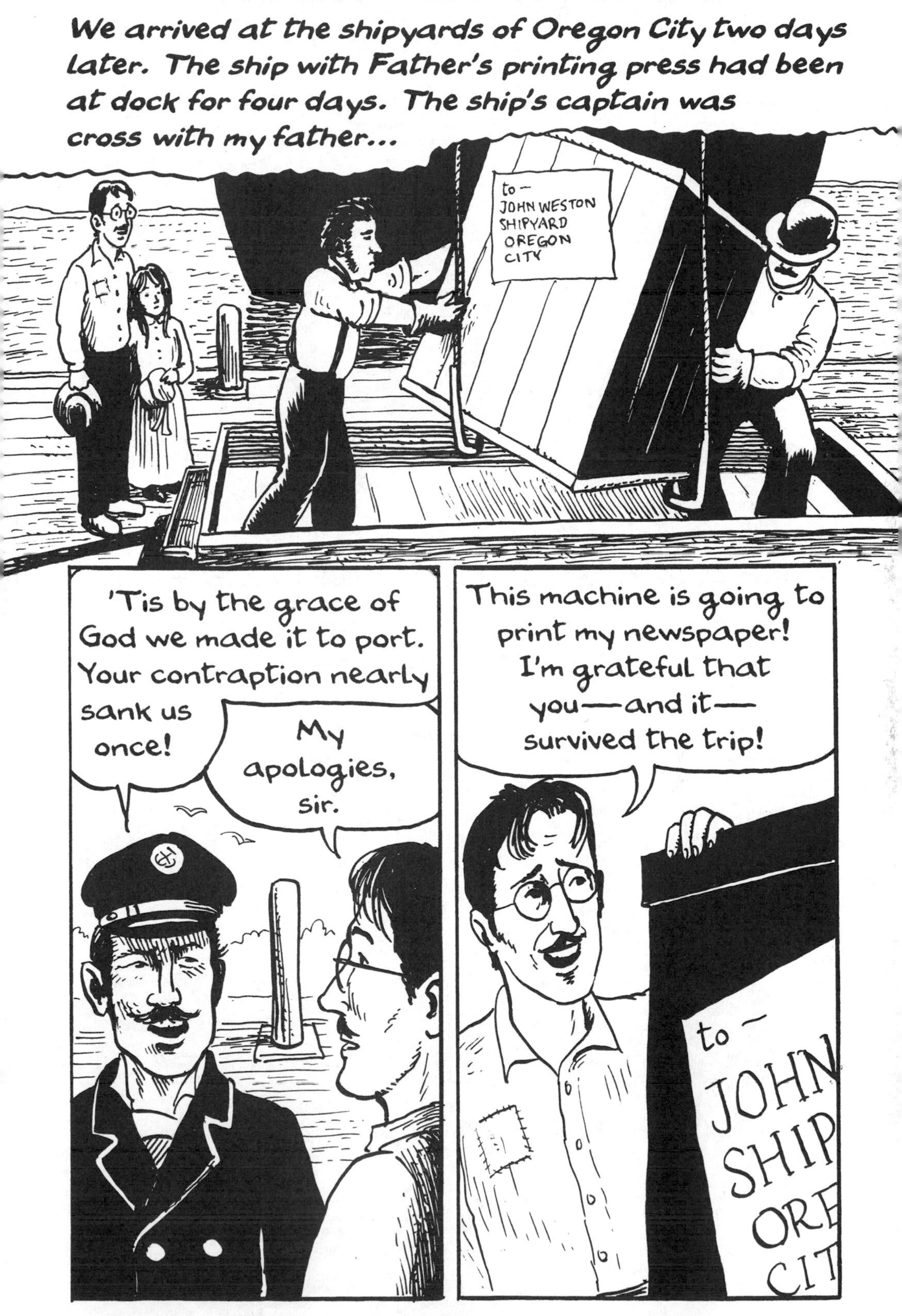
We arrived at the shipyards of Oregon City two days later. The ship with Father's printing press had been at dock for four days. The ship's captain was cross with my father...
to — JOHN WESTON SHIPYARD OREGON CITY
'Tis by the grace of God we made it to port. Your contraption nearly sank us once!
My apologies, sir.
This machine is going to print my newspaper! I'm grateful that you—and it—survived the trip!
to —

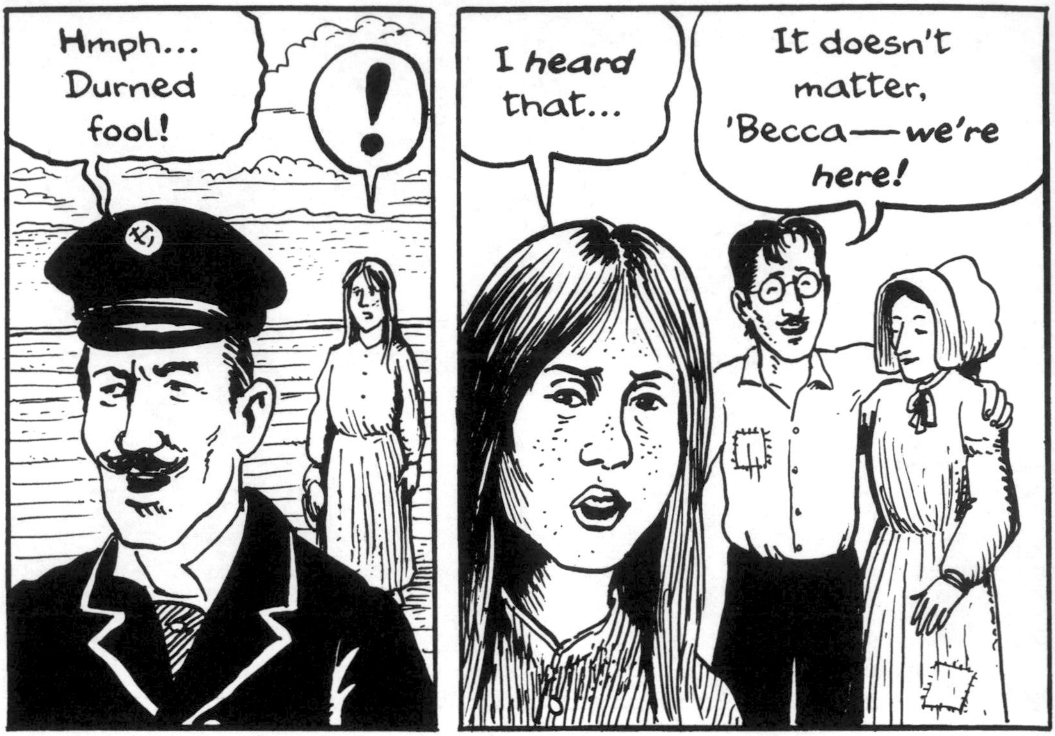
Hmph... Durned fool!
!
I heard that...
It doesn't matter, 'Becca—we're here!

Father hired a wagoner to haul his printing press to our new home. Along the way, I noted with interest the Indian families who lived alongside the new settlers. It was, in truth, their land too...

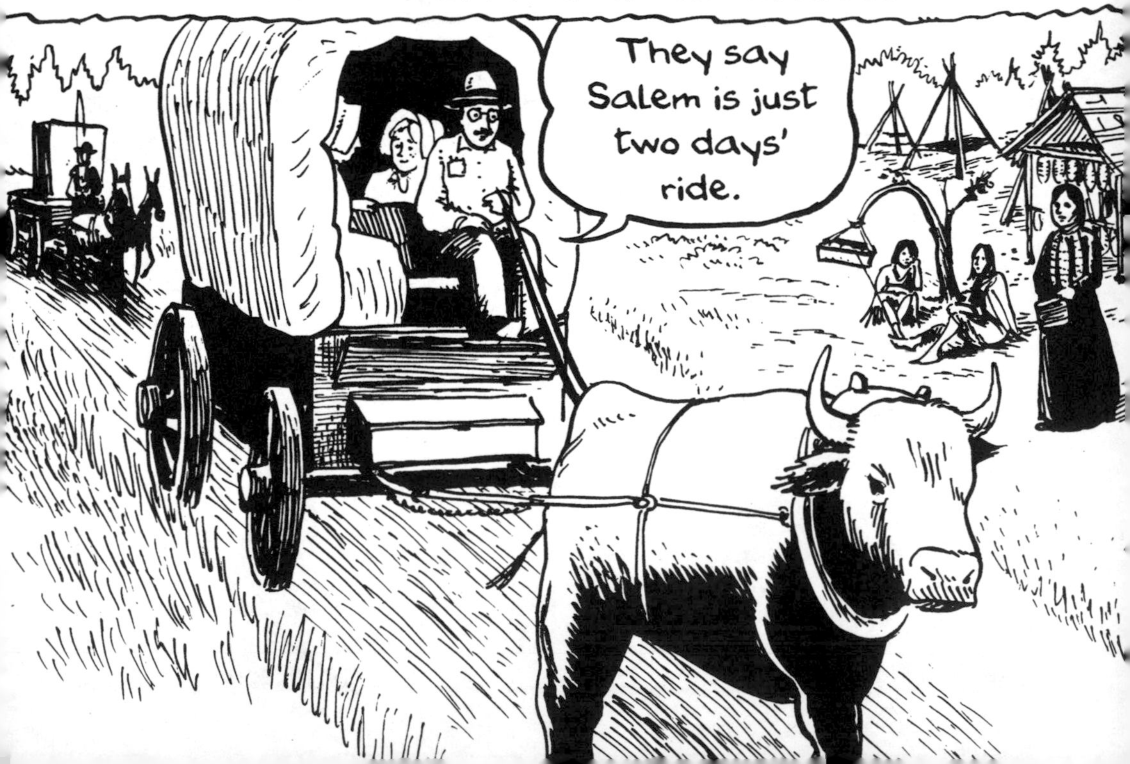
They say Salem is just two days' ride.

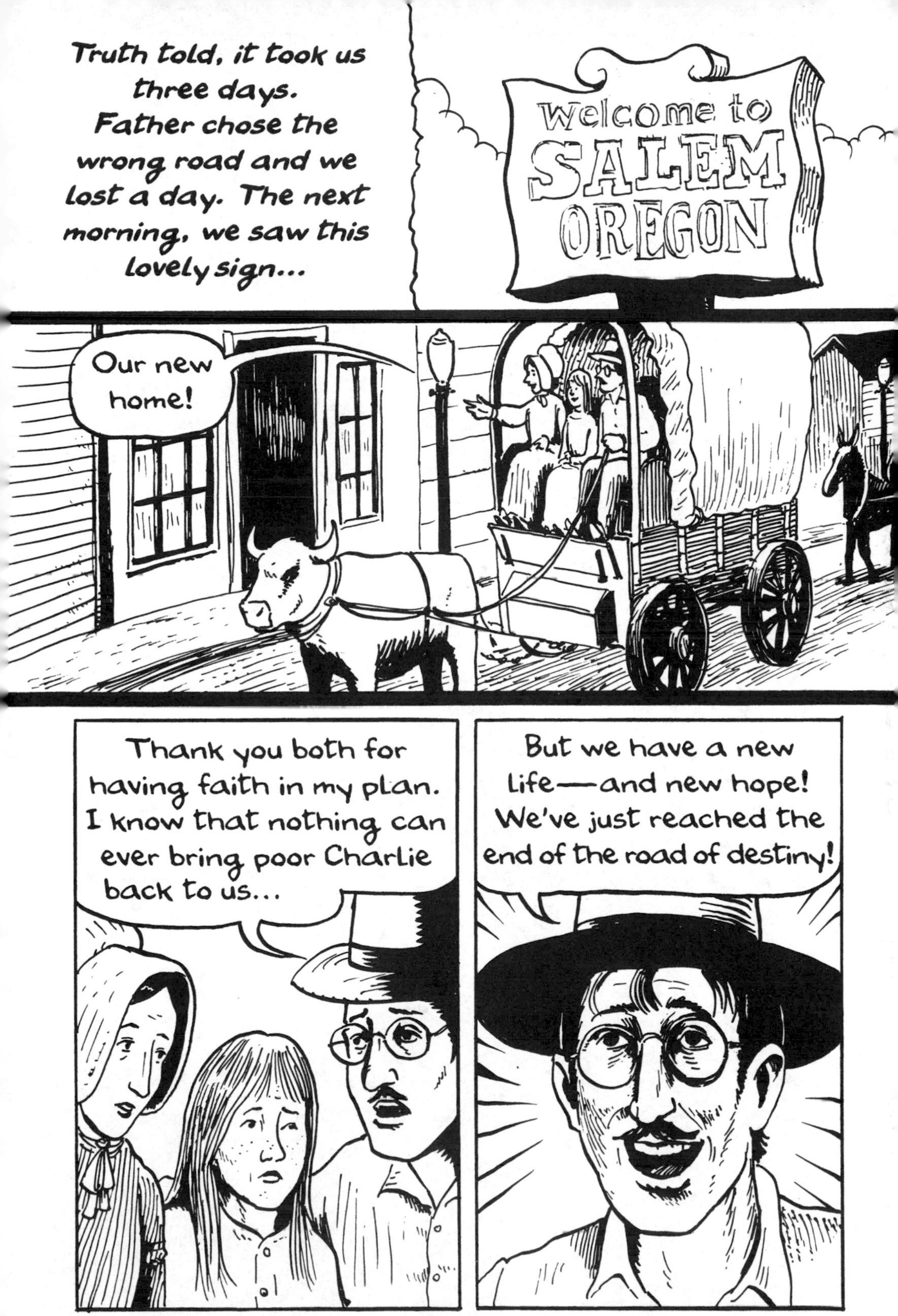

Truth told, it took us three days. Father chose the wrong road and we lost a day. The next morning, we saw this lovely sign...
Welcome to SALEM OREGON
Our new home!
Thank you both for having faith in my plan. I know that nothing can ever bring poor Charlie back to us...
But we have a new life—and new hope! We've just reached the end of the road of destiny!

Salem ~ 1868

Salem Guardian-Post
GOLD DISCOVERED IN CALIFORNIA

Salem Guardian-Post
Portland Incorporated as Township

Salem Guardian-Post
Confederates Fire on Fort Sumter

Salem Guardian-Post
LINCOLN SHOT
President killed at Ford's Theatre

Father's newspaper grew—like the town around us. He once ran for mayor—and nearly won!

This train robbery is Indiana news, Mr. Tumey! What I want is Oregon news!

We built a nice house in the heart of Salem. My mother gave piano and voice lessons in the afternoons.

That's fine, Gloria! You play so well...

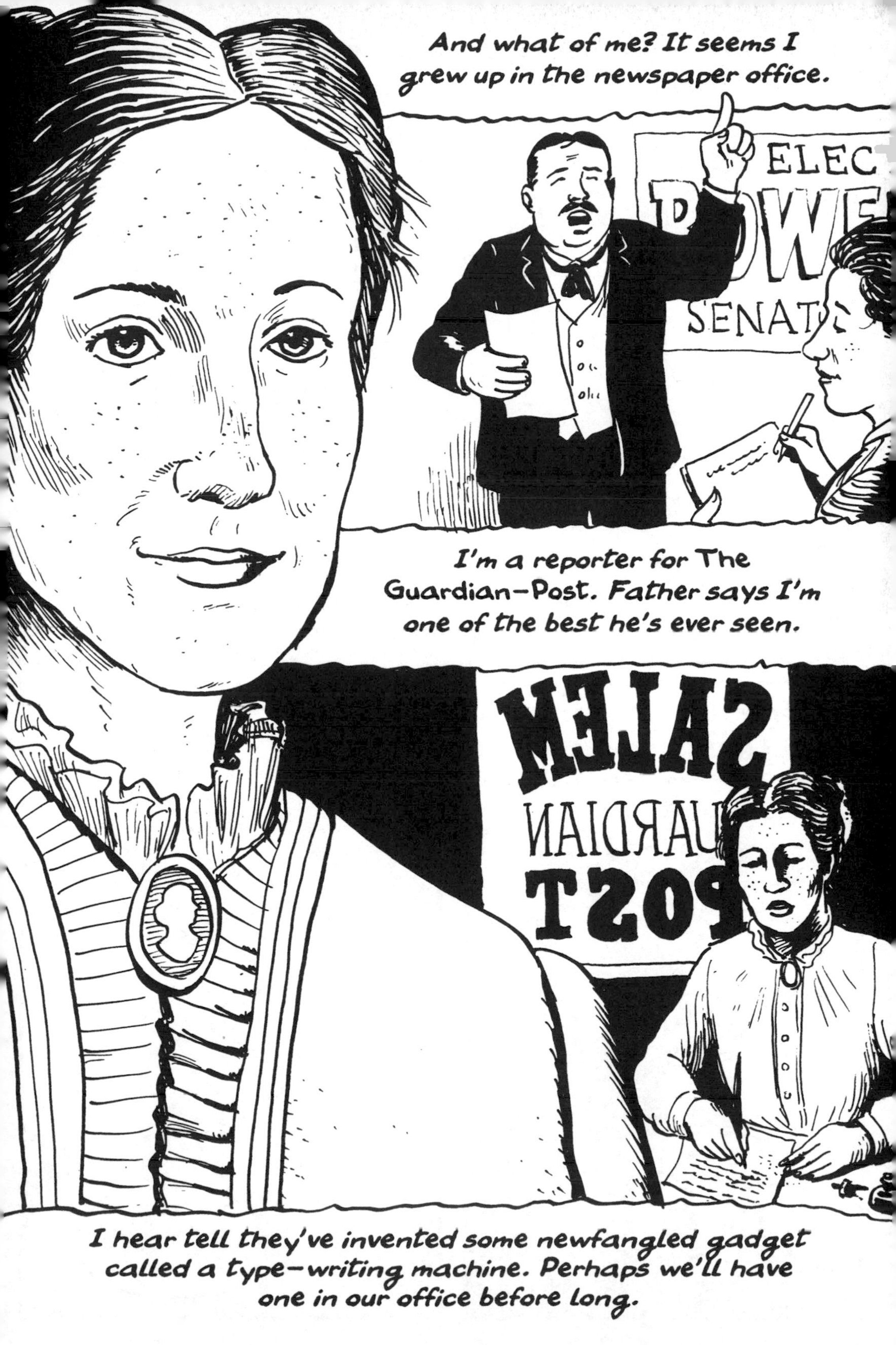
And what of me? It seems I grew up in the newspaper office.
ELEC
SENAT
I'm a reporter for The Guardian–Post. Father says I'm one of the best he's ever seen.
I hear tell they've invented some newfangled gadget called a type–writing machine. Perhaps we'll have one in our office before long.

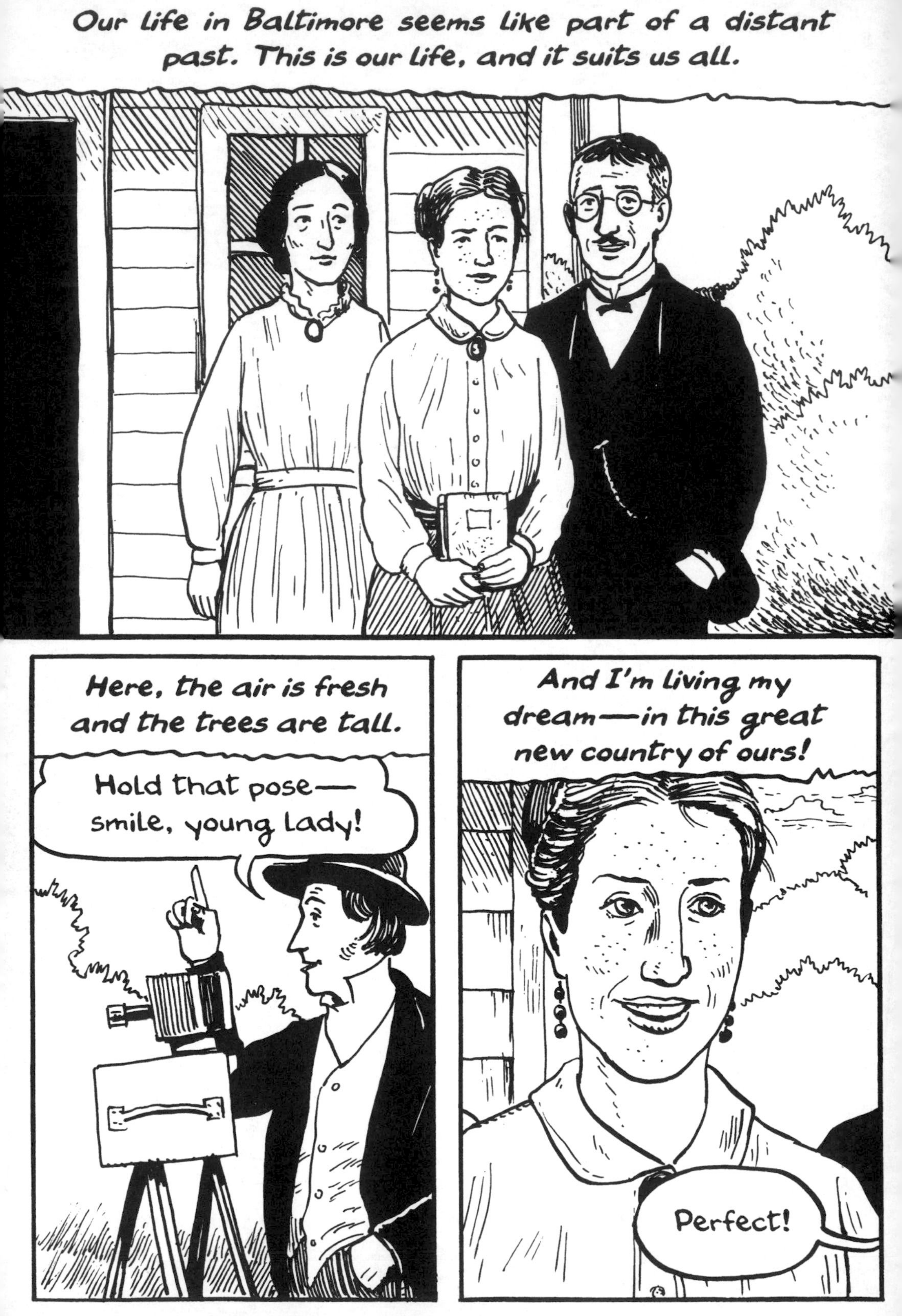
Our life in Baltimore seems like part of a distant past. This is our life, and it suits us all.
Here, the air is fresh and the trees are tall.
Hold that pose— smile, young lady!
And I'm living my dream—in this great new country of ours!
Perfect!

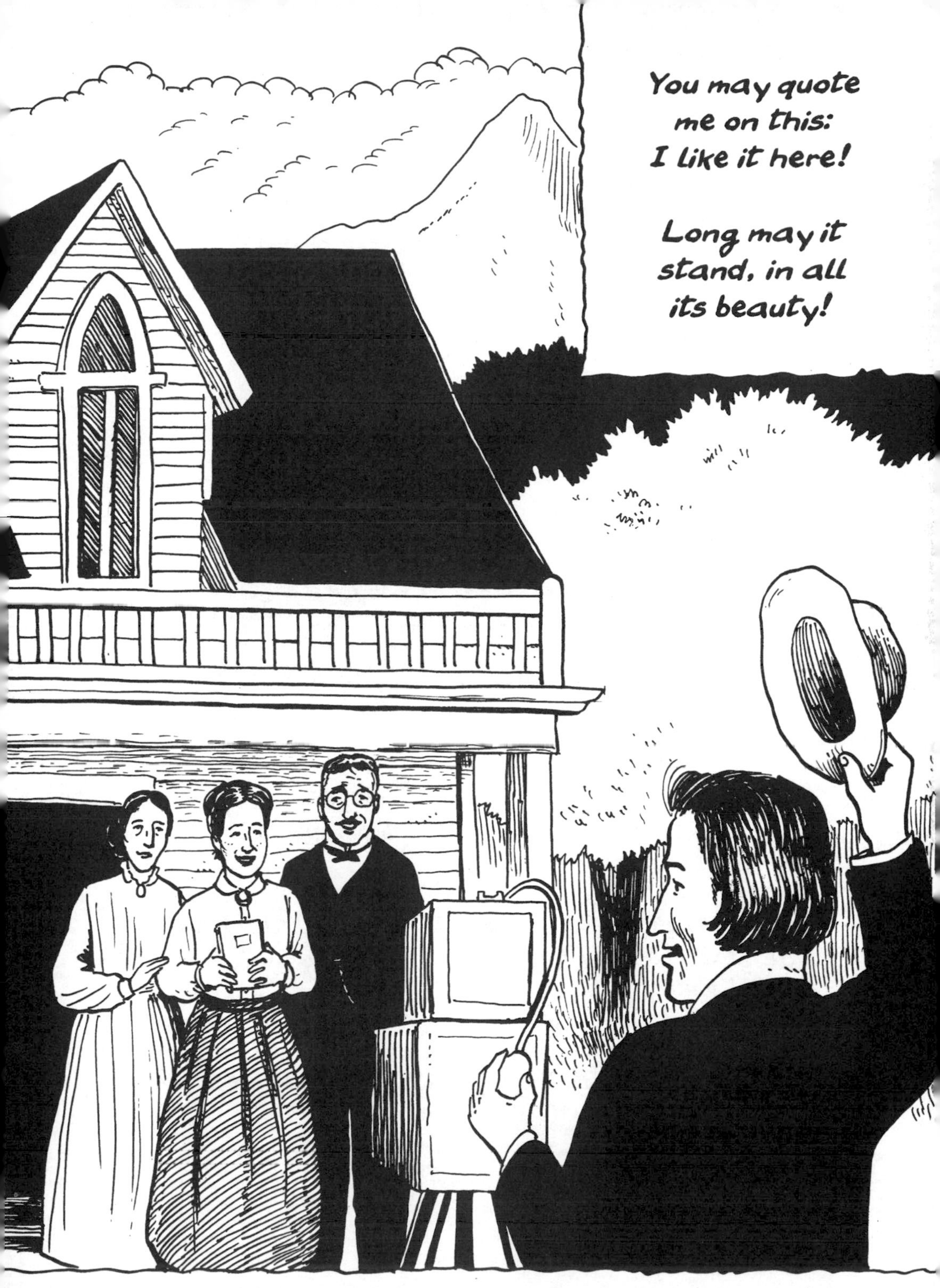
You may quote me on this: I like it here!
Long may it stand, in all its beauty!

The Road To Destiny ~ THE END ~

Bibliography

CORNERSTONES OF FREEDOM: THE OREGON TRAIL
R. Conrad Stein
(Danbury, CT: Children's Press, 1994)

FAR FROM HOME: FAMILIES OF THE WESTWARD JOURNEY
Lillian Schlissel, Byrd Gibbens, and Elizabeth Hampsten
(New York City: Schocken, 1989)

*THE GREAT PLATTE RIVER ROAD: THE COVERED WAGON
MAINLINE VIA FORT KEARNY TO FORT LARAMIE*
Merrill J. Mattes
(Lincoln, NE: University of Nebraska Press, 1987 ed. of 1969 book)

*OREGON TRAIL STORIES: TRUE ACCOUNTS OF LIFE IN A
COVERED WAGON*
David Klausmeyer
(Guilford, CT: Globe Pequot Press, 2004)

THE OREGON TRAIL
Francis Parkman
(Washington, DC: National Geographic, 2002 ed. of 1872 book)

THE OREGON TRAIL: AN AMERICAN SAGA
David Dary
(New York City: Knopf, 2004)

*THE OREGON TRAIL DIARY OF REV. EDWARD EVANS
PARRISH IN 1844*
Edited by Bert Webber
(Central Point, OR: Webb Research Group, 1988)

THE OREGON TRAIL IN AMERICAN HISTORY
Rebecca Stefoff
(Berkeley Heights, NJ: Easlow Publishers, 1997)

OUTLINE HISTORY OF AN EXPEDITION TO CALIFORNIA
"XOX"
*(Lafayette, CA: Great West Books; 1999 reprint of 1849 satirical
booklet)*

THE PAWNEE
Stuart A. Kallen
(Farmington Hills, MI: Lucent Books, 2000)

WAGON TRAIN: A FAMILY GOES WEST IN 1865
Courtni C. Wright; illustrated by Gershom Griffith
(New York City: Holiday House, 1995)

Frank Young is a writer and cartoonist living in Seattle, Washington. This is his first graphic novel in a thirty-plus–year publishing career. Young is also a musician, improv comedian, and comics historian.

David Lasky has been a published cartoonist since 1989. Among his best known work is the award-nominated *Urban Hipster* and *No Ordinary Flu*, in collaboration with King County Public Health. He is currently working on the graphic novel, *Don't Forget This Song*, the story of country music's Carter Family.